S0-ANO-394

# THE NEW AMERICAN EMPIRE

**Causes and Consequences
for the United States and for the World**

# RODRIGUE TREMBLAY

SOME RECENT BOOKS BY RODRIGUE TREMBLAY

*Why Bush Wants War*,
Religion, oil and politics in world conflicts (in French)

*The Way it Is (L'Heure Juste)*,
*The shock between politics, economics and morality* (in French)

*Modern Macroeconomics,*
*Facts and Theories* (in French)

*Africa and Monetary Integration* (in French and in English)

*Introduction to Economics* (in French)

# Rodrigue TREMBLAY

# THE NEW AMERICAN EMPIRE

## CAUSES AND CONSEQUENCES
## FOR THE UNITED STATES AND FOR THE WORLD

Copyright © 2004 by Rodrigue Tremblay

*All rights reserved. No part of this book shall be reproduced or transmitted in any form or by any means, electronic, mechanical, magnetic, photographic including photocopying, recording or by any information storage and retrieval system, without prior written permission of the publisher. No patent liability is assumed with respect to the use of the information contained herein. Although every precaution has been taken in the preparation of this book, the publisher and author assume no responsibility for errors or omissions. Neither is any liability assumed for damages resulting from the use of the information contained herein.*

ISBN  0-7414-1887-8

Tremblay, Rodrigue, 1939-
The New American Empire

1. United States. -2. George W. Bush. -3. Iraq. -4. Religion and Politics. -5. Oil. - 6. War against Iraq. -7. Empires. -8. Western Civilization.
Bibliography and index

Edited by ACHON Books

*Published by:*

**INFIꙨITY**
PUBLISHING.COM

*1094 New Dehaven Street, Suite 100*
*West Conshohocken, PA 19428-2713*
*Info@buybooksontheweb.com*
*www.buybooksontheweb.com*
*Toll-free  (877) BUY BOOK*
*Local Phone (610) 941-9999*
*Fax  (610) 941-9959*

*Printed in the United States of America*

*Printed on Recycled Paper*

*Published  June 2004*

To CAROLE,
for her support and
inspiration

# CONTENTS

# ABOUT THE AUTHOR

Rodrigue Tremblay is a prominent Canadian-born economist with a Ph.D. from Stanford University. He is a former Woodrow Wilson fellow and a Ford International Fellow.

He is now professor emeritus at the University of Montreal, after having occupied the positions of full professor of economics at the University of Montreal, president of the North American Economics and Finance Association, president of the Canadian Economics Society, and advisor to numerous organizations.

He has written 25 books dealing with economics and finance, some also tackling moral and political issues.

Dr. Tremblay has travelled extensively in Europe, in the Middle-East, in North Africa and in sub-Sahara Africa.

# FOREWORD

The adventure of the American-led war in Iraq is far from over. In fact, it may last for many years. In its wake, this episode in international affairs will leave deep cracks in the world geopolitical landscape.

This situation comes at the very end of the long Kondratieff economic cycle, whose stylized length is about 54 years. The last full cycle ran from 1949, with the removal of World War II price controls, to 2003. It is, therefore, a phenomenon that supersedes simple politics and encompasses the entire world economy and the half-century-old movement towards economic globalization.

One can ask if the long and uninterrupted march towards world economic interdependence has reached a zenith and has now begun to regress and could even unravel during the next decades. Indeed, globalization has been a prominent feature of the international economic system following World War II, under the enlightened leadership of the United States, beginning with the much-acclaimed 1948 Marshall Plan, which launched a devastated Europe towards economic integration and economic prosperity. It has been buttressed by strong international and multilateral organizations, such as the GATT/WTO, the IMF, the World Bank, etc.

The adoption of a worldwide imperial doctrine by the Bush administration, in 2002, poses a direct threat to the movement towards economic globalization and to the strengthening of international cooperation. Not only has such a policy served to justify the invasion of Iraq, but it has also marginalized the United Nations and, indirectly, it has weakened all the other multilateral organizations.

Is this a temporary shift in the international world order, before basic beneficial reforms are suggested, or is it a more permanent and dangerous blueprint for the 21st Century?

It is obviously too soon to conclude one way or another. One can nevertheless identify the causes of such a fundamental shift in U.S. foreign policy and its consequences for America and for the world. Indeed, as the pre-eminent superpower, the United States is now confronted by new threats to its security arising, not from hostile established governments, but from an apatrid Islamist terrorist movement. The way it chooses to react to such an unconventional challenge, either unilaterally or multilaterally, will frame the international environment for years to come. This book analyses the causes and consequences, both for the U.S. and for the world, of this new reality.

Rodrigue TREMBLAY
January 2004

# INTRODUCTION

# 1

## INTRODUCTION

*"Nothing is more dangerous than empires that pursue their own interests while pretending to do a service to humanity as a whole."*
Eric HOBSBAWM

*"We may someday look back on this moment in history as the time when the West defined itself for the 21st Century—not in terms of geography or race or religion or culture or language, but in terms of values—the values of freedom and democracy."*
Paul WOLFOWITZ

*"The best guarantee of not being suddenly deprived of an enemy is to make as many enemies as possible."*
Shimon TZABOR

The end of the 20th Century and the beginning of the 21st Century have produced a break in history. Three phenomena, in particular, have provoked a fundamental shift in international relations: the collapse of the Soviet Union and the end of the Cold War in December 1991, the cliffhanger election of George W. Bush to the U.S. presidency on November 7, 2000, and the al Qaeda terrorist attacks against the United States, on September 11, 2001.

These three significant events will influence the world for decades to come. The 9/11 disaster, in particular, with the death of 3,000 innocent victims, was a shock which rivaled other catastrophes of the past, such as the burning of the Karltheater of Vienna, in 1881, when 1,500 people died, or the sinking of the Titanic in 1912, with about the same number of victims, or again, the 1906 San Francisco earthquake with its 450 to 700 deaths; but it did not match the savagery of the atomic cataclysm of

Hiroshima and Nagaski in 1945, which brought 230,000 innocent persons to their fiery death and which are considered to be two of the most monstrous acts of the 20th Century.

At the close of the 20th Century, one could have expected that empires and aggressive wars belonged to a primitive past; but suddenly and without warning, the 21st Century appears to be a throwback to the 19th. Peace, democracy, multilateralism, and worldwide economic integration risk being pushed aside by wars of aggression, political confrontations, international unilateralism, and institutional chaos.

After the catastrophe of September 11, with the support of the United Nations and in collaboration with many other countries, the United States launched a legitimate war against international Islamist terrorism. Why did the U.S. then use this as a pretext—in defiance of the United Nations and almost all other member countries—to undertake a colonialist and imperialist adventure in the Middle East? Imperialist, because the United States occupies and controls Iraq's destiny by force. Colonialist, because the U.S. will be the first to benefit from the take-over and stabilization of the Iraqi oil industry.

What were the influences that prompted the Bush administration to deploy its military might in Iraq, against international law and international public opinion? Why did the administration trade the subtlety of diplomacy for the brutality of war? What were the relative importance of religious considerations, the constraints of partisan politics, and the desire to control the strategic oil-producing region of the Middle East in the decisions of the Bush administration to invade Iraq? What's behind George W. Bush's push for a worldwide American Empire? What are the intellectual roots behind this push toward imperialism? And, most crucially, what will be the political and economic consequences of the American drift towards an emerging American "Imperium", both for the United States and for the world?

In this dawn of the 21st Century, a disturbing wind of religious militancy and a supremacist will to military power blows in certain important circles of American society. That such a regression takes place in the most heavily-armed nation on the planet can only add to the fear that, on the international front, political destabilization and recurrent armed conflicts become an enduring reality.

## America's new imperium

Since the United States of America is the only military superpower remaining after the collapse of the Soviet Union, and since it has no intention to disarm itself, the U.S. will play a central role in future world stability—or instability. The domestic U.S. political market is of great interest to those outside its borders. It is the source of American politicians' primary preoccupations and principle motivations. It follows that in order to understand American foreign policy, one must understand its domestic politics.

In this light, the new "Bush Doctrine" of world supremacy and dominance, and its "America First" policies, proclaimed in September 2002 and applied to Iraq in March-April 2003, will influence political and economic relations between countries for decades to come. Indeed, the Bush Doctrine is a pre-emptive and discretionary war doctrine, and since it has become the cornerstone of U.S. foreign policy, it places America above international law. Armed with this doctrine, if it is not vigilant, the United States could be in the 21st Century what Germany was in the 20th Century, that is, a danger to the world.

Every country should be concerned by the desire for world power that is manifested by American leaders. This is in part a gut reaction to the humiliation felt by all Americans after September 11, 2001. Americans—and in this they mirror their president—desire a military and political victory to revenge and erase the insult of 9-11.

This deep sentiment is found in many American politicians, but also in leaders of various religious organizations and in the mass media. What is worrisome is that the events of recent years have allowed a radical right to take complete control of the U.S. government. Such a development poses a threat to America but also to the world. Indeed, there is nowadays almost a sacred alliance among the religious, media, and political-economic interests urging the United States to use its enormous military superiority to promote these groups' agendas— political, economic and religious. For example, a key policy-maker in the U.S. administration, House Majority Leader Tom DeLay, never misses an opportunity to repeat that he entered politics to promote a *"biblical worldview."*

Since the same messianism is present in President George W. Bush and in his immediate entourage, it can be said that this alliance is now solidly in power in Washington, and especially in the electronic media. Its members harbor no scruples, impose upon themselves no limits, and have no doubts as to the soundness of their objectives. The Republican Party is its political instrument of choice, while the U.S. armed forces are its military instrument of intervention. The world will suffer the repercussions of this American nomenklatura's new imperialism.

Religion, politics and violence

Today, in some respects, the two men who most threaten world stability are the stateless terrorist leader Osama bin Laden and the American president, George W. Bush. Since these two leaders frequently use religious terminology to justify their actions, it is important to understand the relationship that can exist between politics and religion when religion leaves the purely personal domain and invades the public space.

More fundamentally, how have Christian religions evolved, allowing for the emergence of democracy in the West, while a religion such as Islam has remained mired in a paralyzing totalitarianism that refuses the values of democracy and progress? How is Western civilization, which has dominated the world over the past several centuries, indebted to Christianity's acceptance of democracy? And, at the end of the day, how does the current reemergence of fundamentalist religion risk turning America into an imperial power and signal a setback for Western civilization?

In order to better understand the causes leading to the events that are shaking the world order, this book doesn't hesitate to investigate the explosive links between religion, partisan politics, and oil in the motivations behind the desire among American neo-conservatives to create a U.S.-dominated world empire.

When considering the problem of violence and religion, for example, there is always a risk that humanity will fall back into barbarism. Religious or "faith-based" violence is the most dangerous of all, especially when it is unleashed against civilians rather than governments and states. Are men more violent, are they more disposed to excess when they believe that their actions are dictated by God? Are organized religions and wars interrelated?

It is not that the great religious traditions necessarily encourage violence. For most of them, it is rather the opposite. They preach love for others and mutual aid. Nevertheless, without fail, groups which are on the fundamentalist fringe of the great monotheist religions go to the original texts to find odes to violence, providing arguments to support their fanaticism and justify their cruelty toward people who don't think as they do.

Since religious groups seek the support and the following of the greatest number, in certain countries they may act like populist political parties. In fact, they are often substitutes for traditional political parties, proposing various policies and different approaches, and providing a sense of identity and belonging to troubled individuals.

The worst situation is when religious fanatics gain political power in a society. The mixing of politics and religion introduces elements of absolutism and intolerance that can, when taken to the extreme, justify the most terrible transgressions. Throughout history, this distortion of proselytizing and politicized religions has been and continues to be the source of countless human tragedies.

## The politics of oil

Extreme religious motivations are far from being the only explanation for the human tendency toward violence. Economic and political interests play a large role in the initiation of military conflicts and wars. Today, it is imperative to see how economic interests tied to the strategic control of oil reserves influence the politics of war and peace. Indeed, would a war against Iraq have occurred if the White House, in 2003, had been occupied by persons not directly connected to the oil industry?

This mixture of religious motivations, political aims, and economic interests constitutes an explosive cocktail. Add a wounded and humiliated superpower—governed by a single-minded and bellicose leader—and you have the recipe for an explosive double cocktail that threatens to transform the planet.

Oil supply to industrialized countries and to emerging economies plays a pivotal role in this equation. Improved standards of living are always accompanied by an increase in motorized transportation and increasing energy demands. When the developing world trades its bicycles for automobiles—in China, in India, or elsewhere—oil consumption will skyrocket, at the same time as oil production will tend to peak. In the foreseeable future, there are scarcely any sufficiently economic substitutes for crude oil as the main energy source. In this context of world economic growth, those who control oil reserves will indisputably hold a major geopolitical advantage.

Even if Africa and certain former Soviet republics increase their production of black gold, the Middle East will continue to contain the world's principle reserves of oil. Over the next decades, what happens in Saudi Arabia and in Iraq, in particular, will influence not only the Middle East, but also the entire world geopolitical map.

## Empire, legitimacy and democracy

Without any form of consultation whatsoever, the United States *de facto* exerts military, political, economic and cultural power over foreign populations. How can the peoples who are subjected to American power "vote" on how that power is exercised? Is the idea that "Might makes right" compatible with the ideal of an open and democratic society?

An imperial regime is intrinsically undemocratic. It concentrates political power instead of spreading it among the people. In the case in question, only American citizens, and in fact, only those who participate in the electoral system, have a voice in the matter.

This democratic deficit is one of the greatest sources of resentment toward the phenomenon of economic globalization and global interdependence. As long as nation states have a voice in multilateral institutions, such as the United Nations or the World Trade Organization (WTO), globalization retains an aspect of indirect legitimacy. People have the impression that they "vote" through their governments on measures that affect them directly. Multilateralism thus becomes a substitute for a truly democratic world government, which will still be impractical for decades to come.

However, when a country undertakes to dictate its will to multilateral institutions, and even to push them aside in order to follow its own interests, any democratic legitimacy to globalization is erased. Why would the world endorse an international regime unilaterally controlled by one country? Such an arrangement is neither democratic nor acceptable.

By espousing imperial unilateralism, and by embarking upon unprovoked and discretionary wars, the United States under George W. Bush is threatening the progress in international relations that has been made over the last half century. Peoples and countries will be reluctant to accept being subjugated by a power that pursues only its own narrow interests, to the detriment of the rest of humanity. Such an agressive imperial power has no democratic legitimacy and its exercise can only result in chaos and disintegration. In refusing multilateralism, in becoming a world empire, the United States risks causing worldwide unrest and both economic and political regression. A great democracy cannot become imperialistic without destroying itself. Everyone, inside and outside the United States, should think long and hard about the possible consequences of such a mammoth shift of direction in the role of the U.S. in the world.

As the title indicates, the main purpose of this book is not to describe, but to analyse and explain the causes and consequences of the fundamental shift in U.S. foreign policy taking place during the crucial first years of the 21st Century. It explores the functioning of the complex American political market, especially as it relates to the motives and interests of major groups and participants. It then proceeds to integrate the new U.S. foreign policy into the larger geopolitical context of world political stability and economic prosperity and of the future of Western civilization.

# 2

# THE MANICHAEISM OF OSAMA BIN LADEN AND GEORGE W. BUSH

*"Of all deceivers who have plagued mankind, none are so deeply ruinous to human happiness as those impostors who pretend to lead by a light above nature. Science has never killed or persecuted a single person for doubting or denying its teachings, and most of these teachings have been true; but religion has murdered millions for doubting or denying her dogmas, and most of these dogmas have been false."*
George SPENCER, d. 1908, Lyndonville, Vermont, headstone.

*"Power always thinks it has a great soul and vast views beyond the comprehension of the weak; and that it is doing God's service when it is violating all His laws."*
John ADAMS

*"Kill them all! God will know his own."*
Words attributed to Arnold AMAURY, Abbot of Citeaux and papal legate, at the massacre of Béziers, during the Albigensian Crusade, in 1209.

Good and Evil, good terrorism and bad terrorism[1]

To a certain extent, all religions paint the world in black and white.

In 1948, a bellicose evangelist preacher in New Jersey, the Reverend Carl McIntire, became famous when he proposed in a radio broadcast that the United States carry out a "pre-emptive" nuclear attack against the Soviet Union. A religious fundamentalist, founder of the Bible Presbyterian Church, McIntire was persuaded that a worldwide nuclear hecatomb was necessary to "purify" the world of communist countries.[2] He believed that no country should have a system that differed from his own religious model, whatever the cost.

The same extremism and the same quest for absolute virtue are seen in Islamist fundamentalists. In 2001, an Islamist terrorist introduced the notion of "good" and "bad" terrorism into the international political vocabulary. The religious terrorist Osama bin Laden declared in a video message, *"Yes, we kill their innocents and this is legal, religiously and logically...There are two types of terror, good and bad. What we are practicing is good terror. We will not stop killing them and whoever supports them."*[3]

It is clear that this quest for absolute virtue leads naturally to the hatred of non-believers. The worst crimes become acceptable to one whose spirit is obsessed with the utopic Supreme Good. Persuaded that he is acting in the name of God, there is no limit to the extremist's cruelty. Entrenched in his fundamentalist mission, bin Laden wraps his calls to faith-based violence in a prayer: *"I ask God to help us champion His religion and continue jihad for His sake until we meet Him and He is satisfied with us. And He can do so. Praise be to Almighty God."*[4] The line between religious fanaticism and insanity, between religious fervor and pathological delusion, is very thin indeed. The world should take notice when someone with a following, with a fanatic mind and with powerful means, receives his marching orders from Heaven.

As if one extremism elicits another, President George W. Bush didn't hesitate to introduce religion and the dangerous notion of absolute virtue into American politics. When he was governor of Texas, he established an annual "Jesus Day", on June 10th.[5] In his public debates, he also exclaimed, *"Jesus changed my heart!"* And, once elected president, in January 2001, George W. Bush declared September 14 to be a national day of prayer. This is in addition to the permanent prayer day established in 1952 by Harry S. Truman, a day Ronald Reagan, in 1988, proclaimed to be the first Thursday of every month of May.[6]

Bush even opened his administration to a notorious representative of the American Religious Right, Attorney General John Ashcroft. Son and grandson of Protestant pastors, potentially a modern-day Torquemada.[7] Ashcroft declared to a group of students at Bob Jones seminary, *"We have no king but Jesus."*[8] All of these declarations and all of these policies were in violation of a pluralist society's democratic principle of government neutrality in religious matters.

So it was no surprise after the September 11th attacks, when George W. Bush, mirroring his antagonist bin Laden, said that Islamist terrorists and mass terrorism represented "Evil", implying that "Good" and virtue belonged to the United States, and promising to *"rid the world of evil and terror."* [9] This followed a declaration in his "war whoop" speech to Congress, on September 20, 2001, that *"Freedom and fear, justice and cruelty, have always been at war, and we know that God is not neutral between them."* In other words, God is on our side. [10]

Bush concluded this speech to the Congress, by saying, *"May God grant us wisdom and may he watch over the United States of America."* The American president, like some Americans, seems to think that God is an American, and that the United States was created, not by the Founding Fathers (Washington, Jefferson, Adams, Franklin ...), but by God. He came close to making such a solemn proclamation in 2001, when he declared *"Our nation was chosen by God and mandated by history to serve (*the world*) as a model of justice."* [11]

It is ironic that in their public declarations, it seemed to be a contest to see who could be the most pious and mention Allah or God more often, George W. Bush, Osama bin Laden... or Saddam Hussein. Because, even though the Iraqi dictator was not really known for his piety, he resorted to references to Good and Evil to chastise the United States for its *"policies of Evil"*, as he multiplied his incantations to Allah. In 2002, after having been plebicited at 100% by the Iraqi population, Saddam Hussein declared, *"The Iraqi question...is now the center of the battle between Good and Evil."* [12]

In 1996, after his disastrous wars against Iran and Kuwait, Saddam Hussein decided to wage a political campaign with the theme of "faith" or "iman", discarding the secular model that he had espoused until then. In the 1970's and '80's, Iraq, under the Baath Party, had become, with Turkey, one of the most secularized Muslim countries. One result was the emancipation of women, another, the legalization of the sale of liquor. However, after his successive defeats, Saddam Hussein felt politically isolated and saw the need to embrace organized religion. He even ordered the construction of two new mosques in Baghdad, one of which was to be named after himself.[13]

All three leaders—Bush, bin Laden, and Hussein—rely on absolute values with a religious connotation to consolidate their authority and to demonize their adversaries. It is perhaps understandable on the part of bin Laden, a medieval conception of Islam seeming to be the only ideal he has to offer the world. Even a sanguinary dictator like Hussein can be understood, if not condoned, for associating himself with religion and the deity to legitimize his position, after having led his country to ruin.

However, this shouldn't be the case in the United States, the historic example *par excellence*, along with France, of democracy and liberty. In the House of Representatives, there are two life-sized portraits, one of Washington, and one of Lafayette. In other words, France was instrumental in the U.S. gaining its independence, and was therefore present at the birth of the United States. That George W. Bush is not able to articulate fundamental American values without losing himself in conjectures on Good and Evil is a tragedy for the United States, for the West, and for the world. Indeed, one thinks as a totalitarian before acting as one.

What the United States has to offer the world is not a sketchy medieval version of Good and Evil, but a system of fundamental political values that are based upon the right of peoples to self-determination, to a democratic government and the rule of law, on inalienable human rights and individual freedom, on the respect for life, on tolerance, on the basic rights of freedom of thought, of religion, and liberty of conscience, on free enterprise and economic progress through science, industry, and personal effort, and on the right of individuals to seek happiness.

All of these values are rejected by Islam, but George W. Bush is incapable of explaining the contrast between the two civilizations, one founded upon a medieval and totalitarian religion, and the other on a modern and democratic humanism. On the contrary, he gets mired in a role that is not rightly his—that of Chief Theologian—when he takes it upon himself, as president, to judge the relative worth of different religions or the religious status of some people. For this is just what he did when he declared publicly that Islam is a religion *"based on peace, love and compassion"* or when he identified some Americans as "sinners".[14]

## Manichaeism and moral absolutism

The temptation to divide the world between good and evil comes around periodically throughout history. Manichaeism is the doctrine of moral absolutes. The Manichaens formed a religious sect in the 3rd Century. Disciples of Mani (216-277), they believed that the world was irreparably divided between Good and Evil, the darkness of matter obscuring the light of the spirit. The Manichaens were condemned by the Roman Catholic Church at the Council of Constantinople in 381. The same dualist approach, separating the material from the spiritual, was revived under the name of Catharism in the Languedoc region of France, during the 12th and 13th Centuries.[15]

## Political-religious fanaticism

When leaders succumb to a manichaean classification of "Good" and "Evil", it is not only to demonize their enemy— although that can be a prerequisite before killing them or committing atrocities—but especially to assure themselves and their people that the enemy is 100% in the wrong and that they are 100% in the right.

In such a metaphysical context of moral absolutism, the fanatic does not question his basic presumptions, objectives, or the means he employs to divide humanity between Good and Evil. Everything is either black or white. All wrongs are on one side and all the pious justifications on the other. Between friend and foe, between the pious and the infidel, there is no middle ground. There is only a wall of hatred and distrust that violence or warfare help to cement.

The political-religious fanatic harbors no doubt and knows no hesitation. Thinking for himself is anathema. Any compromise, accommodation, understanding or acceptance of others is impossible. Tolerance is seen as weakness or submission and to be avoided at all costs. He despises intellectuals who analyze causes and question ideas, opinions, and philosophies. What he seeks is immediate results, whatever the price to pay by himself or by others.

Above all, he seeks to dominate people and situations, preferably through fear, terror, and violence, and if needs be, war. His ferocity is equal to his convictions. When he kills, it is in the name of God or Allah, which eliminates beforehand all personal guilt and any remorse. He has a mission, and that makes him important in his own eyes, and especially, in the eyes of his relations.

Osama bin Laden, leader of the al Qaeda terrorist movement, could not be more clear: it is in the name of God (Allah) that he kills innocent victims. *"These men* (the September 11th hijackers) *have realized that the only course to achieve justice and defeat injustice is through jihad* (Muslim holy struggle) *for the cause of God* (Allah)."[16] His language is practically identical to that used by George W. Bush after the September 11th attacks.

It is a paradox of the 21st Century, that both Osama bin Laden and George W. Bush apply the same manichaean terminology to describe themselves and their enemies. One seems to be a mirror image of the other. Both refer to Allah or God to justify their political actions. Both believe—or at least claim—that the Divinity is on their side; each thinks he is on the side of Good, while the other is automatically on the side of Evil.[17]

For a manichaean leader, debates and discussions are out. Any policy is justifiable, since the goal is to fight absolute Evil. It is all-out war, *jihad*, with the blessing of God or Allah. An ambitious leader can then put the frosting on the cake by announcing that he was chosen by Allah or God to lead, and the circle is closed.

This is perhaps the fundamental reason for the fanaticism of manichaean religions and why they have for so long been the source of war. They tend to encourage blind obedience and primitive instincts, instead of reflection, study, and dialogue. Whether it be in the Bible or in the Koran, there are many passages that justify violence.

The mix of religious Manichaeism and public affairs is always to be feared. Such a simplistic view of the world is dangerous in several ways. Not only is it a sign of a lack of rational thinking, but it aims to impose an absolute conformity of vision. It is the antithesis of freedom and democracy. Imposed conformity is the enemy of progress in any domain. In the face of fanaticism and irrational terrorism, democracies must defend their values and their principles on a different level than elementary religious manichaeism.

## Religious terrorism

A totalitarian, religious conception of society is the source of today's very real international terrorism threat. It is a vision that knows no respect for individuals, for human life. It follows that political-religious terror challenges not only Western countries, but all populations who aspire to live in freedom and democracy.

For this reason, it is wrong to think that religiously-based terrorism is a kind of modern war of religions pitting Islam against Christianity, or against any other religion. It is rather the extreme reaction of some totalitarian and religious groups who are violently opposed to the humanist values of democracy, freedom, openness, tolerance, and the rule of law; that is to say the values that have dominated in the West for three centuries and are the foundation of its progress.

Religion-tainted, worldwide terrorism is an attack against, and a negation of, these fundamental values, not only in the West, but everywhere. This is perhaps especially true in the countries that are ruled by religious totalitarianism, such as Shiite Iran or Sunni and Wahhabi Saudi Arabia.

# 3

## POLITICO-RELIGIOUS FUNDAMENTALISM IN THE USA

*"To do evil a human being must first of all believe that what he's doing is good... Ideology—that is what gives evildoing its long-sought justification and gives the evildoer the necessary steadfastness and determination. That is the social theory which helps to make his acts seem good instead of bad in his own and others' eyes, so that he won't hear reproaches and curses but will receive praise and honors."*
Alexander SOLZHENITSYN

*"The leader who needs religion to govern his people is weak... We have to rid ourselves of superstition. Anybody is free to believe in anything, but we need freedom of thought."*
ATATÜRK (1881-1938), founder of modern Turkey.

*"The United States has God's special blessing."*
U.S. Attorney General John ASHCROFT, April, 2003.

On November 10, 1620, a group of English families landed at what became Plymouth, Massachusetts. In 1609, they had fled religious persecution in England, and sought refuge in Holland. While living in Holland, their children learned Dutch and adapted to the country's lifestyle, which their parents considered to be frivolous and a threat to their education. They decided to move on, this time to try their luck in the New World. On September 6, 1620, they set sail for New England on the *Mayflower*, taking 65 days to cross the Atlantic Ocean.

The 110 passengers were divided into two groups. One group of 44 people was the more religious. They called themselves the "Saints" and called the other 66 passengers the "Foreigners".

Even before setting their feet on dry land, in order to end the tensions between the two groups, they signed an agreement proclaiming equality among the colonists and the establishment of a *"Civill body Politick"*, governed by *"just and equall Lawes" (sic)*. It was the beginning of the American civil government, born of a compromise between religion and business. The new colonists called themselves the Pilgrims, and their document is known as the Mayflower Compact.

The Plymouth Colony was not the first in the future United States. The first permanent European colony was established by the London Company in Jamestown, Virginia, on May 14, 1607.[18] Captain John Smith was the leader of 105 men, whose mission it was to find gold. From 1607 to 1620, towns were established all along the New England coast.[19]

So among the first Americans, there were those who came to the New World to find riches, and others who sought religious freedom. Historically, these two motivations have always been present in the United States. Later, many American colonists, anxious to preserve freedom of religion, revolted against British rule, especially in Congregationalist New England, when the royal power attempted to establish the Anglican Church as the state religion.

This is why, after the War of Independence against Great Britain, from 1776 to 1783, the leaders of the new nation chose to establish a lay republic. The Preamble to the 1787 United States Constitution states clearly that the new constitution promotes secular political objectives: *"We, the people of the United States, in order to form a more perfect Union, establish justice, insure domestic tranquillity, provide for the common defense, promote the general welfare, and secure the blessings of liberty to ourselves and our posterity, do ordain and establish this Constitution for the United States of America."*

Unlike the constitutions of some other countries, the U.S. Constitution makes no reference to a deity. Neighboring Canada, for example, makes a direct reference to God, declaring that its constitution is based upon *"the supremacy of God and the rule of law"*. The United States Constitution is much closer to the French Constitution, which expressly defines France as a secular nation:

*"France is an indivisible, secular, democratic, and social Republic, assuring equality before the law of all citizens without distinction of origin, race, or religion, and respecting all beliefs."*

The two constitutions, both the American and the French, derive their inspiration from the same democratic principle of government *"of the people, by the people, and for the people".* They proclaim the same important secular principle that all political power emanates from the consent of the people, and that, consequently, it is not in the government's domain to concern itself with religious matters.

While less explicit than the French Constitution, the United States Constitution implies, at least, the principle of laicity and secularism in its First Amendment, which reads *"Congress shall make no law respecting an establishment of religion, or prohibiting the free exercise thereof."* American courts have interpreted this amendment as an obligation, on the part of the government, not to get involved in churches' activities and not to favor any one religion over another.

Therefore, the Constitution guarantees a certain separation between the state and churches, but not necessarily between the state and religion in general. Even though its northern neighbour, Canada, is a constitutional monarchy whose constitution officially recognizes the supremacy of God and whose head of state is also the head of a church (Church of England), it is paradoxically a country that displays a tradition and a political culture which are decidedly more secular that those of the United States.

Indeed, it is relatively easy for a government to violate even the principle of secularism contained in a constitution, if it does not believe in its validity. Public anticonstitutional initiatives, once implemented, take years to be contested and declared unconstitutional by the courts. And even then, slightly modified versions of the original government projects can be initiated to replace the discarded ones. The protection a constitution provides to citizens is only as good as their government. For instance, the former Soviet Union's Constitution was, in theory and on paper, a model of liberty and freedom. In practice, however, the contrary was true: the state made sure that citizens who wanted to fully exercise their rights and freedoms could not do so.

27

## A religious country

Although the United States is in name a secular republic, it is nonetheless a very religious country. In fact, even though the Constitution is a secular document, the Declaration of Independence (1776) makes a direct reference to a heavenly Creator as the source of the new rights and freedoms that the revolutionaries wished to establish: *"...That all men are created equal; that they are endowed by their Creator with certain inalienable rights..."*. And they signed *"...with a firm reliance on the protection of Divine Providence"*.

Actually, the United States has always been a religious country. In fact, the United States is without a doubt the most religious of the Western countries.[20] Americans exercise in great numbers the freedom of religion guaranteed by the Constitution. And just as the Middle East is swept by the sandstorm of Islamic fundamentalism, the United States is the only country in the West to be swept by a strong current of religious fundamentalism. In fact, the two regions where religious fundamentalism is most widespread are the United States and the more extreme Muslim countries (Iran, Afghanistan, Sudan, etc.). It is a strange coincidence that the more the United States becomes a world economic, political, and military empire, the more its citizens embrace the most extreme religious beliefs.[21]

Just as in some Islamic countries, the United States is facing an increasing threat from non-democratic religious fundamentalism. Indeed, this is a country where many religious fundamentalists *de facto* refuse the separation of Church and State, as outlined in the Constitution, and openly propose that the government become actively involved in promoting religion and religious values, using tax monies paid by the entire citizenry. To them, political power in a democracy does not come from the consent of the people but from an abstract Deity that supposedly establishes theocratically the very foundation of a country's laws.

No U.S. politician would go as far as to openly reject democracy in order to embrace theocracy. Nevertheless, it is very difficult, in contemporary America, to pursue a career in politics without paying at least lip service to the religious bent of the country. In the U.S., politicians of every party are expected to mention God and Jesus in their speeches in a manner that is strangely reminiscent of the mullahs in Iran or in Sudan. Others go further and invoke God's powers in their incantations.

Many U.S. religious fundamentalist groups are actively involved in politics and their tax-exempt status makes their influence most welcomed by some, and much to be feared by others. Recently, George W. Bush and some right-wing Republican candidates have received the favors of this growing political block. As a consequence, both the White House and Congress have sponsored measures to bring religion into public life.[22] Even conservative judges, however, have refused to undermine the Constitution and they have, on numerous occasions, enforced the principle of freedom from religion, as a necessary corollary of the principle of freedom of conscience and of religion.[23]

Today there are more than 220 religious denominations and 2,000 sub-denominations in the United States, grouped into 16 large religious families.[24] There are more than 500,000 churches, temples, and mosques. Religion is a very prosperous entrepreneurial industry. While religious organizations enjoy a tax-exempt status, they possess radio and television stations, seminaries, "universities" and enormous properties.

The industry offers many lucrative careers to those who wish to devote themselves to it. Hypnotist-healers have a heyday. Televangelists claim to talk to God and perform miracles in his name. They extort fabulous sums—completely tax-free—from the most naïve and vulnerable members of society.[25]

The U.S. is undoubtedly the only democratic country where so many television stations are controlled by religious enterprises, many of them highly politicized. Day after day, Bible-thumping and pulpit-pounding preachers devote themselves to squeezing the maximum amount of money from a credulous public. Many televangelists are multimillionaires who own grand domains and ranches. Some of their organizations are truly billion-dollar religious-commercial-political empires.[26]

The most popular and growing denominations are promoters of evangelical Protestantism and Christian fundamentalism.[27] Religious fundamentalism is the counterpart of Islam. Just as Islam tends to ascribe a literal meaning to the words and expressions in the Koran, Protestant fundamentalism in the United States considers that all the stories, metaphors, myths and fables found in the Bible are the word of God and, as such, must be understood literally.

Religious fundamentalism is an anti-modern movement that reaches far back in U.S. history. Many preachers have made a name for themselves by promoting the most abstruse and eccentric Bible passages. In the 19th Century, the Reverends John Nelson Darby and Cyrus Scofield developed evangelical ideas based on a theology of despair. They said everything would go from bad to worse until the final Judgement Day, which would arrive in an apocalyptic end of the world.[28] In the 20th Century, during the 1920's, religious fundamentalism resurfaced with the "social gospel" of Walter Rauschenbusch. Today, television screens and radio offer a plethora of evangelical preachers who compete to see who can be the most alarmist and who will succeed in squeezing the most money out of the terrified masses.[29]

Modern technology has changed the way people work, play, and love. It has changed how people are born, become ill, and die. The new religious movement is a reaction against the intrusion of modern technology upon daily life. Religion becomes an escape, a flight from life's reality, and a way to free oneself from the pressures that technology and a competitive economy impose on people. Collective spirituality makes up for a lack of a private intellectual life. Some churches organize huge revivals that are in fact séances of collective hypnotism. In the past, some have even led to collective suicides.[30]

It is in the South that religion is the most aggressive. It is in the South, also, that economic forces seem to leave the poorly-educated individual on his own. There are hardly any structured labor unions able to stand up and face large industrial corporations. The organizations that are ready and able to welcome the distraught individual are religious organizations.

Nowadays, southern politicians and elected judges defy the U.S. Constitution regarding the separation of Church and State, just as they defied the rest of the country regarding the abolition of slavery or the end of racial segregation.

The American population is much less informed than is generally imagined, especially in the South and the rural Mid-West.[31] Many accept the fantasies and myths that these churches, less and less on the fringe, try to sell them. For instance, there are nearly three times more Americans who believe in the virgin birth of Jesus (83 percent) than in evolution (28 percent), even though biblical scholars regard the legend of a virgin Mary, and of her subsequent assumption, to be very shaky myths. Indeed, as fundamentalist evangelicals replace the less mystical congregations, more and more Americans embrace the legendary narratives in the Bible as being real, even though it is widely regarded that the intent of such legends was to serve as illustrative teaching tools, in an ancient world where most people could not read and could not learn by themselves. Notwithstanding, a staggering 36 percent of Americans believe that the Bible is the word of God and should be taken literally. Many Americans place in a big mysterious blackbox called "God" everything around them they do not understand. For them, religion becomes the ultimate intellectual refuge. It can even become a substitute for education. Everywhere, the more man is small, the more the idea of an omnipotent God is attractive.

Indeed, it's hard to understand, in this age of scientific knowledge, how there can still be people who believe the myth that the Earth was created 4,000 years ago, or that there were men on the Earth who were 80 feet tall, or that others, such as Methuselah, lived to the age of 969 (Genesis 5:27)! That the Earth is stationary and the sun revolves around it (Joshua 10:12-14). That one may sell one's daughter into slavery (Exodus 21:7), or that if a man commits adultery with another man's wife, both the adulterer and the adulteress must be put to death (Leviticus 20:9-11), or that a person who works on the Sabbath should be put to death (Exodus 35:2).

Christian fundamentalists and Muslim fundamentalists have the same distorted and mythic vision of the world. Muslim fundamentalists also set the age of the Earth at 4,000 years, as well as believing that the Kaaba sanctuary in Mecca was built by Adam himself.[32]

The fact that so many Americans believe that religious legends are reality is scary indeed. If the U.S. were a remote Third World country, we could dismiss such ignorance as primitive. But the U.S. is the most heavily-armed country in the world and it could really wreak havoc around the world if it chose to do so.

Nowadays, America may be on the same destructive path that the Islamic world took centuries ago, when the latter dismissed its rich intellectual and scientific traditions to embrace religious obscurantism and fanaticism. Such a fateful move plunged Islamic countries into a cultural, social, political and economic crisis that was so deep that even today, they cannot seem to find ways to extract themselves from it.

Indeed, the resurgence of religious myths and the flirting with irrational ideas in the U.S. has had increasing cultural and political consequences. For one, it has created a chasm between the attitudes of peoples in other democratic countries and what Americans think. For instance, Americans tend to believe that religion and morality go together, while in other democratic countries, where numerous religious wars and massacres took place, such a link is rarely made. Indeed, there are numerous historical examples where the more religious the perpetrators, the more ferocious they were in their murderous undertakings.[33] Thus, while 58 percent of Americans believed that it is necessary to believe in God to be moral, only 13 percent of French people believe so.[34]

Similarly, within the U.S., political attitudes are more and more framed by religious considerations. Ultra-religious Protestants are especially attracted to the Republican Party, even more so since George W. Bush has become its leader, while more moderate Jews and Catholics tend to be more frequently drawn to the Democratic Party. As a result, a deep social schism seems to be brewing in the United States, as more and more uneducated Americans embrace religious fanaticism and enter the political arena. Their aim is to change the U.S. Constitution to make it more religious, or at the very least, name to the Supreme Court judges who do not believe in constitutional neutrality in regard to each individual's fundamental freedom of conscience.[35]

When George W. Bush won the November 2000 presidential election, despite having received fewer popular votes than his adversary, Al Gore, it was observed that tax-free religious organizations played a decisive role in that victory.[36] Indeed, it was a veritable *tour de force* for the Republican Party to attract the poor white vote that traditionally has gone to the Democrats, since Franklin D. Roosevelt and John F. Kennedy, but today, because of religion, goes to the Republicans. The Bush administration has succeeded in granting huge tax reductions to the richest Americans, while at the same time retaining the support of the poorest with the lure of a reactionary religious ideology. This polarization of the vote along religious lines instead of socio-economic status is a new phenomenon.[37]

That is why, once George W. Bush squeaked into the White House, he quickly acted to reward the religious groups that had openly supported him, by creating a system of public subsidies for church-administered charitable organizations.[38]

It is estimated that there is a block of some 40 million people who consider themselves "born again" and who express their religious fundamentalism by voting overwhelmingly Republican. In general, they are passionately against the right of women to safe abortions and also against all forms of gun control, even of the most deadly arms.[39] During the 2000 presidential campaign, for instance, it is estimated that white evangelical voters accounted for about 40 percent of the votes that George W. Bush received. And later, it was observed that the religious right had had an unusual influence on the policies pursued by one of the most religious White Houses in American history.[40]

Is it possible that the United States is falling into the Old World pattern of before the French Revolution, when there existed an unhealthy symbiosis between political power and religion? European kings counted on the religious hierarchy to legitimize their absolute power, and, in turn, the kings rewarded the churches by exempting them from taxes and granting them diverse privileges.

The separation of Church and State brought the greatest advance in civilization in the last three hundred years. Democracy and freedom from state intervention in religious matters are the two underpinnings of such a demarcation. It is nevertheless most ironical that many Europeans chose to migrate to the United States and flee a Europe corrupted by this very mixture of state religion and politics. Nowadays, some American religious groups dream of controlling the government apparatus in order to use it as a tool for their apostolic work.

In 1954, Texas Democratic Senator Lyndon B. Johnson added an amendment to a revenue bill in order to prevent nonprofit organizations from taking advantage of their favorable treatment by the IRS. In accordance with this amendment, any group with a nonprofit, or tax-exempt status according to article 501(c)3 of the tax code, is prohibited from endorsing or opposing candidates, or becomes subject to losing its tax-exempt status. The amendment passed by unanimous consent.

Even though this law is frequently violated without raising objections from the IRS, some religious groups are trying to have it repealed. If they succeed, despite the constitutional requirement of the separation of Church and State, they will have accomplished a tremendous political coup.[41]

After the September 11 attacks, some religious leaders lost no time in recuperating the tragedy to serve their own interests. For these religious extremists, it was secondary that the attack was the work of Islamist terrorists, led by al Qaeda, under Osama bin Laden, in retaliation for the pro-Israeli American Middle East policies. In fact, they proclaimed it was really a manifestation of God's punishment.

Two days after the attacks, two of the country's most visible religious leaders—and closest to the Republican Party— repeated the refrain that Americans had themselves to blame for the calamity. Jerry Falwell, of the Moral Majority, and Pat Robertson, of the 1.2 million-strong ultra-right Christian Coalition, declared on Fox TV that the terrorist attacks were God's punishment for the secular character of U.S. society, *"God continues to lift the curtain and allow the enemies of America to give us probably what we deserve. I really believe that the pagans*

*and the abortionists and the feminists and the gays and the lesbians who are actively trying to make that an alternative lifestyle, the ACLU, People for the American Way all of them who have tried to secularize America. I point the finger in their face and say: 'You helped this happen.' " (Falwell)*
*"Well, I totally concur."* (Robertson)[42] [43]

As for Franklin Graham, the son of the famous preacher Billy Graham, and head of the Southern Baptist Convention (SBC) that his father founded, he thought it wise to distance himself from the religious zeal of the Muslim terrorists. *"The God of Islam is not the same God (as that of Christianity). It's a different God, and I believe it is a very evil and wicked religion."* It seems that one fundamentalism mirrors the other.

### American obsession with the end of the world

The most disturbing phenomenon in the United States in this dawning of the 21st Century is the popularity of end-of-the-world scenarios based on the Bible and propagated by several religious denominations. In true Manichaean style, fundamentalists are persuaded that the world seesaws between Good and Evil, and that only at the end of the world will Good triumph. These groups promote popular works of end-of-the-world fiction that use the biblical vocabulary of the Apocalypse and the battle of Armageddon in the combat between Good and Evil.[44]

Two authors in particular have become rich by publishing religious fiction. Tim LaHaye and Jerry B. Jenkins' series of evangelical novels is called "Left Behind".[45] It is a religious fantasy which, because of its supernatural themes, is the adult equivalent of the children's series "Harry Potter".[46] The plot centers on battles between the Antichrist— sometimes presented as the United Nations Secretary General and his "global peace force", sometimes as a leader of the European Union and head of a new Roman Empire—and the religious heroes who fight the unbelievers. With ten books published so far in the series, selling more than 3 million copies each, one can imagine how many Americans are attracted to end-of-the-world scenarios.

These religious novels contain a strong dose of hate propaganda against the United Nations and against anything resembling a system of international or supranational law, and even against Europe. They hawk the ridiculous notion that the creation of the European Union, the "United States of Europe", and the establishment of the European currency, the euro, are signs that the end of the world is near.[47] And since there is a verse in the Bible that says that those who bless Israel will in turn be blessed, these books develop the idea that for the Bible prophesies to be realized, it is necessary that Israel be strong and victorious. The call thus goes out to fundamentalists and evangelicals to do everything in their power to persuade the U.S. government to defend Israel.[48] Such is the wind of religious folly that blows over the United States today.[49]

Such manifestations of paranoia would be of little consequence if it were not for the fact that, since January 2001, the White House is home to George W. Bush, a man imbued with fanatical evangelical religion. Bush has the capacity to act in a manner espoused by the books of the "Left Behind" series. In what measure are the Bush administration's positions on the United Nations, the International Criminal Court, Israel, or Europe, for example, influenced by the fundamentalist religious convictions of Bush and his advisors? As we will see later, there is certainly reason to be concerned, since this small group of people has access to the biggest stock of nuclear weapons the world has ever seen.

The will to power and the law of the strongest:
the world endangered by American religious fundamentalists

In November 1901, an essay by the famous German philosopher Friedrich Nietzsche (1844-1900) was published posthumously and entitled "The Will to Power".[50] The original title was to be "Beyond Good and Evil", which shows that the problem of the distinction between these two notions is not new.

In this book, Nietzsche explains how the will to power originates in the desire for personal freedom, a ruthless freedom won through battle, conflict, and by crushing others for one's own advantage. George W. Bush's policy of "U.S.A. First" seems to be lifted directly from Nietzsche's essay. One might reflect on the fact that, by their actions, some 20th Century leaders, such as Adolf Hitler and Joseph Stalin, also subscribed to this justification of the "will to power" by any means, with disastrous results for their countries and for humanity.

Under certain economic or political circumstances, the will to power can mutate into the collective will to power of a clan, a class, a caste—of a nation or an empire—or of a religion or an ideology, over all others. Add a religious justification for crushing one's enemies, and you have an infallible recipe for declaring war any time it seems advantageous to do so. Throughout history, the very human institution of religion has encouraged the will to power among its followers and, in so doing, has often been the source of war.[51]

### Triumphalism and paranoia in the United States

It is always a danger when too many people in a country earn their living in the industry of war and in the industry of religion. Today in the United States, these two industries are very prosperous. For one thing, all American industry profits from the 300-400 billion dollars and more that the Pentagon injects into the economy each year. For another, more than anywhere else in the West, tax-exempt American religious organizations are *de facto* political organizations, acting in parallel alongside the mainstream traditional parties.

It has been observed that the United States is fundamentally a violent society, by far the most violent of all democratic countries.[52] Since World War II, it seems continually to need an enemy to remain focused: North Korea, China, the Soviet Union, the communist block countries, Cuba, North Vietnam, Iran, Nicaragua, Grenada, Panama, Afghanistan, Iraq. As soon as peace is declared with one enemy, the United States finds another, so that it seems to be in a perpetual state of war. This is neither an accident, nor a coincidence. Its motto seems to be "Perpetual War for Perpetual Peace".[53]

Perhaps not surprisingly, the disintegration of the Soviet Union into fifteen separate countries, in December 1991, was a nightmare for some. The war industry is a much too important part of the American economy. It needs to create a demand for its products, and to do so, the population must be kept on constant alert.

In his State of the Union address on January 21, 2002, George W. Bush's speechwriter had him divide the world between the good guys and the bad guys. Echoing the words of Ronald Reagan, who had dubbed the Soviet Union "The Evil Empire", Bush identified three countries that form what he called the "Axis of Evil": Iraq, Iran, and North Korea.[54] The French Foreign Minister at the time, Hubert Vedrine, labeled Bush's point of view simplistic and dangerous. Mimicking Bush's terms, the terrorist leader Osama bin Laden named the United States and six other Western countries as members of an "axis of evil" and the targets of attacks by the al Qaeda network.[55]

### Shortcomings of the American political system

One of the main weaknesses of the American political system is that every four or eight years, a new team of managers needs on-the-job training. The fact is that when a new president is elected, it is usually someone from outside the federal government, and, moreover, he proceeds to replace all the top bureaucrats—more than 3,000 of them—with newcomers. In other words, the government is decapitated of its most experienced and knowledgeable people, who, most of the time, are replaced by others who have to begin again at zero. The continuity and coherence of American policies cannot help but suffer, especially in the area of foreign policy.

The best example of this lack of continuity in American foreign policy was the little concern on the part of the new Bush administration regarding international terrorism, when they took over the reins of power in January 2001. Sandy Berger, the National Security Advisor in the Clinton administration, took great pains to brief Bush's new personnel and advise them of the possible necessity of launching a major offensive against the al Qaeda terrorist network. The Clinton White House terrorism specialist, Richard Clarke, had prepared a detailed strategic plan for such an offensive.

The plan's objective was to destabilize the terrorist network, not only in Afghanistan, where recruits were trained, but also in other countries such as Uzbekistan, the Philipines, and Yemen, where al Qaeda was solidly established. It envisioned the deployment of Special Forces in Afghanistan and the granting of substantial military and financial assistance to the Northern Alliance, the main bulwark against the rogue Taliban regime in Kabul. The plan proposed sending an un-manned Predator spy plane over Afghanistan to gather indispensable real-time intelligence on the activities of al Qaeda. There was a note of urgency, since 17 Americans had been killed just a few months previously, on October 12, 2000, in Yemen, when terrorists bombed the U.S.S. Cole.[56]

But the new Bush administration had other priorities. Unbelievably, the planned attack against Osama bin Laden's al Qaeda network was shelved. It was not looked at again until the end of April 2001. Four long months later, after the bureaucrats were sufficiently familiar with the plan to present it to the Bush administration on September 4, 2001, it was too late. Undisturbed, al Qaeda had been able to develop its own perverse plan for September 11.[57] The American people paid dearly the inexperience of the Bush administration, let alone the negligence of the previous Clinton administration in fighting Islamist terrorism.[58]

The only true continuity in the U.S. government is the undue clout of the political lobbies, which strongly influence, if not outright control, the government, be it Democratic or Republican.[59]

# 4

# POLITICS AND RELIGION IN THE USA

*"I believe every American should have a religious faith, and I don't care what it is."*
Dwight D. EISENHOWER (1890-1969)

*"A people can be immersed in religion, but religion must never become an affair of state."*
Leo BAECK (German rabbi, 1873-1956)

*"I think that on balance the moral influence of religion has been awful. With or without religion, good people can behave well and bad people can do evil; but for good people to do evil—that takes religion."*
Steven WEINBERG, Nobel Laureate, Physics
("Facing Up", Harvard University Press, 2001)

In 1966, the film "The Russians Are Coming, The Russians Are Coming" captured the imagination of the American public. Based on a novel by Nathaniel Benchley, it told the story of a Russian submarine that was shipwrecked on a New England beach. When word got around that the Russians had invaded a sleepy seaside village, a wind of panic swept the population and its leaders.

It was the heyday of the Cold War, and the country was obsessed with the possibility—more imagined than real—of an armed invasion by the nasty Russian communists. Sometimes, who knows why, a collective psychosis can grab a people and fire their imagination.

In 2002, many Americans' greatest fear was about the battle against Satan. Carolyn Risher, the mayor of Inglis, a little town north of Tampa, made headlines when she issued a municipal proclamation officially banning the Devil from her town.[60] When she was asked why she thought it was necessary for her to use her position as mayor to declare war on Satan, she said that four months earlier, when she was meditating alone in her kitchen, it was God himself who told her to do it.[61] God had dictated the words to her—in English—exactly as she had them inscribed in the municipal proclamation. Of course it isn't the first time that someone hears voices in their head and attributes them to a privileged intervention from extraterrestrial forces.

Nor was it the first time that a state or municipal government concerned itself with theological matters. There is a strong political-religious current that incites governments, now to adopt the Ten Commandments, now to produce license plates reading "God Save America", and even to declare an official "National Day of Prayer".

In 1952, during the Korean War, with Senator Joe MacCarthy's Committee on Un-American Activities holding sway, politicians sought to emphasize the distinction between Americans and communists. It seems that it wasn't democracy or capitalism, but religion; Americans worshiped God, while communists were atheists. On April 17, 1952, President Harry S. Truman approved Public Law 324, which read, *"Resolved by the Senate and House of Representatives of the United States of America in Congress assembled, that the President shall set aside and proclaim a suitable day each year, other than a Sunday, as a national Day of Prayer, on which the people of the United States may turn to God in prayer and meditation at churches, in groups, and as individuals."*

In 1954, with the Cold War against the Soviet Union and other communist countries in full swing, the Catholic Knights of Columbus lobbied Congress to modify the Pledge of Allegiance by adding a direct reference to God. Virtually all schoolchildren begin their morning classes by reciting the pledge, which was composed in 1892, by Francis Bellamy (1855-1931), a socialist. In case one does not remember it, it goes like this: *"I pledge allegiance to the flag of the United States of America, and to the republic for which it stands, one nation, indivisible, with liberty and justice for all."* This version was adopted by Congress in 1942.

During the fifties, however, the civic-minded patriotic oath was not deemed to be religious enough for the national leaders. The Republican administration of Dwight D. Eisenhower and Congress tacked on after the "one nation" just two words, "under God", adding a state prayer to a pledge of patriotic loyalty.[62] Nowadays, there are 35 states that require schools to include recitation of this religious version of the Pledge of Allegiance, while at least 10 others have a pledge for their state flag.[63]

In retrospect, one could say that during the 50's, at the time the U.S. was becoming an economic and military superpower, it came close to changing from a secular republic into a religious one. The fear of communism was at its peak, and politicians seemed to be trying to outbid each other by inserting explicit mentions of religion in public matters. Two years after the modification of the Pledge of Allegiance, on July 30, 1956, and again at the instigation of the Knights of Columbus, Congress adopted the words "In God We Trust" as the official motto of the United States. The slogan had been inscribed on all coins and paper money since being adopted by congressional resolution in 1955.

Originally, the motto "In God We Trust" was inscribed on a coin in 1864, following a campaign by a Baptist preacher, Mark R. Watkinson. The phrase was used progressively, until in 1938, it was inscribed on almost all coins, but not on paper money. The 1955 resolution was to insure that all forms of currency bear the formula.

Before this time, the favorite official motto was the Latin phrase "E Pluribus Unum"—"Out of Many, One"—which refers to the great geographical, racial, and cultural diversity of the U.S. population, diversity that is united in allegiance to one country. It also refers to the 13 original colonies that became states in the larger federation. It is a secular, political motto, lacking in religious overtones. "E Pluribus Unum" was chosen by a committee of the writers of the Constitution—Jefferson, Franklin, and Adams. In practice, it has now been replaced by the more religious motto "In God We Trust".

Another more recent example, among others, of the mixing of politics and religion, is that of the Arizona sculptor who started a movement after 9-11, to enroll 28 million Americans—10% of the population—to pray each day for George W. Bush.[64] One sometimes has the impression that those who have money and power, which is surely the case in the U.S., insist that their good fortune receive the *imprimatur* of a supernatural power.

The most unsettling factor in this mixture of religion and politics is the arrival of George W. Bush, a Texas Republican known for his religious pronouncements, and elected in November 2000 as a minority president, with fewer popular votes than his Democratic rival, Al Gore. Reputed to be relatively lacking in intellectual sophistication, Bush attempts to disguise his shortcomings by adopting the style of a televangelist.[65]

It is the first time in U.S. history that the White House has been occupied by a "born-again Christian", the most fundamentalist and extremist of Protestants.[66] Since his close-call election, George W. Bush has multiplied his sermonizing speeches and public prayers. An example of this was on March 30, 2002, when he declared in a radio broadcast, *"We feel our reliance on the Creator who made us. We place our sorrows and cares before Him, seeking God's mercy. We ask forgiveness for our failures, seeking the renewal He can bring"*.

And he continued: *"Faith brings confidence that failure is never final, and suffering is temporary, and the pains of the earth will be overcome. We can be confident, too, that evil may be present and it may be strong, but it will not prevail".*[67]

And as if to underline the fact that he believes himself mandated by God to wage war, he added, *"In this season, we are assured that history is of moral design. Justice and cruelty have always been at war, and God is not neutral between them. His purposes are often defied, but never defeated."*[68]

In his January 28, 2003 State of the Union address, George W. Bush went even further in his talk of Armageddon and, sounding like an American Ayatollah, he hinted that God may have chosen him for a special mission, *"...But what if God has been holding his peace, waiting for the right man and the right nation and the right moment to act for Him and cleanse history of*

*Evil?"*[69] Does George W. Bush really believe that God has chosen him to lead the U.S. in a worldwide war against "Evil"?

This is not the first time that some people go to war in the belief that they have God on their side. During World War I, German soldiers wore on the buckle of their belt the following motto, *"If God is with us, who will be against us?"*

George W. Bush is incapable of expressing himself publicly without making religious references. Another opportunity was given him on February 1, 2003, when disaster struck the space shuttle *Columbia* that disintegrated upon re-entry into the atmosphere. Bush, prompted by his theologian speechwriter, uttered the following words: *"The Columbia is lost. The same Creator who names the stars also knows the names of the seven souls we mourn today. The crew of the shuttle Columbia did not return safely to Earth but we can pray they are safely home."*[70]

Such religious messages from a head of state resemble and even surpass what comes out of the theocracy in Iran and what came out of the ancient Taliban Afghanistan, before it was deposed. Other than George W. Bush, there is no head of state of a democratic country[71], including Great Britain where there is a state religion, who prays in public and claims to be acting in the name of God in his official duties.[72]

For people who are not Americans, hearing U.S. politicians close their speeches with the inevitable patriotic cry "God bless America" is quite startling. As a Belgian bishop remarked, such an incantation at the end of a political or military speech could really mean *"God bless all of us, but not the others"*. Godfried Danneels, Archbishop of Malines-Bruxelles, noted that *"it is not the first time in history that God has been recruited to favor one side, but it must be understood that this should not be done."*[73]

But it is done in the United States. Similarly, in the U.S., many people do not say "I was lucky", when fortuitous events go their way; rather, they would say "I've been blessed". Problems could arise, however, when people begin believing their own slogans. U.S. President George W. Bush goes even further; he begins his war council meetings with a prayer. Since decisions could be made at these conclaves to bomb thousands of people, one blanches at the thought that a president believes himself to be anointed by God to wage war.[74] In the case of Bush, known for his jingoism, the mixture of religion and flagrant nationalism makes one ponder. As reported by Bob Woodward, the *Washington Post's* veteran journalist, George W. Bush doesn't hesitate to claim openly that he considers the United States to be above international law.

In fact, during a meeting of his war council, on September 15, 2001, George W. Bush is said to have declared the following, concerning the need for America to wage war against terrorism whatever others might say: *"At some point, we may be the only ones left. That's okay with me. We are America."[75]* Secretary of State Colin Powell is said to have remarked that talking big was no substitute for policy.

Mr. Bush's religion strongly influences his international policies. It is said that he feels more comfortable with religious people than with nonbelievers. His close ties with U.K. Tony Blair can be explained partly by the fact that Blair is, as one British columnist put it, *"the most overtly pious leader since Gladstone"*. Bush once astonished the Prime minister of Turkey, a Muslim, by saying: *"You believe in the Almighty, and I believe in the Almighty. That's why we'll be great partners."[76]* He even organizes Bible studies in the White House which everybody is expected to attend.[77]

It is surprising that a country founded by people who wanted to escape the tyranny of the state religions which prevailed in 17th and 18th Century Europe, today has leaders who would like to establish Evangelical Christianity as some sort of a state religion. In the past, empires called on the gods to confirm their supremacy. That is the reason we observe an historical link between organized religions, military conquests and wars.[78] That the United States, the world's only military superpower at the beginning of the 21st Century, seeks the same consecration is another indication that humanity's progress is very slow indeed. What is astonishing is that the U.S. Constitution formally forbids the government from taking a position on religious matters, nor may it declare what is good or bad according to a religious interpretation.[79]

What is the most disturbing for world stability is the American president's double penchant for things religious and for things military. The two together are dynamite. In a speech on April 8, 2002, in Knoxville, Tennessee, George W. Bush voiced his own hubristic vision of the relationship between his religious morality and American military power, *"The best way to fight evil is to do some good. Let me qualify that—the best way to fight evil at home is to do some good. The best way to fight them abroad is to unleash the military."*

Around the same time, Bush's advisors released a political document announcing that the Administration was considering modifying the U.S. policy regarding the future use of nuclear weapons. Under certain circumstances, the old policy of deterrence or dissuasion, which stipulated that the U.S. would not be the first to use nuclear arms, could be replaced by the unilateral use of nuclear weapons.

Thus, in 2003, the Bush Administration announced to an incredulous world that it was getting into the business of producing "mini-nukes" bombs, within its new strategy of military "pre-emptive" attacks. These "mini-nukes" would generate an energy lower than 1 kiloton (the bomb launched upon Hiroshima in 1945 had 18 kilotons of energy), and would be different than the larger nuclear bombs, such as the B53, B61 and B83, which are much more powerful.[80] A *New York Times* editorial found utterly "scary" that the Bush-Cheney-Rumsfeld team in Washington could be planning the use of tactical nuclear weapons against North Korea, risking the possible onset of a new Korean War in Asia.[81]

People with a sectarian and ultra-religious morality, especially if they are in power, are at risk of showing great cruelty towards those who do not think as they do. This is all the more possible if the others are of a different color, a different ethnicity, or a different religion. It is doubtful that Harry S. Truman, in 1945, would have dropped nuclear bombs on European cities, but he did bomb Asian cities.[82] One has to hope that the terrible precedent of 1945 never comes back to haunt the United States in the future.

47

## War as an entertaining sport

The U.S. is so often involved in armed conflicts, war is beginning to be seen as a sports event. For many Americans, starting with George W. Bush, the former owner of a baseball team, a war is a bit like a baseball or football game; the aim of the game is simply to be the strongest and to win. In doing so, the people are entertained and the media are occupied with subject matter to fill their pages and airtime. In the U.S., war is part of the entertainment industry.

An analogy can also be drawn between bloody war and virtual video games. There is a plethora of warlike video games that children play on their computer, games where the good guys win over the bad guys by exacting justice themselves through violence. Do video games make war and violence easier and more acceptable? Hollywood also does its part in promoting and banalizing violence. In the 25 most popular films of all times, there are more than nine billion deaths![83] Are modern electronic wars just a transposition in real time of movies and electronic video war games?

The media also played a central role in the country's war psychosis before the onset of the 2003 war against Iraq. In December of 2002, for example, on the eve of the war, some neo-conservative media gave "pre-game shows". They openly discussed how American forces could or should use anti-personnel mines to secure certain Iraqi territories, or how the threat of using tactical nuclear arms could dissuade Iraq from using arms of mass destruction. They didn't seem to be preoccupied by the fact that the victims of land mines are overwhelmingly civilians, and especially children. As for nuclear weapons, it is too easily forgotten that the U.S. remains to this day the only country that has used them to destroy civilian populations. Morality doesn't seem to count for some people when it comes to the game of war.[84]

## Religion in the classroom

In Tennessee, in 1925, John Scopes was found guilty of teaching Charles Darwin's theory of the evolution of species. At the end of the famous 15-day "Scopes Monkey Trial", he was fined $100. His condemnation confirmed the constitutionality of the Butler Law, which expressly forbid the teaching of evolution in Tennessee schools. Similar laws existed in other states: Oklahoma, Florida, Mississippi, North Carolina, and Kentucky. It was not until 42 years later, in 1967, that the Butler Law was repealed.

Despite the constitutional separation of Church and State, however, American fundamentalist groups have never given up their aim of requiring that the myth of biblical creationism be taught in schools. Creationism is the belief that all forms of life on Earth were created in their present form, in six days, by a divine power. However, scientific research establishes the first appearance of life on Earth at some 3.1 billion years ago, in the form of micro-organisms such as algae and bacteria.

Fundamentalists advance the idea that the Earth was created by God 4,000 or 5,000 years ago, while scientific data put the event at around 4.5 billion years ago.[85] Science points to the randomness of climate change, mutations, and environmental catastrophes as the crucial factors in the appearance and evolution of life on this planet.

The newest tactic of extremist religious groups is to claim that creationism has scientific value. They add the word "science" to creationism, just as they add the title "university" to their seminaries, in order to confound legislators and judges as to their true intentions. They now call religious ideas about creation "intelligent design theory", saying that only a god could create a process that can produce complex organs as, for example, the eyes of humans and animals.[86]

From a logical point of view, however, the following two propositions are equivalent: a) Life on Earth is so advanced that it must have been created by a divine being; b) life on Earth is so advanced that it must have been created by a race of super-intelligent extraterrestrial creatures. Since no one can provide any evidence to support one or the other proposition, both are but pure speculation, without scientific merit.

This doesn't prevent the vast majority of Americans from agreeing with the religious point of view. In fact, most Americans still believe either in a divinely inspired biology, or at least that alternative religious explanations to the concept of evolution and the natural selection of species through adaptation should be a part of the program of studies in their children's schools.

Since they are always seeking votes, from time to time politicians follow the anti-scientific trend by adopting laws that legalize the teaching of religious interpretations of biology. Usually the courts declare such laws unconstitutional.[87] Other laws of the same stripe replace them, in America's never-ending debate on the origin of the Universe.[88]

## American religious propaganda

In the mid-80's, under the Reagan Administration, policy makers thought they had found a magic formula for promoting American interests against the Soviet Union. During the Soviet occupation of Afghanistan, the U.S. furnished Islamic religious schools with free books promoting Islamic militantism—and also to some extent to Pakistani schools during the rule of General Zia—with the aim of encouraging a *jihad* (holy war) against the Russian atheists. The plan of the U.S. Agency for International Development was to provide religious Afghan schools, "madrassas" or Koranic schools, with textbooks written in a language glorifying Islamic law, *jihad*, and the war against infidels, that is, Soviet Communists.

In other words, it was a matter of distributing free books which were actually little catechisms for the perfect Islamist terrorist, ready to sacrifice himself to kill the enemy. Madrassas are, in fact, religious schools that are privileged sites for indoctrination and recruitment of Muslim terrorists. The American catechism for Islamist terrorists contained not only exhortations to holy war, but also many drawings showing soldiers, guns, bullets, grenades, tanks, missiles and antipersonnel mines.

From 1984 to 1994, the "religious aid" program offered a budget of $51 million to the University of Nebraska at Omaha and its Center for Afghan Studies, for the development of textbooks that glorified war and weapons. The militaro-religious manuals were written in Dari and Pashtu, the two dominant languages of Afghanistan and part of Pakistan. These little books became very popular with the Afghan Islamic clergy, and, once in power in 1996, the Talibans adopted them as instruction manuals in militant Islam.

During his weekly radio address on March 16, 2002, George W. Bush announced that his administration would follow in the footsteps of the Reagan administration and that USAID was preparing to distribute 10 million new manuals in Afghanistan. The University of Nebraska-Omaha received $6.5 million to produce a new version. Observers noted, however, that the new propaganda manuals were still promoting Islamic fervor and contained verses from the Koran and other religious teachings related to the Islamic religion.

That didn't prevent Bush from declaring that the new textbooks would teach Afghan children respect for human dignity instead of fanaticism and intolerance.[89] As for the old terrorist manuals, USAID began editing out the passages that were too clearly promoting violence and assassination.

And so, even though the Constitution expressly forbids the government from promoting a religion, and even more from spending money to do so, from 1984 to 1992, the administration of Ronald Reagan and George H. Bush spent millions of dollars promoting Islam and terrorism in Afghanistan and in the adjoining areas of Pakistan. Observers agree that religious fundamentalism was effectively inexistent in Afghanistan and Pakistan before the U.S. government decided to finance them and to furnish ideological and military arms to combat the Soviets.[90]

On September 11, 2001, this public "investment" was repaid with interest when 19 Islamist terrorists—several of them trained in Afghanistan—committed their attacks on American soil, killing thousands of Americans.[91] What is all the more surprising is the insistence of George W. Bush to pursue the same disastrous adventure of such simplistic, antidemocratic religious propaganda in Third World countries.

A new U.S. international Inquisition

In 1998, under President Bill Clinton, the U.S. acquired a new tool to interfere in other countries' affairs: The International

Religious Freedom Act. The new law was introduced by Senator Joseph Lieberman (D-CT) and Senator Don Nickles (R-OK) and was approved by the U.S. Senate by a 98-0 vote. The law was the direct result of the lobbying of the U.S. Congress by many faith-based U.S. organizations during the 1980's and 1990's.

The stated purpose of The International Religious Freedom Act was to identify a wide range of diplomatic and economic tools that the U.S. government might utilize to encourage freedom of religion and conscience throughout the world. In reality, as is often the case in political matters, the "Religious Freedom" Act is really a misnomer. It could easily have been called the "Freedom for America to impose its religion and politics on other countries" Act.

An Office was subsequently created and mandated by the International Religious Freedom Act: The Office of International Religious Freedom, located in the Bureau for Democracy, Human Rights, and Labor of the U.S. State Department (N.B., during the Middle Ages, the Catholic Inquisition was called the "Holy Office").[92] It is headed by an Ambassador at Large for International Religious Freedom and is responsible for issuing an Annual Report on the status of religious freedom and persecution in all foreign countries by September of each year.[93] On the basis of this report, the State Department designates "countries of particular concern" for their "systematic, ongoing and egregious" violations of religious liberty. These countries are then subject to punishing actions, including economic sanctions, by the United States.

It is easy to see how this new American religious messianism could become a new religious McCarthyism. It could become a censorship tool in the government's hands that could taint the entire American foreign policy. The U.S. government could not only sponsor religious freedom and religious tolerance within its borders and abroad, but could embark upon the business of actively promoting religion and violating other countries' sovereignty. A U.S. Religious Chief Inquisitor would roam the world to make sure that American religious orthodoxy is followed in the American way. Religion or the lack of religion could become a political tool to denounce, condemn and attack other countries, outside the framework of international law, and outside the United Nations.

Freedom of religion has a corollary and it is freedom from religion, because each individual has the fundamental right of conscience. Imposing religion is the exact opposite of freedom.[94] It is ideologically totalitarian in nature, as it has been amply demonstrated throughout history. If, under the cover of freedom of religion, the U.S. government were to become a public promoter of religion around the world, it would be doing so in violation of the U.S. Constitution. No public money should ever be used to promote religion.

Already, the U.S. government has denounced countries such as Germany, France and Greece, as being not religious enough, because they don't let some religious cults have complete liberty of action within their borders. A case in point is the U.S.-based and commercially-oriented Church of Scientology, a cult founded in 1954 by U.S. science fiction writer L. Ron Hubbard. In Belgium, France, Ireland, Italy, Luxembourg, Spain, Israel, Mexico and the United Kingdom, the sect pays taxes as a commercial enterprise.[95]

What the U.S. government wishes is to be able to prevent democratic governments in Europe and elsewhere from protecting their countries against foreign invasion by U.S. commercial organizations disguised as religious organizations. All these countries have constitutions that protect freedom of religion and of conscience and do not need a foreign power to teach them lessons on the means to preserve freedom and liberty. In fact, the democratic country which nowadays has the most laws on its books restraining freedom and liberty is the United States of America, with its Patriot Act and similar legislation that suspend the right of Habeas Corpus and even allow the establishment of concentration camps.[96]

## U.S. and worldwide fight against AIDS

In the matter of birth control in poor and over-populated countries, or the promotion of sex education, or the emancipation of women, the religiosity of the U.S. government sometimes leads it to associate with the most repressive regimes. The United

Nations exerts considerable effort in helping the poorest countries control their population explosion and eliminating sexually transmitted diseases such as AIDS. This is a major problem in many poor countries, and especially in sub-Sahara African countries, which are among the world's poorest.

The AIDS epidemic has become an important factor in Third World poverty. According to the United Nations Program on VIH/AIDS (UNAids) and the World Health Organization (WHO), in 2002, there were some 42 million people living with AIDS, while 3 million people die annually from the disease.

Sub-Sahara Africa is especially affected, since it accounted for 70% of the total number of cases, or 29.4 million people. What is more, that region registers 3.5 million more cases each year, or 70% of all new cases in the world. This sexually transmitted disease requires an even more sustained effort to contain the epidemic and reverse its spread.

However, one of the fiercest adversaries of this effort is the ultra-conservative U.S. government, which doesn't hesitate under the circumstances to ally itself with Islamic fundamentalist countries, in order to counter the U.N. efforts. This is another example of the pernicious influence of certain religious fundamentalist groups on American foreign policy.

Thus, during a United Nations summit on children, held in New York in May of 2002, the Bush administration sent the Secretary of Health, Tommy Thompson, to deliver the following message: the fight against AIDS in poor countries must first encourage abstinence and chastity, whether within or outside marriage. Moreover, the United States will not approve any United Nations program that encourages abortion or birth control. The U.S. will not contribute, in any way, to a fight that sees overpopulation as a cause of poverty in underdeveloped countries.

The Bush administration followed through on its threat. On July 22, 2002, it announced that it would no longer make its annual contribution of $34 million to the United Nations Population Fund.[97] In matters of family planning, sex education, and the emancipation of women, it is obvious that the U.S. government is more a part of the problem than the solution.

Paradoxically, it is private American citizens who contribute the most, out of their own personal fortunes, to finance international programs of sex education and birth control. Two of the biggest philanthropists are Bill Gates (Microsoft) and Ted Turner (CNN). These two contributors have given hundreds of millions of dollars to the fight against overpopulation and sexually transmitted diseases in poor countries. It is clear that the U.S. shows two faces to the world in the matter of foreign aid and social policies—that of a Puritan government, prisoner of its prudish electorate, and that of private donors with an open and generous spirit.[98]

# 5

# THE POLITICAL GAME IN THE USA

*"Beware the leader who bangs the drums of war in order to whip the citizenry into a patriotic fervor, for patriotism is indeed a double-edged sword. It both emboldens the blood, just as it narrows the mind. And when the drums of war have reached a fever pitch and the blood boils with hate and the mind has closed, the leader will have no need in seizing the rights of the citizenry. Rather, the citizenry, infused with fear and blinded by patriotism, will offer up all of their rights unto the leader and gladly so. How do I know? For this is what I have done. And I am Caesar."*
Julius CAESAR (101-44 B.C.)

*"With God, all things are possible."*
OHIO state motto

*"Politics is the art of manipulating people."*
*Paul VALÉRY (1871-1945)*

In December of 1998, advisors to the Governor of Texas were preoccupied by the lack of international experience of the man who aspired to become president. Although a half-century old, George W. Bush had never traveled outside the United States, except for visits to Mexican towns across the Texas-Mexico border.

This was in stark contrast to his father, George H. Bush, who became president in 1988, bringing a vast experience in international affairs to the White House. George Sr. had been U.S. Ambassador to the United Nations and Director of the C.I.A. before becoming Vice-President to Ronald Reagan from 1981 to 1988. He never considered himself to be a prisoner of Israel, and when the government of Yizhak Shamir tried to railroad him, he didn't hesitate to retaliate.

In 1992, for example, when the Israeli government threatened to sabotage the Madrid peace process, Bush threatened to suspend the guarantee of $10 billion that the U.S. had promised for the transfer of Russian settlers to Israeli installations in the Palestinian occupied territories. Later, his son, George W. Bush, claimed that his father's firm stand had been a political mistake that cost him his re-election in 1992, by taking away pro-Israel votes. For Bush Jr., it seems that was a mistake not to make again.

George W. Bush could capitalize on the name of his father, but before he arrived in Washington, he was basically ignorant of major world issues. In order to polish his image in the media, his advisors organized a trip to Israel. In December of 1998, Bush was invited by Ariel Sharon to tour the country. Sharon was Minister of Foreign Affairs at the time, but he soon became the leader of the Likud Party and then Prime Minister.

Sharon gave Bush the use of a helicopter to give him a good view of the country. The visit to the holy sites stimulated his religious fervor. Bush tells in his autobiography how impressed he was to see the golden roofs of Jerusalem.[99] Once back home, the presidential candidate was prepared to deliver a speech in front of the powerful super-lobby, the American Israel Public Affairs Committee (AIPAC), where he spoke sympathetically, from personal knowledge, of Israel's narrow territorial limits.[100]

A powerful lobby

In February of 1998, a small group of 40 well-known people formed a cabal, under the direction of Richard N. Perle, an extreme right-wing and absolutist ideologue who presides over the obscure but influential Defense Policy Board. This is a coterie of quasi-official people that usually meets in a room adjacent to the Secretary of Defense's office and advises the latter on defense policy.[101] Perle is often dubbed "The Prince of Darkness" of American foreign policy, sort of an American Rasputin, because of his corrosive influence on the U.S. government. Perle is also reported to be an advisor to the Global Crossing company[102] and some arms dealers in their relations with the Pentagon.[103] In 1998, the group signed an open letter to Bill Clinton, urging him to do everything possible to overthrow the Iraqi regime of Saddam Hussein.

The cabal was publicly supported by Henry Kissinger, former Secretary of State for Richard Nixon and Gerald Ford from 1969 to 1976. Among its members were the former Secretaries of Defense Caspar Weinberger, Frank Carlucci and Donald H. Rumsfeld, and James Woolsey, the former head of the C.I.A., as well as important future undersecretaries such as Paul D. Wolfowitz (Defense), a former dean of the Paul H. Nitze School of Advanced International Studies at John Hopkins University and a pro-Israel hawk, Douglas Feith (Defense), Richard Armitage (State Department), John Bolton (State Department), Paula Dobriansky (State Department), Elliott Abrams (National Security Council), Robert Zoellick (Trade representative), and politicians such as Stephen Solarz (New York), etc.[104] Six months later, President Clinton signed a bill into law called the "Iraq Liberation Act", along with a budget of $97 million destined to aid the Iraqi opposition.

It is important to mention that the leader of the cabal, Richard N. Perle, a Pentagon advisor, and Douglas Feith, one of his former assistants and a future under Secretary of Defense for policy under Donald H. Rumsfeld and Paul Wolfowitz, had written an obscure report, in 1996, entitled "A Clean Break: A New Strategy for Securing the Realm." The 1996 report had been prepared by a Study Group on "A New Israeli Strategy Toward 2000", carried out at the Institute for Advanced Strategic and Political Studies of Washington D.C. and Jerusalem, a think-tank with close ties to the Israeli government.[105]

The group's main purpose was to devise a strategy on how Israel could "transcend" its problems with the Palestinians. Their conclusion was that Israel should attempt to persuade the United States government to change the "balance of power" in the Middle East, and in order to do that, replace Saddam Hussein with a puppet of its own.[106] Indeed, in order to change Israel's strategic position in the Middle East, the U.S. would have to conquer and occupy Iraq, weaken Syria and Iran, and put pressure on states such as Saudi Arabia and Kuwait to curb their support of Palestinian militant organizations, such as Hamas and Islamic

Jihad. Iraq was only the "tactical pivot" within a larger strategy to stabilize the Middle East and to secure American hegemony over the oil producing countries in that region. The two goals could be attained at once. The report was precise in its outline:

*"Israel can shape its strategic environment, in cooperation with Turkey and Jordan, by weakening, containing, and even rolling back Syria. This effort can focus on removing Saddam Hussein from power in Iraq — an important Israeli strategic objective in its own right — as a means of foiling Syria's regional ambitions."*[107]

We have some idea on how successful the group was when one considers the rationale offered officially for the military invasion of Iraq by the National Security Advisor to the President, Ms. Condoleezza Rice, six years later, when she said on October 8, 2003, in a speech before the Chicago Council on Foreign Relations:

*"Terrorists in the Palestinian territories have lost the patronage of Saddam Hussein. Other regimes in the region have been clear — given clear warning that support for terror cannot be tolerated. Without this outside support for terrorism, Palestinians who are working for reform and long for democracy will, over the long term, be strengthened and encouraged."*[108]

For Charles Krauthammer, a member of the cabal in the media, writing in *Time* magazine, the "mission" of the U.S. armies in the Middle East should be—no more, no less—than to bring about the "reformation and reconstruction of an alien culture" and to proceed with the reconstruction of the entire 22 Arab states in the region.[109] Such were the winds of an awesome arrogance and a greatly inflated sense of self-importance blowing in certain corners of American society in the fateful year of 2003. Indeed, this was not without echoing the justification for British imperialism in the 19th Century, as a newspaper had put it, *"The duty of the white man is to conquer and control, probably for a couple of centuries, all the dark people of the world, not for his own good, but for theirs."*[110]

The same group is responsible for introducing "the theory of preemption" in the U.S. political vocabulary.[111] In 1996, its members were proposing that the Israeli government abandon the peace process as a strategy for peace with the Palestinians and adopt a more aggressive strategy that went further than retaliation alone. They proposed that the Israeli government *"change the nature of its relations with the Palestinians, including upholding the right of hot pursuit for self defense into all Palestinian areas and nurturing alternatives to Arafat's exclusive grip on Palestinian society."* In other words, the principle of preemption had to replace the principle of retaliation.

The same new perspective on peace and security, based on military preemption, would find its way, in 2000, into a special report for the *Project for the New American Century,* written by Paul Wolfowitz and Lewis "Scooter" Libby, but this time for the federal government.

Initially, the newly created cabal was devised to implement the 1996 strategy by pressuring the Clinton administration to go along with it. The Clinton administration went only halfway, without committing itself to any military action.

However, when George W. Bush squeezed into power, in 2000, with the help of the U.S. Supreme Court and of his brother Jeb, governor of Florida, the same cabal, using even more pressure, was more successful. It took it upon itself to persuade the new Republican administration that the United States must eliminate the government of Saddam Hussein, presented as a threat to the stability of international oil markets, but also an even greater military threat to Israel.[112]

Its avowed goal was to divert the war against international terrorism and the al Qaeda network, and turn it towards Iraq, its armaments and its oil. Their ultimate goal was to make sure that Israeli foreign policy became U.S. foreign policy.[113] It was an historic opportunity to kill two birds with one stone and to attack a major problem before, they feared, it could become worse.[114]

The trick to draw George W. Bush's attention was to link oil supply security to Saddam Hussein. This was not difficult. The economic justification for the U.S. government's interest in Middle East oil was already present. Indeed, many experts believe that world petroleum output will peak between 2010 and 2020, when half of all exploitable reserves will have been depleted. At that time, the price of the black gold will skyrocket, feeding a worldwide inflation and dislocating industrialized economies. In such a context, if several Middle East countries fell under the domination of fundamentalist and Islamic movements and became extremist religious states, hostile to the West, along the lines of Iran, the resulting world oil crisis could be extremely severe.[115]

That is why, as soon as he took power, it did not take much to persuade George W. Bush that a change of regime in Iraq should be the centerpiece of his foreign policy. However, in so doing, and especially when he refused to impose an agreement in the Palestinian-Israeli conflict, he undermined the efforts of his own government in its war against terrorism aimed at the United States. By threatening to attack an Arab country without visible provocation, instead of discouraging terrorism, the Bush administration actually encouraged Islamist terrorism against the U.S. Was the risk worth it? For the Perle-led super-lobby, it obviously was. It was even necessary: Iraq had to be completely disarmed and the Middle East had to be transformed into a huge oil-producing colony. The two objectives were interrelated.

### The media offensive

Senator Joe Lieberman, an Orthodox Jewish Senator from Connecticut, led the charge of the "Likudniks" in Congress. Lieberman distinguished himself by his firm attitude in exhorting the Congress to give President Bush the necessary authority to act in order to chase Saddam Hussein from power. Interviewed on Fox News, he opined that the U.S. had the strength to get Saddam out and to implement a plan to replace him with a unified Iraqi government. He urged Congress to give President Bush the authority to do *"what American commanders-in-chief are elected for"*.[116]

Also on Fox News, Shimon Peres, the Israeli Minister of Foreign Affairs, demonized Saddam Hussein, which was hardly difficult, and compared Iraq to Nazi Germany, which was a gross exaggeration. The aim was to condition the American public, shaken by the attacks of September 11, to accept that the United States become the aggressor in the Middle East. And for this,

Saddam Hussein had to be presented as the symbol of terror to Americans.

According to Scott Ritter, former head of the United Nations weapons inspection team in Iraq, the claim that it was necessary to attack Iraq because it threatened the security of the United States was a subterfuge.[117] Iraq—poor and isolated—did not threaten the U.S., nor its allies, nor its close neighbors. In fact, Ritter maintained that the Iraqi armed forces represented a threat to no one but to the Iraqi population itself.[118]

Defeated militarily by the allied forces in 1991, subjected to twelve years of economic embargo,[119] exposed to numerous inspections and *de facto* disarmed by the United Nations—in 2002-2003, Iraq was not in a position to threaten its neighbors, much less the United States.[120] It was a country almost completely disarmed in the face of daily air attacks from the U.S.-Great Britain consortium. Moreover, nothing indicated that the policy of deterrence and of containment of Saddam Hussein's Iraq could not continue indefinitely.

In the words of the former U.N. chief weapons inspector, *"Just because Iraq has the capability of reconstituting its weapons of mass destruction doesn't mean it has done so...It is irresponsible in the extreme to say so without providing any evidence. No one...not the U.S. Senate, not the U.S. intelligence community, nor any of the politicians in President Bush's administration have provided anything that remotely resembles substantiated fact to back up their allegations regarding Iraq's current possession of weapons of mass destruction."[121]* All that Bush could say in public was to affirm that Iraq could acquire nuclear arms *"in the not too distant future"*. For Bush, that was enough to crow *"History has called us into action."* [122]

Two conditions must be met for a country to be considered a serious and imminent military threat to another. First, the presumed aggressor must have the military capacity to represent such a threat, and second, the country must have the intention or manifest the desire to attack.

Neither of these conditions prevailed in the case of Iraq vis-à-vis the United States. The third rate military power had practically no air force, and even if it possessed rudimentary weapons of mass destruction, it didn't have the means to deploy them outside its borders. As for the intention to attack the U.S., it was rather English and American planes that bombed Iraqi territory daily, while Saddam Hussein and his clique of relatives had his hands full trying to stay in power after their 1991 defeat.

Despite all the efforts to prove the contrary, no credible link had been established between the al Qaeda network and Iraq, and no military threat had been issued against the United States nor any other country.[123] In a public report, a United Nations inquiry on the subject concluded that there was no evidence linking Osama bin Laden's terrorist group to the Iraqi government.[124] Similarly, during the summer of 2003, when a joint Congressional panel released its 858-page report on the September 11 attacks, the question of possible links between Iraq, the Hussein regime and the al Qaeda terrorists was not even raised. However, twenty-eight pages dealing with Saudi Arabia's involvement in the attacks were obliterated, for "security" reasons.[125] Nevertheless, between an invisible bin Laden, hard to find, and a very present Saddam Hussein, with a mailing address, the choice of those wanting to make an example to the world of American might would be easy. The chosen symbol of terror would be the very visible and rich Saddam, not the invisible Osama, even though there was no obvious link between Iraq and the tragedy of September 11.

But what was behind the cabal in the United States for a war against Iraq? Besides George W. Bush's obvious desire for revenge against the Arab world in general, and against Iraq in particular, a partial and more compelling answer is that this was an attempt by the neo-conservative political lobby in the U.S. to commandeer American foreign policy. This would be quite a political coup! Their primary goal: to preserve at any cost the nuclear monopoly of the State of Israel in the Middle East, to annihilate what was left of the Iraqi army and to make a visible supporter of the Palestinians' cause disappear. The rest of the answer, which is paramount and which we develop in later chapters, concerns the compelling need to pacify the entire Middle East in order to control its vast oil resources, and also, the Republicans' short-term domestic electoral interests for the U.S. elections of 2002 and 2004. As it became abundantly clear, the two official reasons advanced by the Bush administration to invade Iraq, Iraq's alleged links to al Qaeda and its possession of weapons of mass destruction, were bogus.

There is no doubt that, once Iraq was crushed, the leaders of the pro-Israeli cabal would turn their media propaganda against Syria and Iran, the latter country belonging to the "Axis of Evil" identified by Bush in February of 2002.[126] Later, it could be Saudi Arabia, Yemen, Sudan, Pakistan, etc. In truth, this was a coherent plan to use American military might to simultaneously obtain several strategic objectives. In general, one cannot understand U.S. foreign policy in the Middle East without taking into account the political influence wielded by powerful political and religious lobby groups on the White House and on Congress.

The ideological foundation of the new U.S. imperial doctrine

Leo Strauss (1899-1973), a political scientist born in Germany, is the principal guru of many of the supremacist ideologues behind the neo-conservative movement in the United States, and of the most avid promoters of a new American imperialism. Strauss taught at the University of Chicago, where Paul Wolfowitz was his student.[127]

Strauss's political philosophy rests on some quite extreme and repellent ideas: primo, that moral liberalism and moral relativism must be rejected and replaced by some form of moral absolutism and a strategy of permanent confrontation with what is perceived as evil; secundo, religion and faith, as representatives of such moral absolutism, should be put back into politics. In other words, Strauss proposed to reintroduce religious fanaticism into politics, irrespective of the disasters such a recipe has produced throughout history. In so doing, Strauss becomes the anti-thesis of Karl Marx and of his idea that religion is the opium of the masses. For Strauss, religion is necessary to keep social order, even though he himself believed religion to be a "pious fraud" to exert social control.[128] He proposes nevertheless that people should be given their opium in order for them to be guided by an enlightened elite.

Tertio, Strauss rejects individual rights in favor of state power, by arguing that classical and Christian natural law did not impose strict and absolute limits on state power, but that the exercise of such power is better left to the prudential judgment of the wise statesman. From there, quatro, Strauss goes on to become an apologist for a "farsighted" imperialism and for militaristic policies.[129]

Some American ideologues fully embrace Strauss's far right supremacist ideas. For Robert D. Kaplan, for instance, it behooves the United States to become a "Global Empire"; "...*For the time being, the highest morality must be the preservation— and, wherever prudent, the accretion—of American power.*"[130] It doesn't matter if the U.S., in so doing, must put aside its fundamental values, as a republic and as a democracy, and become a militarist power, thus betraying the anti-imperial efforts of its Founding Fathers.[131]

These are the dangerous ideological underpinnings for a U.S. foreign policy aimed at controlling militarily Arab and Muslim countries, in its own interests and in those of Israel. From there also originates the idea that the United Nations should be cast aside, because it is too "obsessed" with the Arab-Israeli conflict.

# 6

# THE INTERNATIONAL CRIMINAL COURT

*"When one kills a man: He is an assassin. When one kills a million men:*
*He is a conqueror. When one kills them all: He is a god."*
Jean ROSTAND (1894-1977)

*"Whether you are powerful or miserable,*
*The courts will find you innocent or guilty."*
LA FONTAINE, Fables

*"War creates more evil-doers than it eliminates."*
KANT (1724-1804)

### Opposition to an international criminal court

The role of the International Criminal Court is to judge war crimes, genocides, and crimes against humanity. On May 5, 2002, the United States government notified Kofi Annan, the United Nations General Secretary, that it was revoking its support for the creation of an international criminal court. Although Bill Clinton had given the measure his approval *in extremis*, on December 31, 2000, this was an unprecedented move.

The Bush administration vehemently opposed the creation of such a court. It much preferred *ad hoc* international military-styled courts, rather than international criminal law courts, for judging war crimes, along the lines of the Nuremberg and Tokyo Trials following World War II. These temporary military courts were created by the United States, under the auspices of the United Nations, with the mandate to judge Nazi and Japanese leaders.

Why, then, a half century later, in 2002, was the U.S. so opposed to the establishment of an international court that most countries considered to be a gain for civilization? There are the official reasons. The United States was afraid that an independent and supranational court, beyond U.S. control, might turn against it. At any one time, the U.S. has some 255,000 troops deployed around the world, pursuing systematically interventionist policies outside its borders. It surely doesn't want to see the day when a U.S. general, or diplomat, or even politician is brought before an international court of justice.[132]

In fact, the U.S. has troops in 120 countries, from Djibouti in Africa to South Korea in Asia, and, under the Bush Doctrine, is bound to be in a state of perpetual war for years to come. In fact, it is easier to identify the countries where the U.S. does not maintain troops than those where it does. It is a country that is going to look more and more like the Israel of today, a country surrounded by more or less hostile nations, with the operating motto of "Damn the rest of the world".[133]

There are also moral reasons. Some U.S. politicians, George W. Bush among them, are close to adopting the Israeli myth of the "chosen people", and consider the U.S. to be the "first nation, under God". This is probably what U.S. Attorney General John Ashcroft implied when he said, on April 2003, that *"The United States has God's special blessing."* Such a mythical and paranoid worldview makes the U.S. a "promised land", unlike any other. This should naturally confer a special international status upon America. It follows that, for Americans who subscribe to these ideas, submitting U.S. actions to the authority of an international court of justice would not only be an abusive limitation of national sovereignty and military superiority, but would be straight out sacrilegious.

So because of its alleged "moral superiority" and its status as the only military superpower left after the downfall of the communist Soviet Union, in 1991, the Bush Administration feels the United States should have a special judicial status among the nations of the world. Its dominant role in world affairs in general, and the war against international terrorism since September 11, in particular, make Americans potential targets, meriting special protection. Consequently, this special country should be able to intervene anywhere in the world, according to a superior international law.

In the recent past, it is true that the United States has not hesitated to intervene militarily in several countries. Most of the incidents were police actions: in Grenada (1983), in Lebanon (1983), in Nicaragua (1981-1990), in Panama (1989), in Somalia (1992-1993), in Haiti (1994-1996), and in Sudan (1998), etc., as well as political interventions in many others. In Iraq (1990-1991) and in Afghanistan (2001-2002), on the other hand, full-fledged wars were fought in response to the invasion of Kuwait by Iraq, under Saddam Hussein, and the attack on U.S. soil by the al Qaeda network of Osama bin Laden.

For geopolitical reasons, the U.S. government opposed the creation of the International Criminal Court and expended enormous efforts to shield itself from its jurisdiction, because it insisted on keeping all the necessary latitude to intervene militarily and politically in the affairs of other countries, whenever it considered that American national interests were at stake.

The International Criminal Court: A reality check

Despite the reticence and the opposition of the U.S. government, the International Criminal Court (ICC) is a *fait accompli*. It came into existence on July 1, 2002. Four years before, 120 United Nations member countries had adopted the convention that created, for the first time in the history of the world, a permanent international court of justice. As of 2003, 138 countries have signed the convention of establishment of the International Criminal Court. The convention was to come into effect in July of 2002, after ratification by at least 60 of the signatories. On April 11, 2002, the decisive number was met when 68 countries ratified the treaty. Since then, numerous other countries have ratified the convention, including most of the large democracies and all of the 15 members of the European Union.[134]

The ICC will have unfettered authority to bring suits against the perpetrators of war crimes and crimes against humanity.[135] In contrast to the International Criminal Tribunal which preceded it, the International Criminal Court does not require the agreement of the five permanent members of the U.N. Security Council to operate. It will be free to try individuals, from any country, who have committed atrocities, unless their country of origin judges them itself. In this case, the ICC will bow to the concerned national system of justice. Only countries, however, can bring a case before the Court.[136]

Despite this large international consensus and faced with the unavoidable reality, the U.S. government tried a last maneuvre to block the creation of the International Criminal Court. It threatened to pull out of all its U.N. peacekeeping operations, if its personnel were not sheltered from international justice. The Bush administration claimed that it was absolutely necessary that Americans—civilians or military—who participated in U.N. peacekeeping missions, be under the unique authority of U.S. courts. Only China was ready to follow the U.S. lead.

This way of reasoning—if such obstruction of the work of international institutions can be called reasoning—was a red herring. It is unimaginable that people sent into a war-torn country on peacekeeping operations fear, even in theory, being accused of genocide, crimes against humanity, or war crimes. The preoccupations of the Bush administration concerning U.N. peacekeeping missions were but a pretext for obtaining a free hand in unilateral American armed interventions.

Still, on July 5, 2002, the U.S. took an action of grave consequence. Democratic countries around the world were indignant when, at the Security Council, the U.S. opposed its veto to prevent the 14 other members from extending the U.N. peacekeeping mission in Bosnia-Herzegovina.[137] As a compromise, the Security Council, by it its Resolution 1422 of July 12, 2003, accepted to exempt from the new jurisdiction the peacekeeper soldiers of countries not signatories of the treaty of Rome establishing the International Criminal Court, for a twelve month period, renewable. If the U.S. were to repeat this kind of blackmail in the future, it could imperil all fifteen on-going U.N. peacekeeping operations around the world, and any future peace mission. The U.S., armed with its veto power, could, in fact, paralyze the United Nations.[138]

Unfortunately, this was not the only time that international attempts to achieve a more civilized world met with U.S. obstructionism. On July 24, 2002, the Bush government allied itself with China, Cuba, Iran, and Libya—all countries that are known for their lack of respect for human rights—to block the adoption of the United Nations Protocol against torture. The U.S. claimed that the Protocol, which was adopted by a vote of 35 to 8 with 10 abstentions by the United Nations Economic and Social Council, would have permitted international visits in prisons where the U.S. government held suspected terrorists. But it came to naught, since such visits were possible only in the countries that had previously signed the Protocol.[139]

In reality, what the Bush administration was trying by all means possible to obtain was the reestablishment of the veto of the five permanent Security Council members on international institutions, especially the International Criminal Court. This would give the U.S. *de facto* a permanent exoneration for all its military activities throughout the world.

John Bolton, the U.S. undersecretary for arms control under Colin Powell, and responsible for implementing the policy of sabotaging the ICC, explained the government's opinion, *"Restraining U.S. military power is the real hidden agenda here."*[140] He was undoubtedly at least partly right. The last thing the 21st Century needs is a roughneck, armed to the teeth, free from the constraints of the Cold War, and who is unhampered by any rule of law. The world does not want the United States to behave as an unleashed pit-bull, attacking any country it does not like, outside of international law.[141]

With or without the U.S. Bush administration, the new and permanent International Criminal Court for dealing with dictators and war criminals formally opened on March 11, 2003, with the swearing in of its bench of 18 judges.[142] It is backed by the full legitimacy of 90 countries, most of them democratic. Dictators and totalitarian countries such as China have not endorsed the International Criminal Court. The fact that the Bush administration decided to side with them only demonstrates the shaky ground on which American foreign policy is being carried out these days.

Of course, there are many obstacles that have to be overcome for any accusations of war crimes to be initiated. First, precautions have been taken to avoid spurious accusations or politically motivated accusations. A group of judges must review all cases before they are officially submitted. Moreover, the

Security Council can delay cases for 12 months at a time. And most importantly, the Court cannot initiate legal proceedings against people who have committed crimes against humanity within their country of origin, if that country has not ratified the treaty, unless that country gives its consent. It doesn't protect them if they commit crimes outside of their country.

It can be argued that since the U.S. government has secured 22 bilateral treaties granting American citizens immunity from arrest warrants issued by the international court, Americans can behave internationally outside of international law.[143] Also, the fact that Congress has adopted legislation empowering the president to use "all means necessary" to free Americans taken into the Court's custody is another layer of protection of Americans accused of war crime activities.

But all that could be irrelevant. Even if the government of Nazi Germany had passed such laws, this would not have prevented the Nuremberg Tribunal from judging the German war criminals who were accused and judged by the special court.[144] The law has long arms and the military power of the accused can only shield him for a while from facing ultimate justice.

# 7

## THE STRATEGIC IMPORTANCE OF OIL

*"Controlling Iraq is about oil as power, rather than oil as fuel. Control over the Persian Gulf translates into control over Europe, Japan, and China. It's having our hand on the spigot."*
Michael KLARE, author

*"Iraq is a very different situation from Afghanistan. Iraq has oil."*
Donald H. RUMSFELD

*"The United States seeks to destroy Iraq in order to control the Middle East oil."*
Saddam HUSSEIN[145]

What is the role of oil, the blood of the earth, in the U.S. hegemony and war policies? This is surely a pertinent question after the Bush administration decided, in March 2003, to go ahead with the military invasion of Iraq. The Middle East has by far the largest pool of cheap oil in the world. Whoever controls it politically will maintain leverage over oil supplies to the rest of the world for decades to come. In the past, this is an area that has attracted outside powers anxious to dominate its vast oil wealth. In this regard there is hardly a dividing line between international oil corporations and their national governments, with the governments undertaking to promote, secure, and protect militarily their oil corporations.

### A military-industrial complex team

Since January 20, 2001, the U.S. has been led by a group of people who, for the most part, come from either the war industry or the oil industry, or in some cases, both. Many come from Texas, known, of course, as a *"macho"* state. These leaders are determined to exploit to the hilt the enormous U.S. military machine at their disposition to promote their vision of American interests. Their motto is surely *"Let us be feared rather than loved, respected rather than admired."* In the words of George W. Bush, *"Let's roll!"* Their decisions, be they good or bad, are of the utmost importance to the stability or instability of the world in the coming years.[146]

Who are these leaders? The chief is of course George W. Bush, a former director of oil companies. His political career is awash with oil and gas. For a dozen years, his main contributor was Enron and its top officials. For a time, Bush was a director of Harken Energy Corp., a Texas company. He sold his participation to Spectrum 7 Energy in 1986.[147]

Vice president Richard "Dick" Cheney was CEO of Halliburton (1995-2000)—a world giant in oil services in Dallas, Texas—and a former Secretary of Defense in the administration of Bush, Sr. (1989-1993).[148]

General Colin Powell, the Secretary of State, is a career-military man responsible for foreign policy. He is a veteran of the Vietnam War, and as the chairman of the Joint Chiefs of Staff, he was in charge of American forces from 1989 to 1993, a period covering the Persian Gulf War against Iraq, in 1990-1991.

Donald H. Rumsfeld, the Secretary of Defense, is also a former Secretary of Defense in the Gerald Ford administration (1975-1977) and a former U.S. ambassador to NATO.[149] Previously, Rumsfeld was an Illinois congressman and also acted as White House Chief of Staff under Gerald Ford (1974-1975). In private life, Donald H. Rumsfeld was CEO of G.D. Searle and General Instruments. He also sat, from 1991 to 2000, on the board of the Swiss company ABB, a company that sold nuclear reactors to North Korea. Rumsfeld's Deputy Secretary of Defense is Paul D. Wolfowitz, a former ambassador to Indonesia, as well as being a "super-hawk" who has openly favored war against Iraq for more than ten years.

The first Secretary of the Treasury in the Bush administration was Paul O'Neill, former CEO of Alcoa. He was replaced in December of 2002, by John W. Snow, president of CSX, a railroad company. The Secretary of Commerce, Don Evans, is a former CEO of the energy services company, Tom Brown. The Director of the Budget, Mitch Daniels, is a former senior vice president of Eli Lilly. The Secretary of the Army, Thomas White, is a former senior vice president of the infamous Texas energy firm, Enron.

Condoleezza Rice is President George Bush Jr.'s National Security Advisor and a member of the National Security Council.[150] She is a university professor who has specialized in political and military issues, especially in the context of the Cold War with the Soviet Union. Previouly, she was a member of the board of directors of oil giant Chevron from 1991 to 2001, and a Special Assistant to President George Bush Sr. from 1989 to 1991.

Elliott Abrams is a former director of the Ethics and Public Policy Center in Washington, DC. He is also a former assistant secretary of state for Inter-American affairs during the Reagan administration, and was indicted for giving false testimony during the Iran-Contra affair. He was pardoned on Christmas night of 1992, by outgoing President George H. Bush. In August 2001, President George W. Bush appointed Abrams to the National Security Council and placed him in charge of the Middle East and in charge of the Palestinian-Israeli conflict. Abrams is regarded as one of the most prominent advocates of the establishment of alliances with evangelical Americans, the Christian groups that most intensely support Israel, in order to cement the alliance between the United States and Israel. He is the author of the book *Faith or Fear: How Jews Can Survive in a Christian America.*

The present U.S. administration is the most hawkish group ever assembled. George W. Bush's cabinet is filled with people from the oil business and from the military. Certain advisors, such as Wolfowitz and Abrams, have a strong bias towards Israel. In this context, it shouldn't be surprising that these three centers of interest (oil, war, Israel) are paramount in the policies of the Bush administration.

The first priority of U.S. foreign policy: security of oil supply

Oil plays an important role in every industrialized economy, and especially in the United States. Indeed, oil enters into virtually all economic activities, either as a source of energy or as a raw material for a host of industries. Economist James Hamilton of the University of California at San Diego has established that nine of the ten U.S. recessions between 1945 and 2003 were preceded by a substantial rise in the price of oil.[151]

Frequently, geopolitical factors have played a central role in perturbing international oil markets. Thus, in November 1956, the Suez Crisis was instrumental in the 10.1 percent decline in oil output. During the fall of 1973, it was the Israeli-Palestinian war that destabilized international oil production, which dropped by 7.8 percent. A few years later, in November 1978, an oil shock followed the onset of the Iranian Islamic revolution, and oil production declined by 8.9 percent. Then in October 1980, the Iran-Iraq war provoked another drop in world oil output, this time by 7.2 percent. Finally, when Saddam Hussein decided to invade Kuwait, in August 1990, world oil production contracted by 8.8 percent. Each time, an economic recession followed. It is an obvious fact that world oil production is closely related to geopolitical instability, especially in the Middle East.

It is therefore understandable that as soon as he took office, George W. Bush made energy policy a priority of his administration. Vice president Cheney immediately set himself to the task by presiding a commission with the mandate to elaborate a new energy policy. The commission consulted many well-known people in the business community, especially from the big energy firms, before tabling its 163-page report on May 16, 2001. The report contained an ambitious plan to insure the security of the U.S. energy supply for decades to come. It ranged from a reform of the electricity markets, following the meltdown experienced in California during the summer of 2000, to the opening of new domestic petroleum sources—both oil and gas—to new measures for economic growth and energy conservation.[152]

The report noted the need to establish new hub-like bilateral agreements with oil-producing countries, notably Canada, Mexico, Venezuela, Brazil, and the African oil producers.

Concerning the stratigic Middle East region, the site of two-thirds of the world's known crude oil reserves, the report recommended that the U.S. encourage Saudi Arabia, Kuwait, Qatar, Oman, the United Arab Emirats (UAE), Yemen, Algeria, and the other producing countries to accept international investments in order to expand their energy sectors.

The report proposed the construction of a pipeline BTC from Kazakhstan, as well as the pipeline Shah Deniz to pump gas from Azerbaijan, via Georgia and Turkey. It also proposed encouraging Turkey and Greece to merge their pipeline systems in order to pump gas from the Caspian Sea to European markets. Discussions had been undertaken with India and Russia concerning energy production in these countries. The report even recommended that the Group of Eight—G8—hold an annual meeting devoted solely to energy issues, so important are these issues to the economic and political stability of the world.

The domestic side of the U.S. energy strategy quickly bogged down in Congress. The Democrats were strongly opposed to opening the oil fields in the Arctic National Wildlife Refuge (ANWR) in Alaska to prospecting. There was no agreement on the new regulatory powers needed to prevent more disasters like the California debacle in 2000. That left the international side of the plan. After the events of September 11, 2001, the strategy for increasing and better controlling world petroleum production took on a whole new importance.

### The all important April 2001 report

Another energy committee, operating in parallel to the intergovernmental commission, and made up of many of the outside experts who had advised Dick Cheney for his own report, also submitted a report of its own, in April 2001. This *cordon bleu* committee of 41 individuals, among them Ken Lay, the president of the energy company Enron, submitted a more detailed and less publicized report on the global strategy that the United States should adopt in order to end the growing deficit in energy resources.[153]

This report entitled *Strategic Energy Policy Challenges For The 21st Century* was written by several people who worked in the energy sector, assisted by academics and representatives of consulting firms and had the backing of James Baker, who was the Secretary of State under George Bush Sr. from 1989 to 1992. Chevron-Texaco, Hess, Shell, British Petroleum and ENI, as well as Enron and Dynegy, and bankers specialized in energy financing were represented.[154]

The report concluded that the U.S. was becoming more and more vulnerable to perturbations in the supply of foreign crude oil, at the same time that known domestic reserves were falling. The U.S. consumes 26% of the world's oil production, but it has only slightly more than 2% of known reserves. In ten years, from 1990 to 2000, U.S. crude oil reserves have gone from 26 billion barrels to 22 billion barrels. This figure contrasts with the 49 billion barrels that Russia is thought to have in reserves.

During the same ten-year period, sanctions imposed against certain oil-producing countries (Iran, Iraq, Libya, etc.), and the dereglementation of energy markets, had resulted in a drop in investments in infrastructures. As a consequence, there was very little excess production capacity in the world's oil industry.

On the demand side, there had been little effort made to encourage energy conservation and the development of alternate energy sources that are less polluting than hydrocarbons. The result was an increase rather than a decrease in the use of crude oil as an energy source in the key sector of transportation. From 1970 to 1995, the use of oil in transportation grew from 52% to 66%, and it is predicted to rise to 70% by the year 2010. American dependence on oil, both domestic and foreign, is high and growing higher. The report concluded, *"If it does not respond strategically to the current energy circumstances, the United States risks perpetuating the unacceptable leverage of adversaries and leaving its economy vulnerable to volatile energy prices."*[155]

Middle East oil policy has long been a priority of the U.S. government. After all, the C.I.A. intervened with the British in Iran, in 1953, in order to overthrow the nationalist government of Muhammad Mossadeq and protect western oil interests, after it had nationalized the Anglo-Iranian Oil Company.[156] During the first oil shock in the early 1970s, when oil prices were quadrupled,

US Secretary of State Henry Kissinger contemplated the possibility of a US takeover of the Middle East oilfields.

In 1980, President Jimmy Carter, in his last annual State of the Union address, outlined a policy toward the Middle East in these terms, *"An attempt by any outside force to gain control of the Persian Gulf region will be regarded as an assault on the vital interests of the United States of America. And such an assault will be repelled by any means necessary, including military force."*[57] Therefore, it is not new that the Pentagon is part of the U.S. energy policy and that the U.S. government declares itself ready to wage war in order to maintain a free access to the Persian Gulf oil. In 2002-03, the Bush administration was even more aware than previous administrations of the strategic imperative for the U.S. to control the Persian Gulf and its oil, and of the need for the U.S. to assume Britain's historic role in that important region.

In 1990-1991, George H. Bush, a former Texas oil man himself, did not hesitate to commit U.S. military forces against Iraq and Saddam Hussein in order to prevent the Iraqi dictator from controlling Kuwait and the other Persian Gulf oil fields. In 2002-2003, the Bush-Cheney administration, heavily loaded with Texan oil people, was also preoccupied with a Saddam Hussein sitting "on a sea of oil" and worried that his calls to use oil as a weapon to bring about a settlement of the Palestinian-Israeli conflict could be heard by the other Arab governments in the region. The war against terrorism offered a cover to secure militarily the entire Middle East region and prevent future disagreeable surprises. Why would anyone think that the Bush-Cheney team, an oil industry duo from Texas, would be less inclined to wage war, in 2003, in order to "liberate" the Iraqi oil fields?

Moreover, oil is a commodity which is sold in U.S. dollars and, as such, it is an integral part of the U.S. financial system. In fact, when the Hussein government started to demand payment for its oil in euros rather than dollars, in November 2000, this raised red flags in New York and Washington. Indeed, the control of oil supplies has to do with a lot more than simply influencing its market price. It is about the security of supply, about the leverage it gives to whomever has the hand on the spigots over the rest of the world, and about the investments derived from the petro dollars.

## The heavy American dependence on foreign oil

According to the U.S. Energy Information Administration, U.S. oil consumption is around 19.8 million barrels per day. That is equal to 26% of the world's production, but domestic production is only 9.1 million barrels a day.

Thus, the United States is in the uncomfortable position of having to import 10.7 million barrels, or 54% of its daily consumption. In 1990, the U.S. dependence on foreign oil was only 40%. Before 1948, the United States was even a net exporter of oil. Things have changed, because the U.S. hydrocarbon reserves have been over-exploited (3,000,000 of the 4,000,000 oil and gas wells worldwide have been drilled in the U.S.).

At the rate the U.S. produces and consumes oil, it is well on its way toward a major energy crisis within a decade. The U.S. exploits its oil reserves with a total production of 3.3 billion barrels a year. Since the known domestic petroleum reserves hardly top 22 billion barrels, if no other large deposit of oil is found, the U.S. will reach the "bottom of the barrel" between 2008 and 2010.

Of course there are the oil reserves in Alaska, but the reserves in the Alaskan public parks are limited. In fact, even if they develop the oil sands in the Arctic National Wildlife Refuge (ANWR), estimated at 10 billion barrels, the U.S. share of world hydrocarbon reserves would go from the present 2.3% to a mere 3.3% in ten years.[158] In other words, the U.S. is in a dangerous position because of its oil deficit, and it will be for decades to come. We can understand why, in Bush and Cheney's minds, the need for a secured access to Middle East oil was not an option, but almost a strategic and economic necessity.

Indeed, such a dependence on foreign energy sources, especially when they are unreliable, gives rise to a significant geopolitical vulnerability. In 2000, the five countries that supplied the most foreign crude oil to the United States were Canada[159] (15%), Saudi Arabia (14%), Venezuela (14%), Mexico (12%), and

Iraq (8%).[160] On a regional basis, 50% 0f American oil imports come from the Western Hemisphere, 24% from the Middle East, 14% from Africa, 9% from Eurasia, and 3% from elsewhere. The U.S. has a vital interest in expanding and diversifying its oil supply sources, if not actually controlling them.[161]

In 2002, Sunni and Wahhabi Saudi Arabia produced 7.1 million barrels of oil a day—almost 10% of world consumption. However, it has an excess daily capacity of around 3 million barrels. This permits Saudi Arabia to play a stabilizing role on world prices within the Organization of Petroleum Producing Countries (OPEC), an international cartel which was founded in Baghdad in 1960, and which it dominates.[162] The United States has traditionally counted on Saudi Arabia to stabilize world oil prices and to soften OPEC's more threatening positions.[163]

In particular, Saudi Arabia has spent a growing portion of its oil revenues on social and political objectives, investing little to increase its productive capacity. Worse, since September 11, 2001, and in the face of the growing intransigence of Israel in the Palestinian-Israeli conflict, Saudi Arabia, like the other producers in the Persian Gulf, has fewer and fewer domestic and foreign interests that coincide with those of the United States.[164]

In the future, the strong current of anti-Americanism in the Gulf region is liable to prevent governments, including Saudi Arabia, from collaborating fully with the United States. The report clearly identifies the causes of the fissure that has appeared between the U.S. and the Arab oil producing countries:

*"Bitter perceptions in the Arab world that the United States has not been evenhanded in brokering peace negotiations between Israel and the Palestinians have exacerbated these pressures on Saudi Arabia and other Gulf Cooperation Council (GCC) countries and given political leverage to Iraq's Saddam Hussein to lobby for support among the Arab world's populations."[165]*

In theory, Russia, which does not belong to the 11-country OPEC club (including Iraq), and which produces around 6.9 million barrels of oil a day, could increase its productive capacity by 50%. In this way, it could reduce somewhat the Saudi influence on the world crude oil market.[166] Indeed, according to a June 1,

2003, US-Russian agreement, some 13 percent of US oil imports should come from Russia by the year 2010, reducing the OPEC input from 51 percent of US consumption to 40-42 percent in 2010. This hinges on the completion of the colossal Murmansk Project that entails the building of a major new pipeline to ship West Siberian crude through a deepwater terminal near Murmansk inside the Arctic Circle, from Russia to North America. However, this would require substantial investments to repair the deplorable state of Russia's oil pipelines and ports.[167]

Concerning Iraq, a country that *"floats on a sea of oil'* according to US Deputy Defense Secretary Paul Wolfowitz,[168] the April 2001 report made the general observation, *"The resulting tight markets have increased U.S. and global vulnerability to disruption and provided adversaries undue potential influence over the price of oil. Iraq has become a key "swing" producer, posing a difficult situation for the U.S. government."*[169]

After Saudi Arabia, Iraq's known crude oil reserves are the second largest in the Middle East. With 115 billion barrels in proven oil reserves, or 11% of known world reserves, and 17% of Middle East reserves, Iraq remains a major source of oil supply.[170] Saudi Arabia, with 265 billion barrels of reserves, possesses 25% of world reserves, while the United Arab Emirates and Kuwait each possess around 9% of world reserves. In other words, the region controls two thirds of world reserves.[171] If we add the oil from the Caspian Sea basin, the region holds three quarters of known world reserves.[172]

Undeveloped oil reserves in Iraq are presumed to be even more important. According to Richard Spertzel, former Chief Inspector for the United Nations for biological weapons in Iraq (1994-1998), these undeveloped reserves are the largest in the world. According to other specialists, in fact, potential Iraqi reserves are on the order of 220 to 310 billion barrels—some estimates running as high as 400 billion barrels[173] —since Iraqi territory is relatively unexplored because of the many years of war over the last quarter century.[174]

It is estimated, in fact, that only 15 oil fields are developed and producing out of the 73 that have been discovered. Iraq's oil fields located along the north-south border with Iran, from the

Kirkuk fields in the north to those of Basrah and Rumaila in the south, have been producing for decades. However, there are numerous discovered fields in the western desert, near Jordan, which are still to be explored.[175] If this were to be confirmed, Iraq could become an oil pump as important as Saudi Arabia, perhaps even more. For someone who has already "tasted" oil, it is enough to make him lick his lips!

Because of this enormous potential, the productive capacity of Iraq, evaluated at some 2.8 million barrels a day, could easily rise to 6 million barrels a day and more in a few years, and possibly to 10 or 12 million barrels a day. Two ifs: if the country's internal and international political situation stabilizes and if foreign oil companies, anxious to invest, can do so.

This was not the first time that the U.S. government paid attention to Iraqi oil. In December 1983, for instance, Donald Rumsfeld met with Saddam Hussein in order to persuade him to let the Bechtel Group of San Francisco—whose former president was Secretary of State George Shultz—build an oil pipeline from Iraq to the Jordanian port of Aqaba, near the Red Sea. It was a billion-dollar project and the Reagan administration wanted Saddam Hussein to sign off on it. But Iraq turned down the project, because it feared Israel could too easily destroy the proposed oil pipeline.[176]

### Saddam Hussein's threats to U.S. allies and to international oil markets

Regarding the United States' vulnerability to a disruption in the oil supply originating in Iraq, the all-important April 2001 report specifically targeted Saddam Hussein as an obstacle to US interests, because of his control of Iraqi oil fields. The report also announced things to come and suggested the use of "military intervention" as a way to access and control Iraqi oil fields and help the US out of its energy crisis:[177]

*"Iraq remains a destabilizing influence to US allies in the Middle East, as well as to regional and global order, and to the flow of oil to international markets from the Middle East....*

*"Saddam Hussein has also demonstrated a willingness to threaten to use the oil weapon and to use his own export program to manipulate oil markets. This would display his personal power, enhance his image as a 'Pan Arab' leader supporting the Palestinians against Israel, and pressure others for a lifting of economic sanctions against his regime....*

*"The United States should conduct an immediate policy review toward Iraq including military, energy, economic and political/diplomatic assessments....*

*"The United States should then develop an integrated strategy with key allies in Europe and Asia, and with key countries in the Middle East, to restate goals with respect to Iraqi policy and to restore a cohesive coalition of key allies."*

In the eyes of the authors of the April 2001 report, the United States will never be "energy independent" and is becoming too dependent on foreign powers for supplying it with oil and gas. Therefore, the Administration has no choice but to put oil at the center of its preoccupations and proceed toward *"a reassessment of the role of energy in American foreign policy".*

The greatest weakness of the April 2001 report was its insistence that the United States persist in its pretense that oil policy and foreign policy had to be kept separate, and that the Palestinian-Israeli conflict had no bearing on the issue:

*"While moving to defuse tensions in the Arab-Israeli conflict through conflict resolution and negotiations, [we recommend to] maintain energy and political issues in U.S.–Middle East relations on separate tracks.*

*"The timing might not be appropriate for a major initiative to solve the Arab-Israeli conflict in a comprehensive manner, but it is important to reduce immediate tensions and violence in that conflict.*

*" While this is a tenet of U.S. foreign policy for other reasons, it can also be helpful to the oil situation in ensuring that the two issues do not become linked and are kept on separate tracks."*

In reality, these two questions are closely interrelated. In the Middle East, the United States cannot ask for a secure access to its oil resources and be seen, at the same time, as the unconditional sponsor of the Israeli government. This was clearly demonstrated by the following event.

On April 8, 2002, as if to confirm the fears raised in the April 2001 report, Saddam Hussein made a fateful nationally-televised speech that deeply horrified and traumatized the oil-obsessed Bush administration. He announced his intentions to use oil as a political weapon against Israel and against the United States.

Indeed, the Iraqi president had decided to cut all oil exports for 30 days or until Israel withdrew from Palestinian territories. No oil would flow through the pipelines in the direction of the Turkish ports and of the southern ports for a month. Not only that, but Iraq was making calls on other Arab oil-producing states also to cut oil exports, as a way of pressuring the United States into forcing Israel to end its military incursions into Palestinian territory.

Only Libya supported Saddam Hussein's call for an oil embargo, even though Iran's supreme leader, Ayatollah Ali Khamenei, called on Arab states to launch a one-month "symbolic" oil embargo against Western countries to pressure them to stop supporting Israel.

Not since 1973, had oil been used for such an overtly political aim. In the aftermath of the Arab-Israeli war (the 1973 Yom Kippur War)[178], the Organization of Petroleum Exporting Countries (OPEC), led by Saudi Arabia, boycotted oil exports to western countries, in retaliation against the West and the United States for their support of Israel.[179] The embargo caused a global energy crisis and quadrupled world oil prices from 1973 to 1974. This in turn precipitated the 1973-1974 recession, the most serious since the 1929-1939 depression.[180]

Since then, the world's 26 wealthiest nations have created the International Energy Agency to provide a cushion against any similar disruption. Based in Paris, the IEA can tap into 4 billion barrels of strategic oil reserves maintained by its member countries. Such a reserve, although quickly available and large, being equal to 5.5 years of Iraqi oil production, represents no more than one quarter of the yearly oil consumption of the United States, and only 114 days of oil imports by its member nations. Therefore, oil-consuming nations remain vulnerable to dislocations in oil supplies, even though in November 2000, Saudi Arabia promoted the adoption by the Organization of Petroleum Exporting Countries and other major exporters, of a pledge that oil would not be used as a political weapon.

Nevertheless, what Saddam Hussein, and others such as Osama bin Laden, would like to see is a repeat of the 1973 oil embargo by Muslim countries. If they were to succeed in putting politics ahead of economics and reasserting a tight Arab control on oil supplies, the world economy could be thrown into turmoil. In this sense, Iraq and Saddam Hussein did pose an economic threat, not only to the United States, but also to the world.[181] Would such a threat be serious enough to constitute, by itself, a *casus belli?* This is something that the United Nations will surely have to decide in the future.

### The rush to oil contracts

There is a long list of oil companies that have signed contracts for the prospecting and development of Iraqi oil fields, or have begun negotiations with the Iraqi government to do so.

As early as 1995-1996, French oil companies had already signed the largest contracts for drilling and working the oil fields.[182] The French giant Total SA holds the largest position in Iraq, having obtained the exclusive rights to develop the Majnoon fields, situated 30 miles north of Basrah, at the Iraq-Iran border, in southern Iraq. The estimated reserves in this area were on the order of 10 billion barrels. These wells, plus those of the smaller field of Bin Umar, would permit Total SA to produce 400,000 barrels a day of Iraqi crude.[183]

The contracts between the Iraqi government and the French companies were of the type called "production sharing agreements" (PSA), which permit the companies holding them to include the reserves they control in their annual statements. Accounting methods consider these rights of prospecting and drilling to be tangible assets.[184] It is easy to understand why the government of Jacques Chirac tried to play both sides during the discussions at the United Nations, when the United States and Great Britain clamored for severe anti-Iraq resolutions.

Italian and Russian companies were also well-positioned to profit from the coming Iraqi oil boom. The Italian consortium ENI/Agip is presumed to have concluded a deal to develop the oil fields of Nassiriyah, at a cost of $1.9 billion, with reserves that could reach 2 billion barrels. After a meeting with George W. Bush at Camp David, Prime Minister Silvio Berlusconi declared that Italy was with the United States, whatever it did, and that American bases in Italy could serve during a military campaign in Iraq.

Iraq owed Russia a debt of $8 billion U.S. (as well as $3 billion to France), dating from the Persian Gulf War of 1990-1991. Not wanting to be left out, Russia negotiated with the Bush administration in order to recoup its due.[185] There was also the splinter in its foot of the anti-terrorism war in Chechnya. The hostage crisis in the center of Moscow itself, in October of 2002, and the frictions with Georgia which harbored Chechen terrorists, had intensified Russian repressive actions in that part of the world.

Could Russia be persuaded to exchange its reticence about an Anglo-American attack against Iraq for assurances that the U.S. would protect Russian economic interests in Iraq and wouldn't bother the Russian government in its own anti-terrorism battle? Could Russian President Vladimir Putin succeed, as did Ariel Sharon in Israel, to solve some of his domestic political problems by hitching up with the Americans' international war on Islamist terrorism?

Whatever the case, a consortium of Russian companies, under the direction of the Russian AOA Lukoil, in association with the companies Zarubezneft, Mashinoimport and Tatneft, had signed an array of U.N.-approved contracts worth $3.5 billion, over a period of 23 years, to renovate several Iraqi oil installations. In addition, the consortium had maneuvered to develop the West Qurna oil fields, situated 62 miles northwest of Basrah. They were capable of generating 7.5 to 15 billion barrels of oil, perhaps even 20 billion barrels.[186]

Even China has interests in the development of Iraqi oil resources. The China National Petroleum Company held contracts enabling it to tap some 2 billion barrels of oil.[187] All these countries wanted to partake of Iraq's remains, after George W. Bush's successful plan to invade and bring about an "imposed regime change" in this Middle East country.

The major American and British oil companies were the odd men out in the list of companies poised to exploit Iraqi oil. As a result of the U.N. sanctions, but especially because of the sanctions the U.S. and British governments themselves voted against Iraq (as well as against Iran and Libya), their own companies risked being overtaken on the world crude oil market by rival companies. Many of the American and British oil companies had their core assets in the North Sea, in Alaska and in the shallow waters of the Gulf of Mexico. These were all areas where production was declining.

The Anglo-American companies were encouraged, however, by the declarations of Ahmed Chalabi, a former banker in Jordan and a protegee of Richard Perle since the early 1990's. According to Chalabi, a member of the Iraqi National Congress and of the Iraqi opposition in exile, after an overthrow of Saddam Hussein, the new Iraqi regime would work only with American companies. And, as if to spite Russia, he added that the new government in Baghdad would not have the resources to pay the $8 billion debt that Iraq owed Russia.[188]

James Woolsey, a former Director of the C.I.A., was candid in his assessment of the oil situation when he explained to the *Washington Post* that France and Russia should understand that if a new regime is installed in Baghdad, the U.S. would do its best to be sure the Iraqi government will work closely with American oil companies, *"It's pretty straightforward, France and Russia have oil companies and interests in Iraq. They should be told that if they are of assistance in moving Iraq toward decent government, we'll do the best we can to ensure that the new government and American companies work closely with them."[189]*

A former advisor to the U.S. Department of Defense, Charles V. Peña, Director of Defense Policy Studies at the Cato

Institute in Washington D.C., made it even clearer, *"Oil is at the centre of our Middle East policy. Everything we do in the region is ostensibly to ensure ourselves a cheap supply.*[190]

It was therefore a hard reality that neither the Exxon-Mobil/Chevron-Texaco/Valero Energy/Conoco, etc., nor the British Petroleum/Royal Dutch-Shell were among the companies that had obtained development contracts for Iraqi oil fields.[191] Unless there was a political change in Baghdad, imposed by force, American and British companies would be obliged to join existing consortia in order to participate in investments and production. The overthrow of Saddam Hussein's government by force promised to open the doors for them.

It was not surprising that the exiled leaders of the Iraqi National Congress (INC), led by Ahmed Chalabi, a Shia Iraqi who had left his country when he was 11 and who had not returned in 45 years—a man especially close to Vice President Dick Cheney—were discretely courted by Exxon-Mobil and Chevron-Texaco. Chalabi was particularly useful, because as head of the London-based INC, founded in 1992, he had spent more than a decade lobbying the U.S. government to overthrow Saddam Hussein, and would surely be part of a new Iraqi government. At the same time, the Bush administration, especially the Pentagon, used Chalabi as its single most important source of intelligence to build its case to go to war against Saddam Hussein's Iraq.[192] It was particularly important to prepare the terrain for the oil negotiations that would follow Saddam's overthrow.[193]

If the United States was ready to attack a sovereign country without evident provocation, it wouldn't be a much of a stretch to suspect George W. Bush and his vice president Dick Cheney—both veterans of the oil industry—of wanting to control all Iraqi oil reserves, both developed and undeveloped, according to a new American energy policy applicable to the entire world. One might think that what the U.S. leaders wanted to do was to establish a *"Pax Americana"* in the Middle East. The goal would be to facilitate the prospecting, production, and transport of oil from the region, but also from central Asia, beginning with the Caspian Sea and countries such as Turkmenistan, Uzbekistan and Kazakhstan,[194] and even including Azerbaijan and Russia.[195]

In order to build the necessary pipelines needed to reach the Asian and European markets, the entire geopolitical map of the Persian Gulf and central Asia had to be controlled and stabilized.[196] It would be easier to control Riyadh, Damascus and Tehran, went the theory in Washington, if we controlled Baghdad first.

It was clear that Saudi Arabia was a key country in the U.S. government's hidden agenda. Once Iraq was under their control, they would pressure Saudi Arabia into following a more pro-American policy. At the same time, American control of Iraqi oil would weaken OPEC and the cartel's ability to impose oil embargoes, such as the one in 1973, when the price of oil shot up from $3 to $12 a barrel. This could also mean the break up, once and for all, of the Arab-dominated cartel organization.

In 2002-2003, it was obvious that the Bush administration's energy policy aimed to stabilize the Middle East, militarily, and sought to insure the control of enormous crude oil reserves, both known and unexplored, not only in Iraq, but throughout the Middle East. With the Cold War over, the United States had the military means to "re-colonize" the region of the Persian Gulf, beginning with Iraq. Indeed, it was evident that installing a pro-US regime in Iraq would open up lucrative possibilities for American oil companies and guarantee the United States an easy and long-term access to cheap and abundant oil reserves. This was known to most people around the world, but many commentators in the U.S. were in the slough of denial.

The planning was well advanced. As early as July, 2002, *The New York Times* divulged a government document titled "CentCom Courses of Action", which contained a plan for a military campaign against Iraq. It enumerated ongoing U.S. preparations for the massive bombing of thousands of sites— airports, roads, and communication centers—as soon as the occasion was right.[197]

On January 17, 1961, President Dwight D. Eisenhower (1890-1969) made a farewell speech that has lost nothing of its relevance. In his historic speech, Eisenhower, a former general, warned his countrymen against the military-industrial complex, *"In the councils of government, we must guard against the acquisition of unwarranted influence, whether sought or unsought, by the military-industrial complex. The potential for the disastrous rise of misplaced power exists and will persist. We must never let the weight of this combination endanger our liberties or democratic processes. "*

If Eisenhower were to come back today, he would be stupefied to see how great an influence the military and industry wield in the government. The central U.S. policies are strongly tailored to the interests of the military-industrial complex, all wrapped up in a blatantly religious rhetoric.[198]

# 8

# PREPARATIONS FOR THE 2003 WAR AGAINST IRAQ

*"I know not with what weapons World War III will be fought, but World War IV will be fought with sticks and stones."*
Albert EINSTEIN (1879-1955)

*"No sensible man prefers war to peace, since in war, fathers bury their sons, while in time of peace, it is the sons who bury their fathers."*
HERODOTUS (c.484-425 B.C.)

*"No enterprise is more likely to succeed than one concealed from the enemy until it is ripe for execution."*
MACHIAVELLI (1469-1527), from *The Art of War*

In 1941, Japan's militarist government, thinking that Hitler was winning the war in Europe, and wishing to consolidate its expansionist positions in Asia, decided to launch a surprise preventive attack against the United States. December 7, 1941, stands in history as the date of the infamous Japanese attack on the Hawaiian port of Pearl Harbor.

It follows that the United States should understand that nothing galvanizes a proud population more than being attacked and humiliated by another country. Despite this, the Bush administration was persuaded by the cabal led by Richard Perle and by some self-interested Iraqi exiles that *"people will be dancing in the streets of Baghdad the day the United States invades Iraq."*[99] As if Americans wanted to dance in the streets when Japan attacked the U.S. in December 1941.

Nevertheless, throughout the summer and fall of 2002, headlines trumpeted, *"Israel's Sharon urges U.S. not to delay attack against Iraq"*.[200] Or, heading an article by former Secretary of State Henry Kissinger, *"Delaying Iraq decision could hurt U.S."*[201] Or, after a public intervention by the National Security Advisor, Condoleezza Rice, *"U.S. Makes 'Moral Case' for War"*. And again, as if to support the hostile intentions of the Bush-Sharon tandem, *"Tanks sent to the Persian Gulf"*,[202] and *"Bush given detailed plan for attacking Iraq"*.[203]

As time passed, war preparations intensified. *"58,000 American Soldiers deployed in the Gulf"*, or again, *"When Americans approach, the Iraqi regime will fall"*.[204] It was truly a concerted plan, concocted some time before, for exercising strategic control over Iraq's destiny and establishing a puppet Iraqi government. All done to be able to dole out the country's oil reserves, and push aside the French, the Russians and the Chinese.

Whether the source be Ariel Sharon, Henry Kissinger,[205] or Condoleezza Rice—not to mention the plethora of neo-conservative journalists[206]—a never-ending stream of propaganda and disinformation blitzed the American public. It was a public still smarting over the September 11 attacks, a public ready for vengeance.

The empire of the press mogul Rupert Murdoch, *"the most dangerous man in the world"* according to Ted Turner of CNN and AOL Time Warner, distinguished itself by its aggressiveness and its partiality in its pro-war stance, in the three English-speaking countries that were to become directly involved in the war—the USA, Britain and Australia. In the U.S., Murdoch's main tools were The *New York Post, The Weekly Standard* magazine and, above all, the Fox News network, all owned by Murdoch, which were continuously calling for the "liberation" and for the military invasion of Iraq, a country where children account for half of the population. The president of Fox News, a hawk from the Reagan era, even wrote George W. Bush to tell him that his network would strongly support him in his war plans. They were joined by the conservative *National Review* and the *US News & World Report*, and occasionally, by national newspapers such as *The New York Times, The Washington Post, The Washington Times* and *The Wall Street Journal*.

94

In the U.K., where Murdoch controls 40 percent of the press, his tools were *The Sun, The Times, The Sunday Times* and *News of the World*. Murdoch asked Tony Blair how he could be useful to the imperial cause. The answer was to attack the French! In Australia, where Murdock and his News Corp. control three quarters of the media, the partisan onslaught was even heavier in favor of the coming war. Such a pro-war media push explains, at least in part, why the support for the war of aggression against Iraq was less severely criticizised in these countries, especially in the United States, than in the rest of the world.[207] Many U.S. news media have abdicated their responsibility for critical inquiries into government affairs and have become instead an integral part of the government propaganda machine.

At first, however, the response to this war propaganda was lukewarm and mitigated. Even though there was no sympathy for the dictator, in power since 1979, the average American realized that the proof that Saddam Hussein was a strategic and immediate threat to the U.S. was not forthcoming. People were profoundly divided on the advisability of a unilateral American attack on Iraq.

Polls by CNN/USA Today/Gallup showed that the support for an invasion of Iraq by American troops fell from 70% in December, 2001, to only 51% in August 2002. Support for the war fell to levels seen during the Vietnam War—33%, if the war were, hypothetically, to make 5,000 American victims. Worse, only 20% of respondents thought that the United States should proceed against Iraq without the support of its allies. This was not far from the support for an invasion as polled in Great Britain, 19%. In fact, the American people never demanded that their country go to war against Iraq, just as Americans never demanded that their country be transformed from a respected democracy into an interventionist empire. Both were imposed upon them by a small group of far-right neo-conservative ideologues.

As the war plans proceeded, some level-headed Americans, well-known and possessing vast experience, began to intervene publicly against the plans of the neo-conservative "hawks" who were advising the president. These men had seen war first-hand and were better able than less experienced people to weigh the risks and the costs of war.

Republican Senator Chuck Hagel, a member of the Senate Foreign Affairs Committee, and a veteran of the Vietnam War— another senseless, discretionary imperialistic war, in which 58,209 young Americans were uselessly sacrificed because of the tragic decisions of a handful of politicians—resumed the issue, *"It is interesting to me that many of those who want to rush this country into war and think it would be so quick and easy don't know anything about war. They come at it from an intellectual perspective versus having sat in jungles or foxholes and watched their friends get their heads blown off. I try to speak for those ghosts of the past a little bit."* [208]

His words were echoed by General Anthony Zinni, former Chief of the U.S. Central Command and special envoy to the Near East, *"Attacking Iraq now will cause a lot of problems... If you ask me my opinion, Gen. Scowcroft, Gen. Powell, Gen. Schwarzkopf, Gen. Zinni, maybe all see this the same way"*. He added that *"it might be interesting to wonder why all the generals see it the same way, and all those that never fired a shot in anger and really hell-bent to go to war see it a different way. That's usually the way it is in history."* Other generals, such as Norman Schwarzkopf, head of "Desert Storm" against Iraq in 1991, and Wesley K. Clark, former Commander-in-Chief of NATO, also publicly agreed.[209]

Brent Scowcroft, another former general, and in fact, a former National Security Advisor for George H. Bush, reminded George W. Bush that a preemptive war against Iraq would weaken international support for the war on terrorism and would cast the United States in the role of aggressor for the first time in its history. It would be the best way to antagonize all its friends, to intensify the political instability in the Middle East, and to damage long-term U.S. interests.

For William Cohen, former Secretary of Defense in the Clinton administration, *"Saddam Hussein is not more of a threat today than yesterday"*. Cohen doubted that it was necessary to attack Iraq in order to protect the United States.[210]

James Baker was Secretary of State in the administration of George Bush, Sr. from 1989 to 1992, and thus served during the Gulf War of 1990-91. He urged George Bush, Jr. to be prudent.

Baker presided over a coalition of 40 countries that participated in the operation to expulse Saddam Hussein from Kuwait—declared by Hussein to be Iraq's 19th province. Eleven years later, Baker opined that in short-circuiting the U.N. Security Council, the U.S. would succeed only in isolating itself and undermining its moral position in the world.

Former Secretary Baker proposed instead to incite the Security Council to adopt a resolution enjoining Iraq to accept U.N. inspections at any time, in any place, and without exceptions, as well as authorizing the use of force if necessary in order to carry out the inspections.[211] Moreover, he urged Bush to put all the weight of the United States behind the search for a solution to the Palestinian-Israeli conflict, and thus to restore America's credibility.[212]

All these admonitions, coming from experienced Republicans, as well as urgings from senators Bob Graham (FL), Arien Specter (PA), and Richard Lugar (IN), not to mention Dick Armey, Republican House Majority Leader, and a fellow Texan, as well as Lawrence Eagleberger, Baker's successor at the State Department, rattled Bush. They somewhat neutralized the combative influence of Cheney, Rumsfeld, and Rice in the confrontation with Secretary of State Colin Powell. For Congressman Armey, it was clear that *"the United States has no justification for attacking, if there is no Iraqi provocation."*[213]

On September 1, 2002, Secretary of State Colin Powell, a former general, spoke publicly of his disagreement with his colleagues, saying that he believed the Iraqi crises could be defused if the U.N. resumed arms inspections.[214] A cabinet that can't convince the only general in its midst of the soundness of its military policy must really be out of good arguments.[215]

One might expect that the opposition to Republican George W. Bush's militarist stance would come from the Democratic Party. However, after Al Gore's heart-breaking loss in 2001, the most visible Democratic standard-bearer in Washington was his running mate, Senator Joe Lieberman (CN). Lieberman is a politician who is on the right of Bush, besides being completely devoted to the interests of the Israeli government.[216]

Other Democratic leaders were much less critical than certain Republicans. They didn't dare confront both Bush and Lieberman, choosing to support the objective of overthrowing Saddam Hussein, while hoping that Congress would be consulted as to the means. The Democrats in Congress, in the words of Tom Daschle, the Senate Democratic leader, wanted to *"move on to other things"*.[217]

Former President Jimmy Carter (1976-1980), Nobel Peace Prize laureate in 2002, was practically alone when he denounced the dangerous tack taken by the Bush administration and its withdrawal from its traditional defense of human rights. Concerning the cabal in favor of war, Carter repeated what should have been evident, *"Baghdad is not now a threat to the United States"*.[218]

But the Democratic Party, under the informal direction of Joe Lieberman, had joined the anti-Iraq cabal.[219] Lieberman exclaimed, without fear of being contradicted, *"We (the Democrats) feel that the president should be authorized to take military action without the U.N. if the U.N. will not do it."*[220]

It was only after a strong intervention by Al Gore, in a speech in San Francisco on September 23, 2002, that the Democrats emerged from their lethargy. With firmness and clarity, Gore exposed the reasons that the United States should not violate the U.N. Charter and launch a unilateral war. In the days that followed, other Democratic figures, among them Senator Ted Kennedy, raised their voices.

The fact remains that on questions of war and peace, as on many other issues, in the words of writer Gore Vidal, the U.S. is not far from having a one-party system...with two right wings.[221] This is perhaps the reason why so many Americans feel disfranchised and that less than 4 out 10 bother to vote in mid-term elections, and only 5 out of 10 vote in presidential elections. This is the lowest participation rate of any democratic country. Since abstentionism is a form of protest vote, one can say that there exists in the U.S. a fair amount of political alienation. American democracy is deeply unbalanced, even if the powers to be would deny such an assessment.

Faced with the ambivalence and the diffidence of the Democratic opposition, Bush could ignore his critics and the isolated calls for caution and devote himself to war preparations. The day after James Baker's declaration, Vice President Dick Cheney refused Baker's advice and publicly reiterated the need for the U.S. to launch a "preventive" war against Iraq. The reason, he said, was because one day, Saddam Hussein might take control of the Middle East and of *"a large part of the world's oil reserves"*.

Alberto R. "Al" Gonzales, the Administration's attorney, argued that the president could declare war against Iraq without the approval of Congress, despite the fact that the Constitution says otherwise, and despite the "War Resolution Act of 1973", which, since the Vietnam War, forbids any president from deciding, by himself, to go to war.[222]

For his part, the Secretary of Defense, Donald H. Rumsfeld, acting as the true Secretary of State, multiplied his appearances before congressional committees and in the media to promote the idea that the U.S. should attack Iraq. No one knew who—Colin Powell or Donald H. Rumsfeld—was really in charge of American foreign policy.[223] Worse, when the time came to prepare a resolution for Congress to give its approval of a "preventive" attack against Iraq, it was the study of attorney Gonzales that was asked to write it.[224]

The war against terrorism marks time

While George W. Bush and his advisors set their sights on Iraqi oil, the war to eradicate the al Qaeda terrorist network marked time. For one thing, the anti-terrorist operation the United States had begun in Afghanistan after September 11, 2001, was far from complete. True, the Talibans had been ousted, the al Qaeda training camps had been destroyed, and a provisional Afghan government had been formed under the leadership of President Hamid Karzaï.

However, the anti-terrorist battle itself had slowed down. Neither the al Qaeda leader, Osama bin Laden—the man George W. Bush wanted "dead or alive" after September 11—nor his right-hand man, Ayman al-Zawahiri, had been captured. The Taliban leader, Mollah Mohammed Omar, was still at large. Many

Afghan Islamist terrorists were hiding in Islamic enclaves in neighboring Pakistan. And President Hamid Karsaï, whose authority hardly extended past the confines of Kabul, was often the target of assassination attempts.[225]

What was perhaps even more dangerous for the future stability of Afghanistan, the reconstruction aid that had been solemnly promised arrived in a trickle.[226] The democracy that George W. Bush claimed would be established in Iraq was not apparent in Afghanistan. Women were still oppressed, although the girls' schools were finally opening, while the "warlords" were again masters, as before, and controlled most of the country outside the capital. A report published by Human Rights Watch (HRW), in November of 2002, commented that Afghanistan was still a divided country, ruled by clan warlords who intimidate and repress the local population, and deprive them of elementary rights.

It was evident that the political, social, and military situation in Afghanistan was far from stable. The country was hardly a model of liberty and democracy for the region. Afghanistan was even at risk of once more becoming a hornet's nest of Islamist terrorist activity. Even though other NATO countries, such as Germany and Canada did step in, the United States was nevertheless in danger of getting bogged down in Afghanistan just as Russia had been a dozen years before, when it was the U.S. who supplied weapons and aid to the Talibans to fight the "infidels".

The ravages of Islamist terrorism touched the whole world and upset the stability that is necessary for the freedom of movement of people and commerce. Now it was a French oil tanker that was the target of terrorists off the coast of Yemen. Then again, it was hundreds of young Westerners who were burned and mutilated in a Bali tourist center in Muslim Indonesia.[227]

It was common knowledge that the war against al Qaeda, Osama bin Laden, and Islamist terrorism did not really involve Iraq, a less religious country, relatively untouched by Islamist extremism. There were many people in other countries, however, beginning with Pakistan, Iran, Saudi Arabia, Sudan, Yemen,

Indonesia, Malaysia, East Africa and Chechnya, who were actively supporting Islamist terrorist groups. It was these countries who should have been the first—well before Iraq under the dictatorship of Saddam Hussein—to be summoned to cease their support of terrorism.

If Saddam Hussein's Iraq, or any other country, were actively encouraging international terrorist groups, the entire world community, and not just the United States, would be justified in condemning that country and ordering it to put an end to its support, under the threat of military sanctions and being put under the protectorate of the United Nations. This was the case in Afghanistan, when it accepted to become a haven for the al Qaeda training camps. No one objected to the right of the United Nations and of the United States—the country that had suffered an attack—to take military action against Afghanistan. Put simply, if Saddam Hussein were an international terrorist, he would lose his legitimacy, and the United Nations, through a coalition of volunteer countries, would be thoroughly justified in taking the necessary steps to overthrow him.

In 2002-2003, this was not the case. It could be argued that the dictator Saddam Hussein was a hypothetical threat, given his past animosity against Israel and the United States. However, there was no direct link between the Iraqi regime and international Islamist terrorism. Hussein was suspected of being sympathetic to international terrorism, and even of supporting it in secret. The U.S. government alleged that Iraq had furnished nerve gas to al Qaeda, but it never furnished any proof of its claim.[228] Without such proof, it is not difficult to imagine that such accusations were made to demonize Hussein and his government, by knowingly exaggerating their perceived threat.

Despite this, after having begun a legitimate and necessary anti-terrorist war in Afghanistan, the Bush administration seemed all too happy to abandon the job only half-done and to launch an operation of military aggression against Iraq. As a result, they risked unduly intensifying hatred for the United States and the West, and increasing terrorist attacks.[229]

It was an historic occasion to "invade Iraq no matter what". The Bush White House thought it could put its hands on "the Iraqi oil pump"[230] at small a cost.[231] The November 5, 2002, mid-term elections could be fought on the popular theme of a foreign war to insure *"America's security"*. The pro-Israel lobby would abandon the Democratic Party and support Republican candidates, with the possibility of a Republican sweep of the government (White House, Senate, House of Representatives, Supreme Court). It would be the first time in 80 years that one party controlled the entire government. The government of Ariel Sharon in Israel could stall the establishment of a Palestinian state, while all the attention was concentrated on Iraq.[232] And, not the least, the Pentagon and the U.S. war industry could test new sophisticated weapons.[233] Civilization's vital and indispensable war—the war against terrorism—could wait.

# 9

## WAR AND PARTISAN POLITICS

*"It is not in a climate of anarchy that tyrants are born. You only see them rising, hiding behind laws and finding justification in them."*
Marquis de SADE (1740-1814)

*"Truth is always the first casualty of war."*
Rudyard KIPLING (1865-1936)

*"Nobody ever went broke underestimating the intelligence of the American people."*
H. L. MENCKEN

*"God is always on the side of the biggest battalions."*
King FREDERICK II "the Great" of Prussia (1712-1786)

Karl Rove, an extreme-right Republican, is George W. Bush's chief political advisor, head electoral strategist, and patronage czar. In January of 2002, he told Bush that the Republicans would *"create a favorable context"* for the November 5th, 2002, mid-term elections. His objective was for the Republicans to regain control of the Senate, the key to controlling the composition of the Supreme Court.[234]

Historically, the party that controls the White House loses ground in the mid-term election. Since 1860, with only two exceptions, the president's party has lost seats in the House when the president is not risking his office. In fact, since 1945, the presidential party has lost an average of 27 seats in the mid-terms. This is a source of much preoccupation for the party in power. In 2002, the Republican Party held only eleven more House seats than the Democrats. The Democrats could realistically hope to regain control of the House, especially since the state of the economy favored them.

It was glaringly obvious that the Republicans couldn't run on their economic and legislative performance to retain control of the House, nor take control of the Senate, which was lost when the Republican Senator Jim Jeffords (Vermont) became an Independent. The stock markets were greatly depressed since their winter 2000 highs.

After the tax breaks George W. Bush had given and was planning to give to the richest taxpayers, and the huge planned increases in military expenditures, the federal budget had gone from a $100 billion yearly surplus under the Clinton administration to a projected $400 billion annual deficit, in 2003, and was expected to balloon to a record $480 billion and more in 2004 in the aftermath of the war against Iraq. Fiscal deficits and an expanding public debt were projected for the next eight years. In fact, there should be a cumulative federal deficit of $1.4 trillion for the 2004-2013 period, pushing the national debt to $7 trillion by 2013, just as the 77 million American baby boomers begin their retirement. A fiscal disaster is therefore looming on the horizon.

Indeed, when Mr. Bush took office, the 10-year budget projection showed a $5.6 trillion surplus. This was a public sector savings earmarked to cover the projected Social Security deficit when baby boomers start to retire. In 2001, the Bush administration went to work to erase the projected surplus. Even with rising post-9/11 costs, it presented a first tax cut which brought the projected surplus down to $1 trillion. This was a tax cut that delivered about 40 percent of its benefits to the richest 1 percent of American families. In 2003, even with new homeland security expenses and those expenditures connected with the war against Iraq, the Bush administration went ahead with a second tax-cut package that turned the 10-year fiscal projection into a $4 trillion deficit, largely financed by borrowing money from Japan and China.[235] It can be said that George W. Bush turned the 10-year federal budget around on the order of $10 trillion, a tremendous shift in fiscal matters.

This alarmed Alan Greenspan, the Federal Reserve chairman, who warned that U.S. budget deficits could spiral out of control, bring the U.S. dollar down, force an increase in interest rates and damage the economy. In particular, the Fed Chairman bluntly challenged the Bush administration's contention that exploding budgetary deficits pose little danger or that the government can largely offset them through faster economic growth. In Greenspan's words, "... *faster economic growth alone is not likely to be the full solution to the currently projected long-term deficits.*"[236] The International Monetary Fund was not too thrilled either to see worldwide long term interest rates being pushed upwards by the huge U.S. Treasury borrowings.

And, sign of the times, the word "propaganda" was used more and more often in relation to the Bush administration. Under George W. Bush, it seems the entire governmental apparatus was placed under partisan political control. Basic information regarding government policies were kept secret or distorted when made public. A good case in point was the tremendous fiscal impact of Bush's tax cuts. Even though such a misguided economic policy did not produce any jobs, while creating a $400 billion-plus deficit, U.S. Treasury's simulations showing how the top 1 percent of families profited immensely from the measure were never made public. In the past, such analyses were routinely made public. No intelligent democratic debates can take place without this basic information. Democracy is distorted and bad decisions are made.[237]

Moreover, the daily business scandals among Bush's closest supporters highlighted the unbelievable greed of a large part of U.S. corporate management. Consumer confidence was in free fall, and the massive layoffs in the strategic communications and technology sector threatened to send the economy back into recession in a not-too-distant future. Already, in less than three years, 2 million jobs had been lost since George W. Bush's arrival in power.

George W. Bush's dubious policies, conceived in an intellectual vacuum, were high-stakes gambles that could seriously damage the international political order but, also, the international economy. Indeed, a weak U.S. dollar meant that all other currencies were appreciating. Economic stagnation, such as prevalent in Europe and Japan, could turn into a worldwide recession. Domestically, everything was going wrong and risked getting worse. That is why Richard "Dick" Gephardt, the House Minority Leader, could wish out loud that the Democrats would win 40 new seats and take control of the House.

It is easy to see why the Republican strategists were preoccupied with the coming mid-term elections. Since all 435 members of the House and one third of the Senate were up for election, they were especially anxious that the election not be fought on the financial scandals, job losses, or the stock market slide. If it were, the Republicans would lose their shirts.[238] No, the election had to be fought on the themes of patriotism and war.

They held a trump card. The president's approval rating was between 60% and 70% when he talked about the war against terrorism and war plans to invade Iraq. Americans listened when Bush talked about Saddam Hussein and the need to destroy his installations for producing weapons of mass destruction (nuclear, biological, and chemical). The November 5, 2002, elections would be about war, not about the economy.[239]

It was hard to fight an election against Osama bin Laden. No one could find him. Instead, why not center the election on that Arab bogeyman Saddam "Satan" Hussein, the Persian Gulf War enemy who, more than ten years later, taunted the son as he had taunted the father. An election about al Qaeda and Osama bin Laden was not an option. Not only was he still at large and able to plan more attacks against the U.S., but he was a symbol of government failure, while Saddam Hussein had been defeated in 1991, and was a much more visible target.

Even if Saddam Hussein had nothing to do with the terrorist attacks on September 11, 2001, he was an easily identifiable symbol of terrorism and the perfect enemy—an Arab dictator with a reputation for cruelty against the Kurdish and Shiite minorities in his country. What is more, he was sitting on the world's second greatest known reserve of crude oil.

Despite all this, when Al Gore declared that the most important thing was the war against Islamist terrorism, the Administration hastened to put out an argument tying the al Qaeda terrorists to Baghdad, without offering any credible proof of their allegations.[240] Such accusations were even more suspect when

Donald H. Rumsfeld repeated Winston Churchill's quip that "*In war-time, truth is so precious, she should always be attended by a bodyguard of lies*".[241]

The tactic of George W. Bush's strategists in 2002, could have been lifted from the satirical movie "Wag the Dog"[242]. In the film, which highlights cynicism in politics and in the electronic media. Just days before an election, a president's strategists invent a totally ficticious conflict to distract voters' attention from domestic political scandals. Except this time, it was for real.

When the Democrats understood the scope of the Republican's electoral strategy—and after George W. Bush himself lit the fire by declaring that, "*The Senate is more interested in special interests in Washington and not interested in the security of the American people*"—they were forced to attack Bush on his own ground.[243] But it was too late.

A *Washington Post-ABC* poll, conducted in early Fall 2002, showed that the attention given Iraq and terrorism had helped the Republicans.[244] As a rule, voters who were more preoccupied by the economy favored the Democrats, but those who thought that terrorism was the greatest threat tended to endorse the Republicans.

Democrats found some comfort in the ambivalence shown by many Americans in the face of a possible invasion of Iraq, especially in the absence of the usual U.S. allies. Even though a majority of Americans (61%) had been persuaded that it would be acceptable to use force to overthrow Iraq, without the presence of allied countries, that support fell to 47%, compared to 46% who were against the use of force.[245]

The resolution George W. Bush sent to Congress on September 20, 2002, asking for advance authorization to attack and invade Iraq, allowed the Democrats to show their unease with the Administration's strategy. Bush asked for Congress to approve the use of "*all necessary means, including force...to reestablish international peace and security in the region.*" The Democrats succeeded in limiting congressional authorization to Iraq, and not to the entire Middle East.

But the horse was out of the barn. Although lacking the legitimacy of the United Nations, Bush had that of Congress. He could thus pursue his military crusade against Iraq, and especially against Saddam Hussein.

## 1964: The Gulf of Tonkin Resolution

It wasn't the first time that on the eve of an election a president asked for a blank check to make war. In August, 1964, less than a year after he became president following the Kennedy assassination (November 23, 1963), Lyndon B. Johnson was seeking his first electoral mandate. It's a well-known fact in political circles that the best stance for a sitting president at election time is to appear before the electorate in his role of Commander-in-Chief.

Three months before the election, Johnson found the pretext he was searching for to make the Vietnam War the main issue. The war had not yet produced the devastation we now know was to come and still enjoyed solid support among the general population. Johnson had wished for some time to enlarge the war against communist North Vietnam. At the time, the war was conducted more or less successfully by the armies of South Vietnam and Laos, with the aid of American "advisors".

Johnson's political and military strategists invented outright a scenario aimed at provoking North Vietnam into attacking U.S. forces. The U.S. conducted reconnaissance and spy missions in order to coordinate attacks by the South Vietnam and Laotian air forces. The U.S. battleship Maddox was dispatched close to the shore of North Vietnam. When the North Vietnamese tried to chase the ship away, the United States claimed it was an unjustified and unprovoked attack, and that the Maddox was a peaceful ship sailing in international waters. Years later, Robert McNamara, the Secretary of Defense at the time, tearfully admitted that it was all a hoax aimed at escalating the war, so that Congress would approve the deployment of troops to Vietnam.

The media, whether gullible or in connivance, immediately headlined that an American ship had been attacked by Vietnam on the high seas, without provocation. President Lyndon B. Johnson, somber and serious, appeared on national television and announced his decision to respond to the attack. In a move that hugely expanded the war, he authorized the direct bombing of North Vietnam. At the same time, his advisors quickly sent Congress a resolution that authorized the president to step up the war by using *"all necessary means, including the use of armed forces"*, to respond to the North Vietnamese aggression.

The Tonkin Gulf Resolution was adopted by the Senate, on August 7, 1964, three months before the presidential elections, by a vote of 98 to 2. The resolution gave President "L.B.J." the authority to go to war without having to ask Congress for a formal declaration of war, and it allowed him to go before the electorate in the uniform of the Commander-in-Chief. The resolution remains one of the best examples of political lies and manipulation ever imagined to influence public opinion.

In November of 1964, Lyndon B. Johnson was elected president by a landslide against his right-wing Republican rival, Senator Barry Goldwater. By the time the discretionary Vietnam War ended ten years later in an American defeat, 58,000 young Americans had lost their lives and more than a million Vietnamese had perished. All for nothing, except for the 1964 election of Lyndon B. Johnson.

## The United Nations resolution

Thirty-eight years later, in November of 2002, it looked like history would repeat itself with another Texan president. A few short weeks before an important election, George W. Bush's October resolution to Congress had a strongly partisan domestic flavor. Moreover, the resolution contained a double goal: the disarmament of Iraq and the unconditional overthrow of Saddam Hussein's government. The first objective was in accordance with international law. The second was not. In fact, it was blatantly obvious that the second objective was illegal from the point of view of international law.

The French foreign affairs minister, Dominique de Villepin, took it upon himself to remind Bush *"The struggle against the proliferation of weapons of mass destruction—that is the priority...but an action that has as its objective a regime change goes against the rules of international law and would open the door to the worst transgressions.* " [246]

What George W. Bush and his strategists wanted from the Security Council was a resolution similar to the one given him by Congress on October 11, 2002. In the event that Iraq was found to be in "material breach" of the terms of the United Nations resolutions on weapons inspections, Bush wanted a resolution authorizing an automatic resort to force, according to American objectives, without having to go back before the Security Council.

Simply put, what the Bush administration wanted was a blank check from the U.N. allowing the U.S. to launch a war against Iraq on the flimsiest pretext. Moreover, the U.S. would be the sole judge of what constituted "material breach". There was no doubt that such a pretext would be easy to find. The Bush government would then consider that it had the green light to overthrow Saddam Hussein—its real objective—and the United Nations would serve as its legal cover.

### The French approach

The progressive, two-step, approach proposed by the French government was much more respectful of United Nations prerogatives. It was also more logical, even though at the same time it was less severe toward the Iraqi dictator. Contrary to the American project, it proposed an initial Security Council resolution that added no new requirements nor specific threats. Rather, it required Iraq to open its territory to the U.N. inspectors with no restrictions and reminded Iraq of its obligations concerning their mission. This first resolution would have no explicit mention of an automatic use of force in the case non-compliance on the part of Iraq. [247]

As a second step, if Iraq did not respect the terms of inspection and disarmament, and following an inspectors' report of non-compliance, the Security Council would evaluate and debate the measures that should be taken. The Council might authorize the use of force, but would not necessarily do so, and not before serious discussion. Under the French resolution, the Security Council would retain the unique decisional authority to prescribe or not a military attack against Iraq.

Of course, this approach displeased George W. Bush immensely. Indeed, it went against all his military plans, since it would require the U.S. to go back to the Security Council to obtain the explicit authority to attack Iraq. He would lose precious time, besides the fact that the U.S. would be at the mercy of the veto of the Council's other permanent members. The entire American plan of a concerted attack against Iraq could collapse.

In order to open hostilities against Iraq in February or March of 2003, when the climate would be favorable to military operations[248], some semblance of legitimacy from the Security Council was needed, even if the Council wished later to resume discussions on whether or not to join the U.S. in deposing Saddam Hussein.[249] The whole debate was over the necessity or not for the U.S. to come back before the Security Council to get explicit authority to attack Iraq, in the case of a report of non-compliance by the U.N. inspectors. Bush wanted the Security Council to give him enough legal cover to be able to attack Iraq at his own discretion, in case the Security Council, after receiving a circumstantial but inconclusive report from the weapons inspectors, refused to authorize the use of force.

On November 8, 2002, just three days after the Republicans' electoral sweep, the Security Council, with unanimous approval (including Syria, the only Arab country on the Council) adopted a harsh resolution enjoining Iraq to open its doors to the U.N. inspectors and to accept disarmament. For a while at least, George W. Bush had obtained the legal camouflage that he sought in order to enable him to attack, bomb, and invade Iraq on the smallest pretext. Similarly, the wishes of the U.N. Secretary General, Kofi Annan, had also been temporarily granted. The game was on.

The Bush administration finally got much of what it wanted. The United Nations would not have a formal veto on the eventual use of force by the U.S. against Iraq. In the end, France and Russia accepted a single Security Council resolution, couched in ambiguous and coded language, stipulating that Iraq would face *"serious consequences"* if Saddam Hussein refused to disarm or if he obstructed the work of the weapons inspectors. But what would happen if Iraq collaborated with the U.N. inspectors and proceeded to disarm itself? Would not the Bush administration be in a quandary?

In the end—and that could be the essential point—France and Russia didn't insist that the Security Council expressly define what would constitute the "serious consequences" referred to in the U.N. resolution. The only thing they achieved was the more or less firm promise that the U.S. would "consult" the Security Council before embarking on military operations in Iraq, once the report of the weapons inspectors was received and debated.

The two recalcitrant countries had won the battle of words and diplomatic procedure, but lost the battle of events. It appeared that France and Russia saved face, but the U.S. got at least partly what it wanted. The U.S. could, so it thought, decide alone if the "serious consequences" would mean a military attack or not, after having advised the Security Council and considered their opinions. For the first time, for better or for worse, Security Council Resolution 1441 consecrated the United States' preeminent role in the 21st Century's new world order. The United States had placed itself above the veto of the other four permanent members on the Security Council.

As in the case of the deliberations of the Security Council concerning the NATO attacks against Serbia in March of 1999, the Security Council could not oppose a veto to U.S. armed attacks against Iraq, nor propose alternative sanctions. All the council could do, with a more or less divided vote, would be to disapprove the U.S. attacks. It could not stop them.

Nevertheless, for George W. Bush, the operation had not been easy. After accepting to seek United Nations approval, France's firm position confronted him with two choices. Either he accept a fairly restrictive compromise on a single Security Council resolution, which gave him only an implicit, not an automatic, permission to attack Iraq and to effect regime change, or he could resign himself to an impasse at the Security Council, and in so doing, hope that he could block the return of U.N. inspectors to Iraq. That way, he could gain time, and, at the slightest pretense and outside of U.N. control, he could set in motion the military operations to attack Baghdad that were already being prepared.

In the first instance, and supposing that the U.N. inspectors confirmed Iraq's collaboration toward disarmament, Saddam Hussein could stay in power for years and George W. Bush would lose face. In the second, Bush would carry the blame for an unauthorized war of aggression, as well as having contributed to undermining the legitimacy of the United Nations. Indeed, if Bush invaded Iraq even before the U.N. inspections and Iraqi disarmament were completed, or even worse, if he was responsible for subverting the inspection process, he would be unanimously denounced throughout the world as a saboteur of the United Nations, an impatient aggressor pursuing his own shameful objectives.

The Bush administration's initial strategy was to use the Kosovo precedent to intervene in Iraq. Relying on past resolutions, the plan was to bypass the need for a specific U.N. resolution.[250] In this case, Bush only seemed to be trapped by the diplomatic procedures at the U.N.

France and Russia's quiet capitulation at the U.N. allowed Bush to return to his initial project, since he had implicitly received Security Council authorization to use military force against Iraq, by virtue of the "serious consequences" clause. He could act at the moment he judged propitious, (provided he received some collaboration from the U.N. inspectors regarding a non-compliance on the part of Saddam Hussein), without having to return to the Security Council.

In fact, in the Administration's mindset, it was not even certain that they needed a pretext.[251] Two short days after the Security Council adopted Resolution 1441, *The New York Times* headlined *"War Plan in Iraq Sees Large Force and Quick Strikes"*.[252] The article reported that Bush had approved a detailed plan for the invasion of Iraq by 250,000 G.I.s, following the model for the occupation of Japan in 1945. The long debate in the U.N. had all the appearances of a charade.[253]

Nevertheless, the U.N. Resolution 1441 was a double-edged sword; it could be a bane or a bust for the Bush administration. The "serious consequences" were implicitly to ensue only if the U.N. inspection process did not produce results. However, if it were to succeed or give the world the impression

113

that it was succeeding, and if the chief inspectors were confirming it, what would happen to the Bush administration's strategy? How could they decently go to war in such circumstances? Wouldn't they have painted themselves into a corner?

This was the principal weakness in the American strategy to use the United Nations to condone going to war. All along, the Bush administration had assumed that the U.N. inspectors would either be rebuffed by the Iraqi government or that they would find evidence of weapons of mass destruction, in which case the language of Resolution 1441 would legally justify the U.S. in going to war against Iraq.

What the Americans had not planned for was the possibility that the inspection process would be inconclusive and, unhampered by an established timetable, could go on indefinitely with the support of world opinion. In such an instance, all the war preparations that Bush had made according to the first scenario would place him in front of the dire choice of either losing face and recalling the troops, or proceeding without the U.N. approval and risking to be seen as an unlawful aggressor.[254]

Moreover, and unknown at the time, British Prime Minister Tony Blair, Bush's principal ally, would feel the political need to come back to the U.N. for some sort of explicit approval, before invading Iraq. Indeed, just as in the rest of the world, public opinion in the U.K. was increasingly set against Bush's war of aggression and the prospect of killing ten of thousands of Iraqis in order to establish an American puppet government in Baghdad. As more and more Britons saw Blair as George W. Bush's "lap-dog", his approval ratings plummeted. In January 2003, his overall popularity had fallen to 33 percent, while his handling of the Iraq crisis received only a 26 percent approval, and public support for the war was less than 20 percent.[255] Many Britons thought that their prime minister had betrayed his country to "a Texas gunslinger", as writer William Rees-Mogg later put it.

In practical terms, that meant that the Bush-Blair duo would have to come back to the U.N. and try to obtain some additional legitimacy for their war plans. If they were not successful and decided to proceed nevertheless with a military invasion of Iraq, the road to Iraq's oil riches would surely be paved with the remains of the United Nations. In the eyes of the world, the two colonial powers would look like two rogue states going to war in defiance of the United Nations' Charter.

## George W. Bush's partisan military strategy

Just as for Lyndon B. Johnson with the Bay of Tonkin resolution in 1964, George W. Bush's partisan military strategy paid royally on November 5th, 2002. Bush knew what he was doing when he introduced a war psychosis into the political arena. He was preparing the way for an overwhelming Republican victory in the mid-term elections. During the campaign, there would be no talk of the economy, of financial scandals, or of any other bread-and-butter issue. It would be war, patriotism, and the flag! The very day of the election, Republican strategists arranged for newspapers to headline terrorism and the war. *USA Today* titled, *"U.S. kills al Qaeda suspects in Yemen"*.[256]

The election results fulfilled the fondest hopes of Bush and the Republican strategists. Instead of the average loss of 27 House seats, Republicans won five additional seats. Even more important, given the Senate's role in approving Supreme Court nominations, Republicans took back control of the Senate by winning two new seats. All together, Republicans won 51.6% of the popular vote, even though only 39.3% of eligible voters went to the polls.[257]

The Democrats had let themselves be hoodwinked by George W. Bush. Their "me, too" strategy had backfired. Instead of criticizing and proposing alternatives to their opponents' propaganda, the Democrats had strengthened Bush and the Republican Party's main electoral theme. What was worse, they did not rally as a team. Former President Bill Clinton resumed the situation when he commented about the state of mind of Americans after September 11, *"They prefer to have someone who is strong, even if he is wrong, rather than someone who is weak, even if he's right."* Consequently, in remaining silent on the question of national security, the Democrats committed a major political blunder.[258]

In the fall of 2002, the Democrats were drubbed. The success of Bush and his "Let's go to war" party was complete. On several occasions, Bush displayed his worst character traits. He didn't hesitate to use demagogy to further his aims—demagogy against Saddam Hussein, demagogy toward Democratic candidates, demagogy against the United Nations—so much so that it seemed to become a habit. Who could seriously claim that the politics of war and patriotism *à la Bush*, is not a winning tactic in the U.S.?

# 10

## THE AMBIGUITY OF INTERNATIONAL LAWS

*"Nothing discloses real character like the use of power. It is easy for the weak to be gentle. Most people can bear adversity. But if you wish to know what a man really is, give him power. This is the supreme test."*
Robert INGERSOLL

*"The argument of the strongest is always the best."*
LA FONTAINE, Fables, "The wolf and the lamb."

*"Laws are silent in time of war".*
CICERO (106-43, B. C. )

The great social and political progress in the 18th Century came when it was discovered that parliaments and independent judicial courts were essential for establishing and preserving freedom by curbing executive power. No one can take justice into his own hands, and the arbitrary use of force is forbidden and replaced with due process. This is the foundation of liberty in our democracies.

No such progress has been attained on the international scene, where the strongest can indeed take justice into their own hands. We are still at the primitive level of the belief that "Might makes Right" and that arbitrary force can be used without the legitimacy of a world parliament or of a world court. The body of international laws and rules originates primarily in the treaties and protocols that have been signed in the past by sovereign states. This is the case of the conventions that have established international institutions, such as the United Nations, since 1945. However, since there is no world government, in order to be operational, international laws and rules must be voluntarily recognized by national governments.

The basic issue of the legality and the legitimacy of war is still nebulous. Certainly, there has been an improvement since the 19th Century, when empires decided unilaterally if and when their interests would be served by going to war. However, there is still a general climate of world anarchy, especially when heavily armed countries are involved.

## The United Nations' pacifying role

After World War II (1939-1945), it was believed that the creation of the United Nations would prevent senseless wars. In fact, the principle judiciary organ of the U.N. is the International Court of Justice, which has the mandate to settle differences between countries. In reality, however, the United Nations General Assembly is like a parliament with no true power. The real powers of intervention are vested in the U.N. executive, the Security Council.

As a consequence, nothing prevents an empire or a superpower holding a veto in the Security Council from illegally declaring war on another country, unless it be pressure from the other permanent members of the Council. Even though the rules of the United Nations forbid a country from exacting justice on its own, these rules hardly apply in practice in the case of the five powers who hold a veto in the Security Council, and, by extension, for the countries under their protective umbrella. By exercising their veto, these countries can prevent the U.N. from condemning armed aggressions by one country against another.[259]

## The Kosovo precedent

In March 1999, in the middle of the Kosovo crisis in the former Yugoslavia, the Security Council established an historical precedent when it implicitly accepted that NATO, not the U.N., launch punitive air attacks against Serbia. During 78 days, NATO forces directed a bombing campaign against Serbia, until Slobodan Milosevic was evicted from power.

The United Nations Charter admits only two circumstances in which one country is allowed to use military force against another:

- when a country must defend itself against an attack from another country;
- when the Security Council authorizes the use of military force against a country that is in violation of the principles of the U.N. Charter.

In the case of Serbia and Kosovo, it was not a situation of legitimate defense, neither for the United States, nor for any of the other NATO countries. Moreover, Kosovo was legally part of Serbia, which had attacked no other country. Nor had the Security Council explicitly authorized the use of an external military force. Indeed, even though a resolution Russia had presented seeking to condemn the NATO attacks against Serbia was defeated by 12 to 3, this was only an indirect and not a direct authorization to use force against a sovereign country.

The United Nations could have authorized such a breach to national sovereignty by invoking Article 2.7 of its Charter that says that the principle of non-interference in matters that are essentially within the domestic jurisdiction of any state shall not prejudice the application of enforcement measures under Chapter VII of the Charter. That Chapter relates not only to acts of aggression but also to threats to the peace and breaches of the peace, whether they are domestic or external. Previously, it had been implicitly assumed that such threats to peace and security must be to outside the borders of a country.

On April 5, 1991, however, the U.N. Security Council adopted Resolution 688, which described the Iraqi repression of the Kurds and Shias as a threat to international peace and security. As a consequence, France, followed by the U.S., Great Britain and a number of other countries, intervened with ground and air forces in order to compel the Iraqis to desist. The concept was that the sovereignty of a nation-state implies a responsibility to protect the human rights of its citizens, failing which, the international community would be justified in violating that sovereignty and in intervening to protect the embattled populations from the actions of their own government.[260]

Therefore, the principle that the international community has the right to resort to armed intervention in the internal affairs of a sovereign state, even against the wishes of the government of that state, in order to prevent widespread death or suffering amongst the population, seems now to be solidly part of international law.

But, in 1999, there was another complication. The majority of the Security Council deemed that the government of Slobodan Milosevic had not respected the previous Council resolutions in September and October of 1998, enjoining the Serbian government to respect the human rights of their Kosovar minority. Thus, the aggression against the Kosovars and the non-abiding of the Milosevic government of previous U.N. resolutions were considered as sufficient justification for the intervention by NATO, without an explicit authorization by the Council under Chapter VII. This was a completely new concept, that is that "humanitarian" intervention could be carried out by a group of countries without the explicit authorization of the United Nations, but only if previous U.N. resolutions enjoining a government not to persecute a minority of its citizens had not been heeded.

Since this precedent-setting intervention on "humanitarian" grounds, on the basis of numerous previous U.N. resolutions, the rule requiring a clear situation of legitimate defense for adopting a Security Council resolution authorizing one country to attack another seems to have been replaced by two rather ambiguous principles:

*First, that an attack against another country would be justified if that country had systematically ignored previous Security Council resolutions, most notably, when it is a case of protecting persecuted minorities, and this without specific Security Council authorization;*

*Second, that one country could intervene militarily against another if that country posed an exceptional and imminent threat, according to the threatened countries own appraisal, and this without the necessity of a formal Security Council resolution.*

The first principle follows directly from the Kosovo precedent, but not the second one. The first new principle justifies international interventions to protect victims from governmental persecution by virtue of a "humanitarian right of intervention". The second principle seeks to justify a military intervention by one country in the affairs of another, by virtue of its own unilateral view of its vital national interests.[261]

This second new principle makes everything a question of unilateral discretion. If this new precept came to be accepted on the international scene, the world would not be far from reverting to the anarchy of the 19th Century. Questions of war and peace between countries would be decided in a completely arbitrary manner. It would be as if the United Nations were rendered insignificant. The very institution the U.S. helped to create, it is now trying to neutralize—if not actually sabotage. Under this new doctrine, any country which has the means to do so could launch an attack against another, on the simple basis of a violation of previous U.N. decisions, or if there is a perceived threat to itself, or even to a third country. The United Nations would not have to vote an explicit authorization for the use of force.

## The case of Iraq

The Kosovo precedent has important consequences. It is this precedent that George W. Bush cited to justify his intention to invade Iraq on his own. He argued that the Iraqi government had not respected several Security Council resolutions demanding the elimination of all weapons of mass destruction and the return of U.N. weapons inspectors. Bush also claimed that Iraq was a threat to the United States and to its allies, without, however, furnishing any proof. The fact that Saddam Hussein had persecuted the Kurdish and Shia minorities was scarcely mentioned to justify an intervention, since the Bush administration had already officially taken a position against political independence for either group. Later, Deputy Secretary of Defense Paul Wolfowitz would publicly admit that no U.S. troops would have been committed to defend the Iraqi population.[262]

On September 12, 2002, George W. Bush addressed the United Nations General Assembly. He presented his view of the United States' role as world policeman in these terms, *"The*

*Security Council resolutions will be enforced."* His intentions were even more limpid when he delivered an ultimatum to the U.N.: either you force Iraq to respect the previous relevant Security Council resolutions, or the United States, and its military, will do it for you.[263]

In other words, the United States under George W. Bush was summoning the United Nations to adopt any resolution proposed by its government...or else. By threatening unilateral military strikes against another sovereign country, was George W. Bush, in 2003, risking being perceived as about to violate international law, just as Adolf Hitler had done in Poland and Czechoslovakia in 1938-39, the Soviet tandem of Nikolai Bulganin and Nikita Khrushchev in Hungary, in 1956, or as Leonid Bresznev did in 1968 by invading Czechoslovakia and as in 1979, when the Soviet Union invaded Afghanistan?

In fact, such a precedent and the U.S. ultimatum went farther than many—including perhaps George W. Bush himself— might wish. Bush's foremost lack of credibility on the international scene comes from the fact that he chooses which U.N. resolutions must be obeyed and which ones can be ignored with impunity. He seems to have a morality *à la carte*, since he doesn't demand that all Security Council resolutions be respected for fear of sanctions, or even military attack. For example, since the Israeli government has ignored dozens of General Assembly and Security Council resolutions, would the new interpretation of international law permit a country such as Russia or Egypt to attack Israel and force a regime change?

## Bush's objectives

For a moment on September 16, 2002, the world thought that the Bush administration's war preparations would be halted when Iraq unconditionally assented to U.N. weapons inspections to verify that there were no weapons of mass destruction on Iraqi territory.[264] The same hopes arose on October 1st, when Hans Blix, the U.N. chief weapons inspector, announced that an agreement had been reached with Iraq on the conditions for the return of the inspectors.[265] The Security Council's central objective was unconditional inspections in Iraq and its disarmament of all weapons of mass destruction. This mirrored the recommendations of the former Secretary of State, James Baker.

However, it was not the true goal of George W. Bush. Some people, such as a *New York Times* editorialist, wondered out loud about Bush's true objectives, noting that at the United Nations, the U.S. spoke only of the effective disarmament of Saddam Hussein, while in his electoral speeches, Bush spoke endlessly of the overthrow of the "Iraqi dictator".[266]

The link with oil was rarely mentioned, if at all, even though it is most doubtful there would have been a war against Iraq if the White House had been occupied by a president and a vice-president who had not come from the oil industry.[267] Indeed, disarming Iraq wouldn't lead to direct control of the Iraqi government, so in order to sign contracts for oil prospecting and production, the Hussein government had to be replaced by a more accommodating one.

It was not at all evident that George W. Bush really cared if Iraq respected the U.N. resolutions or not, nor if the world was assured that Saddam Hussein no longer possessed weapons of mass destruction. As if to confirm that the objective was really to take strategic control of Baghdad, some anonymous government officials told *The New York Times* that, in the event Saddam Hussein were to be overthrown even before the American strikes, the U.S. could still intervene, in order to "liberate" and "pacify" the country.[268]

In other words, even if Iraq had completely disarmed in obedience to the United Nations, and even if Saddam Hussein had been overthrown or pushed into exile by the Iraqis themselves, George W. Bush would not be have been satisfied. The U.S. administration had to seize the Iraqi government and use it for its own ends.[269] As history will later record, the entire "weapons of mass destruction" pretext was a scheme to dupe domestic and international audiences and a smokescreen for an undisclosed agenda (see chapter 15 below).

Bush's real objectives were clear. First, to be sure that the U.S. controlled the Iraqi government and ultimately the entire supply of Middle East oil; and second, that Iraq cease to be a threat of any kind to Israel.[270] For that to happen, the U.S. had to set up a puppet regime with which lucrative oil contracts could be negotiated. As an indication that the Administration's war plans were highly detailed, even before the U.S. invasion of Iraq, Halliburton, a Texas company connected to Vice President Dick Cheney who was its chairman until 2000, obtained a contract from the Pentagon for advice on rebuilding Iraq's oil fields after the planned war.[271] The Bush administration had decided that it wanted to take control of Baghdad, but what right did it have to do so?

Bush and international law

Did the Bush administration have the right under international law to invade a sovereign nation? The U.S.-led invasion of Iraq was not formally approved by the United Nations. If changing the governments of member countries is not one of the prerogatives of the U.N., changing the governments of sovereign countries is even less a prerogative of the United States of America.

The United Nations Charter, which every member country must respect, is very clear. It outlines the cardinal rule of international law that the territorial integrity of all states must be respected. No international order is possible without this principle.

Article 2.3 and Article 2.4 of the Charter stipulate that:

2.3. All Members shall settle their international disputes by peaceful means in such a manner that international peace and security, and justice, are not endangered.

2.4. All Members shall refrain in their international relations from the threat or use of force against the territorial integrity or political independence of any state, or in any other manner inconsistent with the Purposes of the United Nations.

In arrogating the right to overthrow the Iraqi government and depose Saddam Hussein by force, the Bush administration was prepared to violate international law and the United Nations Charter.

Until the Kosovo precedent of "humanitarian international military intervention" within a sovereign state to protect basic human rights of minorities (but not to overthrow its government) specialists in international law knew only two exceptions to this comprehensive prohibition of state-sponsored violence.

The first exception is every state's natural right to self-defense (Article 51 of the Charter). The second exception concerns the collective coercive measures of the United Nations according to articles 42 and 53 of the Charter. Accordingly, the U.N. Security Council can allow certain member states or regional alliances to use force if a country is in clear violation of the U.N. Charter. This is the reason the U.S. and British governments were anxious to obtain a majority support from the 15-member Security Council. Having failed to win such a seal of approval, the U.S.-led invasion of Iraq appears to the rest of the world to be an illegal and illegitimate act of aggression to replace its government with one of the aggressors' liking.

But, under international law, no individual country can legally use force against another outside of the above narrow situations, without provoking *ipso facto* a return to international anarchy.

## The U.S. and international law

Why then was the U.S. government determined to undermine the international legal system, as it did when it declared itself ready to go to war alone against Iraq? There is no other country in the world that benefits more from the system of international law than the United States of America. American economic and financial interests are substantial and worldwide. The last thing the U.S. needs is a regression of international relations towards anarchy and the rule of brute force.

It would be a terrible mistake for the Bush administration to be so shortsighted as to believe that the U.S. will be able to prosper in a world devoid of international legal order, relying solely on its military might to defend its legitimate interests. If the Bush administration's planners follow the dangerous precedent that others before them have applied with disastrous results (for example, Hitler's Germany, Mussolini's Italy and Krushchev's

Russia), they will be launching the United States on a mine-filled journey it will sooner or later deeply regret.

Other nations in the future, when they become powerful enough, will inevitably attempt to follow in Bush's footsteps and invoke his own precedent for unilateral military action, against any sovereign nation they choose. Where would the world be then? Back to the 19th Century, and possibly, back to the middle of the 17th Century, before the Treaty of Westphalia, which was signed after the end of the European Thirty Years (religious) War!

The Treaty of Westphalia incorporated four basic principles: 1—The principle of the sovereignty of nation-states and the concomitant fundamental right of political self-determination; 2—the principle of (legal) equality between nation-states; 3—the principle of internationally binding treaties between states; and, 4—the principle of non-intervention of one state in the internal affairs of other states.

That is why the Treaty of Westphalia (1648) is so crucial in the history of international political relations. This important treaty formed the basis for the modern international system of independent nation-states. In fact, it marked the beginning of an international community of law between sovereign states of equal legal standing, guaranteeing each other their independence and the right of their peoples to political self-determination. The two most innovative principles being proclaimed were the principle of sovereignty and the principle of equality among nations. They were truly political and legal innovations for the time.

Thus, the Treaty defined these new principles of sovereignty and equality among states in order to establish a durable (eternal) peace and friendship among them, within a mutually acceptable system of international law, based on internationally binding treaties. This was a revolutionary approach to international relations because, for the first time, it established a system that respected peoples' rights and that relied on international law, rather than on brute force and the right of the strongest to regulate interactions between states.

A fifth principle was also present in the Treaty of Westphalia of 1648, and it is the idea that in order to achieve an enduring peace, magnanimity, concessions and cooperation had to be shown by the victorious parties.[272] It was the beginning of a genuine international constitution for humanity, the advent of a new international order and a big step forward for civilization.[273]

After the Thirty Years War, religion became less and less a politically motivating force behind conflicts between European states, being replaced by considerations of national interest. In a way, after 1648, international affairs became "secularized" and somewhat devoid of religious considerations.

If the United States, under George W. Bush, were to declare itself to be *de facto* above international law and claim the right to provoke regime changes in other sovereign countries, this would be an illegal and illegitimate objective. Regime change as a goal of military intervention violates the system of international relations, not only since the advent of the United Nations, but also since the Westphalia Peace Treaty of 1648.

The Medieval concept of "Just War" or of "just cause"[274]

People with a religious bent sometimes refer to the ancient and medieval concept of "Just War" or "righteous war" when they want to justify an offensive and aggressive war. Crafted at a time when the technology of violence was much less advanced than today, the concept of "Just War" pertains to justifying war along Christian moral principles.[275] In reality, the Christian "Just War" concept is the equivalent of the Muslim "Jihad".

Since war's central action is to inflict suffering and death on other people, and since religions purposefully forbid doing to others what one does not want to be done to oneself, or that, as in St. Paul's writings, one must not render "evil for evil", but overcome it with good (Rom. 12:17, 21), it is not easy to justify war and military murder in the name of religion. Nevertheless, historically, some religious scholars, especially after the Church became identified with the Roman Empire, attempted to devise pragmatic arguments to justify wars under certain conditions, from then on considering religion as a stalwart supporter of public authority.

Aurelius Augustinus, better known as St. Augustine of Hippo (354-430), the originator of the Just War Theory, contended that there was a difference between individual morality and public morality. For the individual, even in cases of self-defense of one's life or property, there was never a justification for killing one's neighbor. For a government, however, the Christian morality was more elastic when it meant killing other human beings.

For Augustine, if Christianity were to become an integral part of the Roman Empire, it had to cease being a pacifist religion and stop being opposed to all wars and all killings. Indeed, notwithstanding the Christian precepts of "*Thou shall not kill*" and Jesus Christ's clear message against war and conflict in his admonition to "*turn the other cheek*" and his order to Peter, "*Put up thy sword into the sheath*" [John 18:11], Augustine, following Paul of Tarshis before him, believed that the rulers of nations have an obligation to maintain peace, and to do so, they may engage in wars and killings...under certain circumstances. For Augustine, however, there were very few instances when one nation is justified in attacking another. A government, and therefore its citizens, can wage war only when it is absolutely necessary to defend the nation's peace against serious injury.[276]

In general, the Just War Theory for waging offensive wars of aggression characterizes a war between two sovereign nations as being "just" if it meets three main classical criteria:

- The war must be waged with the *right intention* and for good reasons; that is to say, it cannot be undertaken for revenge or for economic gain and to acquire territories or riches, but to restore peace and not be carried on for the sake of pursuing a victory won by violence ;

- the war must be authorized and declared by a *legitimate authority*, that is, an emperor or a king. Today, when considerations of international peace and good order are paramount, war can only be authorized by an international authority, either an international organization or an international court of justice;

- the war must be undertaken for a *just cause*. It must satisfy the principle of proportionality between the force used and the injury

128

suffered, as well as of discrimination between aims and means in order to defend the nation's peace. To protect itself against serious injury, a nation must not use excessive force. Military force may be used only to correct a grave threat, where the basic rights of a whole population are at stake.

During the Middle Ages, scholastic philosophers such as Thomas Aquinas, Francisco Suarez and Francisco de Vitoria, further developed the Just War Theory, not on the basis of the teachings of Jesus, but on account of natural law.[277] For them, a war of self-defense needed "no special moral justification." However, an offensive war should be viewed only as a defensive measure and needed to be justified by two additional principles, besides the three main criteria already outlined:

- The war must be fought as a *last resort*, after all avenues of peaceful negotiations have been exhausted; and,

- the war must be carried out in a *proper manner*, without killing innocent people indiscriminately.

Nowadays, with the tremendous and awesome destructive power of modern weapons, such principles of "Just War" are irrelevant and cannot be invoked to launch aggressive wars. It is obvious that the use of nuclear weapons, tactical or otherwise, is morally prohibited under any circumstances, because they are designed to kill innocent people indiscriminately.[278] Even the so-called "smart" bombs that certain U.S. military people boast about are morally indefensible and unjust. According to the Pentagon itself, such "smart" bombs miss their targets more often than they hit them.

Such is also the case with cluster bombs,[279] at least five percent of them explode days or weeks after impact, and are often picked up by civilians or unsuspecting children. The same can be said about land mines that kill more non-combatants than combatants. The moral conclusion is clear. Sophisticated modern weapons have rendered modern warfare obsolete because it is no longer waged between armies, but against civilian populations.[280]

Political thinkers who say aggressive wars are justified in theory and in practice are misguided. There cannot be a "Just War" under modern conditions and circumstances. In the aftermath of World War II, Pope Pius XII declared that *"the enormous violence of modern warfare means that it can no longer be regarded as a reasonable, proportionate means for settling conflicts."*

Pope John XXIII's encyclical "Pacem in Terris" (1963) also condemned wars of aggression when he stated, *"Therefore in this age of ours, which prides itself on its atomic power, it is irrational to think that war is a proper way to obtain justice for violated rights."* For this humanist pope, war is not a legitimate instrument of justice and it must be rejected as a viable modern political option. It should be replaced, sooner or later, by some form of legitimate global government.

Regarding the 2003 War against Iraq, Pope John Paul II took upon himself to send a special emissary, Cardinal Pio Laghi, to meet with the president and to tell George W. Bush that his planned aggressive and unjustified war against Iraq did not meet the criteria of a just war and would therefore be immoral. In a letter pleading against war, Pope John Paul II asked Bush "to spare humanity another dramatic conflict".[281]However, White House Press Secretary Ari Fleischer said that his boss wouldn't be influenced by the Pope. National Security Advisor Condoleezza Rice went even further and declared that she could not understand how anyone could consider a war against Iraq immoral.[282]

One can safely say, therefore, that the Just War Theory has been completely eliminated from religious or, for that matter, from humanist and secular morality.[283] What is left is the moral concept of self-defense and defensive wars, but then, only when there is a proportionality between the needs to secure a country's peace and the means to do so.

In regard to Bush's 2003 war of invasion against Iraq, it can be said that such a war violated all five main criteria for a "Just War". First, notwithstanding the denials, the desire to control Iraq's riches in oil reserves, as it has been amply documented in this book, was a paramount preoccupation with the Bush-Cheney administration. This violated the first condition for a just war. Second, this war was not authorized by the United Nations or the International Court of Justice, and therefore it violated the second condition for a just war. Third, it was not a just war because it was not a war of self-defense, but an offensive war "on suspicion", a war of revenge and of retribution to make a statement and to avenge the Islamist terrorists' attacks of September 11, 2001. Fourth, this was not a war of last resort since Bush's war against Iraq was launched without having given sufficient time to the United Nations inspectors to complete their work of inspection and of disarmament of Iraq. Fifth, Bush's war against Iraq involved long range bombings, missile launchings and tank blitzes that could kill thousands of innocent human beings.

Not only, therefore, are the five main principles of the "Just War Theory" obsolete for justifying modern offensive wars, but the Bush administration was violating all five moral conditions for a just war in lauching an offensive war against Iraq. The United States was not only going against international law, it was also going against recognized international morality in its military ventures.

In conclusion, when the Bush administration develops arguments to launch aggressive wars on its own all over the world, it cannot do so according to the basic principles of international law, nor can it do so according to fundamental principles of morality and justice. If it were to pursue this course, it would truly transform the United States into an international rogue state.

# 11

## THE "BUSH DOCTRINE" AFTER WESTPHALIA: A SUPREMACIST POLICY

*"Bush wants to divert attention from his domestic problems. It's a classic tactic. It's one that Hitler used."*
Herta DÄUBLER-GMELIN, German Minister of Justice[284]

*"The United States is in the process of becoming a new Mongol empire, whose interest is less to govern the world than to dominate it by force."*
Shintaro ISHIHARA, Governor of Tokyo[285]

*"It is in general a condition of free institutions that the boundaries of governments should coincide with those of nationalities."*
John Stuart MILL (1806-1873)

*"It is a big mistake for us to grant any validity to international law even when it may seem in our short-term interest to do so—because, over the long term, the goal of those who think that international law really means anything are those who want to constrict the United States."*
John BOLTON (Asst. Secretary of State for International Organizations)

President James Monroe (1758-1831) outlined a new foreign policy in a speech before Congress, in December of 1823. The U.S. government feared that European powers wanted to take back their lost territories in the Americas, especially in South America. The new foreign policy was later called the Monroe Doctrine.

In the North, Russia, which owned Alaska, claimed a territory stretching to the 51st parallel, all the way to Oregon, passing through what is today the Canadian province of British Columbia, but which at the time belonged to Great Britain. In

South America, it was feared that the Holy Alliance among Austria, Russia, and Prussia would help Spain recover its former colonies. Most of these lands had revolted against Spain, following the U.S. example, and had won their independence.

Under his new Doctrine, Monroe warned the European powers not to meddle in the affairs of the Western Hemisphere. In return, he promised not to meddle in European affairs.[286]

Now, back to the 21st Century. On June 7, 2002, George W. Bush delivered a speech to the West Point cadets. He reassured the world that *"America has no empire to extend or utopia to establish."*[287] Three months later, he seemed to have changed his mind. The expansion of American imperialism would be the mark of his presidency. On September 19, 2002, only three days after Iraq informed the U.N. Secretary General that it would readmit the weapons inspectors without condition, George W. Bush sent a 31-page message to Congress. The foreign policy document was entitled *"The National Security Strategy of the United States."*

### "The Project for the New American Century": the neo-conservative imperial project

Condoleezza Rice, a former political science professor and Bush's National Security Advisor, was responsible for the committee which penned the foreign policy document. Inspired by the neo-conservative approach to U.S. foreign policy, it aimed at projecting, as far as possible into the future, the "unipolar advantageous position" that the United States inherited after the break-up of the Soviet Union, in December 1991. The neo-conservative ideologues wanted to tap U.S. military superiority, not for the benefit of mankind as a whole, but purely for narrow American advantages. They believed the United States was "unique" in terms of military, economic and political power, and that it should "use" this power as its leaders see fit. A special think tank project was even created in order to provide the intellectual support for this new aggressive U.S. foreign policy called *"The Project for the New American Century"*.

*"The Project for the New American Century"* was established in the spring of 1997. It is a non-profit, educational organization whose goal is to promote American leadership and

interests in the world. William "Bill" Kristol, a contributor to *The Weekly Standard* and Fox News, is chairman of the Project, and Robert Kagan, Devon Gaffney Cross, Bruce P. Jackson and John R. Bolton serve as directors. Gary Schmitt is executive director of the Project. Its declared objectives are as follows:

*"As the 20th Century draws to a close, the United States stands as the world's most preeminent power. Having led the West to victory in the Cold War, America faces an opportunity and a challenge: Does the United States have the vision to build upon the achievement of past decades? Does the United States have the resolve to shape a new century favorable to American principles and interests?*

*[What we require is] a military that is strong and ready to meet both present and future challenges; a foreign policy that boldly and purposefully promotes American principles abroad; and national leadership that accepts the United States' global responsibilities. Of course, the United States must be prudent in how it exercises its power. But we cannot safely avoid the responsibilities of global leadership or the costs that are associated with its exercise. America has a vital role in maintaining peace and security in Europe, Asia, and the Middle East. If we shirk our responsibilities, we invite challenges to our fundamental interests. The history of the 20th Century should have taught us that it is important to shape circumstances before crises emerge, and to meet threats before they become dire. The history of the past century should have taught us to embrace the cause of American leadership."[288]*

In the fall of 2000, before George W. Bush's election, Paul D. Wolfowitz, the future deputy secretary of defense, and Lewis "Scooter" Libby, Vice President Dick Cheney's future chief of staff, streamlined this strategy of world hegemony for the United States in a little-known 90-page study, sponsored by the neoconservative think-tank Heritage Foundation and carrying the loaded title, *"Rebuilding America's Defenses: A Report of The Project for the New American Century".*[289]
Their report proclaimed:

*"At no time in history has the international security order been as conducive to American interests and ideals. The challenge for the*

*coming century is to preserve and enhance this 'American peace.'*
"

This was an echo of a Pentagon's policy document of 1992, entitled "Defense Planning Guidance, on post-Cold War strategy", written when Dick Cheney was Defense Secretary under George H. Bush. The document's chief drafters were Paul Wolfowitz, then Undersecretary of Defense for policy in the first Bush administration, Lewis ('Scooter') Libby and Eric Edelman. Its main theme reverberates today:

*"Our first objective is to prevent the re-emergence of a new rival, either on the territory of the former Soviet Union or elsewhere, that poses a threat on the order of that posed formerly by the Soviet Union."*

What it meant was that the United States would not try to reap any post-Cold War "peace dividend", but would build up its forces to the point where it could attack any country on Earth, whenever it sees fit to do so, and without fear of significant retaliation.

Now it was September 2002, and the same belligerent policy and the same ideological messianism was put forward by a committee chaired by Security Advisor Condoleezza Rice. Her committee issued, and President George W. Bush approved, a document drawn directly from Wolfowitz's 1992 philosophy and from the *2000 Project for the New American Century*. On September 20, 2002, the White House released the document entitled "The National Security Strategy of the United States". Its content was clearly inspired by Wolfowitz and Libby's blueprint for U.S. world domination. Literary in tone, the document bears the stamp of people profoundly obsessed and infatuated with America's military might. In fact, the words "force" and "military forces" appear in it more than 30 times. The whole operation, however, became a mammoth public relations disaster, provoking an international outcry against the United States, as never before seen.

Through this provocative document, the Bush administration was extending the Monroe Doctrine to cover the entire world, irrespective of widely accepted international law.

The application of American influence was to be wherever and whenever the U.S. president decided, even though nobody ever elected Mr. Bush President of the World. This new Monroe Doctrine could have been titled *"Plan to Consolidate the Worldwide Hegemony of the United States of America"*, or even *"The American Plan to Dominate the Planet"*. The new Bush Doctrine was based upon unilateral interventionism by the U.S. superpower—militarily, economically and politically. In reality, it was an example of voodoo foreign policy based on the fallacious principle that a different law could apply to one nation to the exclusion of all the others, on the sole basis of its military strength.

Never before has an American government presented to the world such a clearly and willfully imperialistic doctrine. For the first time since 1776, a country that was founded in reaction to the British Empire and imperialism in general, a country respectful of a certain historic isolationism, expressed its intention to expand itself into a world empire.

The new Bush Doctrine was at once a battle plan against international terrorism, a solemn warning to rogue states, and practically a suspended declaration of war against the world, or any country that might dare oppose the U.S. objective of transforming the international scene into its image for its own purpose. The United States, through the Bush administration, was announcing that it rejected the ideology of "benign hegemony" and of cooperative world leadership, and was expressing its preference for unilateral military dominance and its will to impose a worldwide exploitative system according to U.S. national interests.

The Bush administration did not see the path to America's national security in the improvement of other countries' and other peoples' conditions. It was satisfied merely to police aggressively the frontiers of hostility at home and abroad. It proposed an "America First" doctrine, based not upon modern international law, but rather on a solipsistic approach to American interests and the elementary principle of brute force.

Some thirty-five years later, the "Bush Doctrine" was a near identical reenactment of the infamous 1968 Soviet Union's "Brezhnev Doctrine", which challenged the United Nations and which had purported to justify in retrospect the Soviet invasion of Hungary in 1956, paving the way for the invasions of Czechoslovakia in 1968, and even Afghanistan in 1979.

Now, echoing his neo-conservative advisors in 2002, George W. Bush was saying that if it became necessary, his newly-discovered empire could disregard international law and, just as in a *coup d'état*, declare its own proprietary law based on the right of the strongest. It would be a reversion to the "gunboat diplomacy" of the 19th Century. At that time, Western colonial powers "cloaked in moralistic righteousness" used their overwhelming military advantages to intimidate and subdue helpless remote countries that could not defend themselves, and to impose their rule.[290]

This new United States world sovereignty project was comprised of 10 main points.

Unilateralist hegemony instead of multilateralism:
"Preventive" wars and wars "on suspicion"

The most important—and the most troubling—aspect of the new doctrine was the shift toward unilateralism in international affairs. The U.S. government no longer believed in the multilateral approach to resolving conflicts. Rather, George W. Bush expressed the wish to return centuries into the past, to a time when a country could exact justice on its own by launching preventive attacks against others, whenever it felt threatened or thought its national interests were at stake.[291]

Bush's declared intention was to return to a pre-World War II, and even pre-World War I, environment. *"For centuries, international law recognized that nations need not suffer an attack before they can lawfully take action to defend themselves against forces that present an imminent danger of attack."* George W. Bush and his entourage adopted the old militarist conception of international relations, *"To forestall or prevent such hostile acts by our adversaries, the United Staes will, if necessary, act preemptively."*

The new Bush Doctrine of "preventive" and unilateral military intervention goes against modern international law.

138

Article 2.4 of the United Nations Charter clearly states that *"All Members shall refrain in their international relations from the threat or use of force against the territorial integrity or political independence of any state, or in any other manner inconsistent with the Purposes of the United Nations."*

There is also Article 51 of the U.N. Charter, which stipulates that it is only in the case of legitimate self-defense following an armed attack, that a country may attack another, and only *"until the Security Council has taken measures necessary to maintain international peace and security."* The doctrine of "preemption" and of "war on suspicion" is not a part of the United Nations Charter. In the past, it has always been considered contrary to international law.[292]

At the beginning of the 21st Century, the second Bush administration claimed that the global military context has changed and that international law must change too. During the period from the advent of atomic weapons at the close of World War II, up until the collapse of the Soviet Union, there existed a "balance of terror" between the major powers that contributed greatly to the preservation of peace over a half century.

During this period, each of the potential belligerents—and particularly the United States and the Soviet Union—possessed enough weapons of mass destruction to enable them to respond in case of an attack. Military strategists call this a second strike capability. It requires each country to over-invest in military installations in order to be certain that its nuclear arsenal can survive an offensive attack. In such a context, no sane person can entertain the dream of world conquest. Even a very powerful country could not chance attacking another by declaring a "preventive" war, since it risked nuclear annihilation at the hands of its enemy. The only example when nuclear arms were used against civilian populations was in the summer of 1945, when the United States held a monopoly of such arms.

Because of this balance of terror, such weapons of mass destruction were not used. Indeed, during the 1970's and the 1980's, an American-Soviet showdown was out of the question since it would have meant the death of between 120 and 180 million Americans, and probably of as many Russians, in the initial nuclear exchange alone. Therefore, as long as the world was militarily multi-polar, the balance of terror and the mutually assured destruction was *de facto* a force of deterrence from war and a factor favoring world peace. The United Nations, the seat of international law, operated under the same multi-polar model, with five countries, all of them nuclear powers, each holding a veto in the Security Council. Therefore, it can be said that deterrence has worked very well in the past in maintaining world peace and is likely to work in the future, provided no single country obtains such a military superiority in destructive technology that it can be lured into believing in its own invulnerability and invincibility.

### *De facto* neutralization of the United Nations in a uni-polar world

In 2002, George W. Bush observed that following the collapse of the Soviet Union, the United States had a "surplus of military power" which protected the U.S. from nuclear reprisals. In his mind, the U.S. was thus free to revisit the possibility of unequal "defensive wars", since some potential adversaries did not possess weapons of mass destruction, and thus had no second strike capability. It seemed logical to him that the United States could launch "preventive" attacks against countries that were a possible threat before they acquired weapons of mass destruction themselves and, with them, the capacity for second strike reprisals.

But there was a rub. This unilateral strategic approach went against modern international law, which requires that the use of force be legitimized by the international community's authority vested in the United Nations. In adopting a strategy of preventive strikes, the Bush government had to push aside the United Nations, or at least neutralize the international institution.

This is why, in its strategy document, the Bush administration adopted the same hostility toward the United Nations that has always been the hallmark of the religious and neo-conservative right in the U.S. It proposed a radical change in the role of the United Nations in its worldwide peacekeeping duties.[293] In fact, George W. Bush stated clearly that he wished to return to the era before the creation of the United Nations, and even before the League of Nations and the International Court of

Justice, in 1919. As far as the principles went, his new policy was, at the very least, a throwback to the 19th Century.

He was not far from concluding that the United Nations was useless, and even detrimental to American interests. Bush seemingly had decided that American military might was so superior to all others that the United States could get along very well without the United Nations, or in any case that it could ignore the U.N. and its rules against attacking other countries. Indeed, in 2003, the then number three at the U.S. state department, John Bolton, was quoted as saying, "*There is nothing as the United Nations (sic)... only the international community, which can only be led by the... remaining superpower... the United States.*"[294] For a partisan of a U.S. monopoly superpower status in the world, the United Nations even appears to be a competitor and a nuisance.

If the world were to accept the Bush Doctrine as it stands, and the new international order it presents, it would mean a *de facto* neutralization of the United Nations, at least concerning the U.S. superpower. In fact, the U.S. could bypass the U.N. to wage a unilateral war, not only against stateless terrorist groups, but also against sovereign states, each time the government thought it was necessary for the defense of America's national interests. But, once the United Nations is eclipsed, who will be left to prevent war?

It would be a return to 19th Century anarchy, when heavily armed empires ruled the world. It would truly be a step backwards for civilization. The right of might would replace democratic rights. To justify attacking another country simply because one day that country might, hypothetically, pose a threat, is imperialist reasoning. It is an argument that could justify almost any invasion, rationalize any war, encourage the worst adventures.

What George W. Bush was really looking for was the right to hold a super-veto at the United Nations. If that right was not recognized, by openly refusing to abide by the articles of the U.N. Charter, would the Bush government go as far as to pull the U.S. out of the world's only peacekeeping organization? Why did the American government want to weaken the United Nations? Was the Bush administration trying to promote mayhem in order to better dominate the world?

In the spirit of the new Bush Doctrine, it was obvious that the war against international terrorism offered a strategic opportunity to promote American interests around the world. *"This strategy will turn adversity into opportunity."* Between the politico-religious violence of the terrorists and the imperial violence of the U.S., there wouldn't be much of a place for an international organizations such as the United Nations to act as a legitimate international policeman, dedicated to preventing regional or worldwide homicidal conflicts.

Moreover, in officially refusing to recognize the jurisdiction of the new International Criminal Court in the case of American citizens, the Bush administration dismissed all attempts to establish an effective system of international law to promote world peace. Under the Bush Doctrine, the only peace that would reign would be a "Pax Americana", imposed through brute force according to American objectives and interests, and not in function of international laws.[295]

## Interventionism and resolution of international conflicts by force

Under George W. Bush, the United States declared, *grosso modo*, that as the only world superpower state, it was effectively above international law and could claim the right to provoke regime changes by force in any other sovereign country. Of course, this was an illegal and illegitimate objective. Regime change as a goal of military intervention violates the system of international relations, not only since the advent of the United Nations, but also since the Caroline Clause of 1837 in international law, and even since the Westphalia Peace Treaty of 1648.

Therefore, in 2003, the second Bush administration was threatening to push the world back, not one half century before the creation of the United Nations in 1945, but three centuries and a half to 1648, when the system of international law between nation-states was first established.[296] Similarly, the terrorist leader Osama bin Laden was also turning the world back some three and half centuries by re-introducing religion as a central factor in international conflicts.

Using a step-by-step strategy, President Bush professed to be relying on an American law adopted at the request of the Republican-controlled Congress and signed by President Bill Clinton in 1998, and which had been advanced by the Perle & Co. cabal, as a legal basis for his plans for unilateral military action against Iraq. Under the "Iraq Liberation Act", indeed, Congress gave the Clinton administration encouragement in seeking ways to provoke a regime change in Baghdad and voted funds towards that goal. However, the Bush administration was conveniently ignoring the last clause in the 1998 law, which read, *"nothing (in this law) authorizes the use of military force."*

In the hands of the new Administration, therefore, the "Iraq Liberation Act" was amplified from a simple political intention to encourage regime change into an instrument to justify a "preventive" military attack on Iraq in order to overthrow its government. This was a gigantic political step forward or backward, depending on how one looks at international law.

An imperial *"Pax Americana"*

Armed with the newly-crafted Bush Doctrine, the United States commandeered the right to be the world's policeman, punishing the "bad guys" and rewarding the good—all this outside the legal framework of the United Nations and international law. The general objective was expanded. *"As we defend the peace, we will also take advantage of an historic opportunity to preserve the peace."*

And, more precisely, the United States claimed the right to judge which countries were acceptable and which were not. *"We must be prepared to stop rogue states and their terrorist clients before they are able to threaten or use weapons of mass destruction against the United States and our allies and friends."*

The rejection of deterrence and containment

The doctrines of strategic deterrence and containment of communism were adopted by the administration of Harry S. Truman, in 1947, to stop the expansion of the Soviet empire. In collaboration with the United Nations, this policy was successful for a half a century. But today, now that the Soviet empire is a thing of the past, and the U.S. aspires to become an empire itself, the Bush administration no longer wants to be constrained by multilateralism and by the four other veto-holding countries at the United Nations. The Bush administration considers that the U.S. should never again be deterred by any other military power. And, what's more, it does not feel bound by any international rule from intervening in other countries' affairs, when and if it is in its own interests to do so.

Evidently, this new imperial ambition, espoused by the second Bush administration, flies in the face of modern international law, which accepts the use of force only in the case of self-defense in the presence of existing threats, not potential ones. It also goes against classical geopolitical realism. George W. Bush was persuaded that military offensives should replace a defensive stand in international relations. It was no longer a question of encircling adversary countries, but of invading them and toppling their governments.

Bush and his advisors seemed incapable of understanding that it is impossible to obtain the collaboration and the support of other governments by cannon-fire. Could they not see that the U.S. cannot export democracy and justice by dropping bombs on people at thirty thousand feet of altitude? Did it not cross their collective mind that military force is not a substitute for intelligence, generosity, and the necessary confidence that must prevail between nations?

## The worldwide crusade for freedom

The interventionist document that George W. Bush presented to the world resembled a quasi-religious mission. It was an apology for the American version of freedom. *"Today, humanity holds in its hands the opportunity to further freedom's triumph over all these foes. The United States welcomes our responsibility to lead in this great mission...the United States will use this moment of opportunity to extend the benefits of freedom across the globe."*

The strategic document affirms that the great battles of the 20th Century have ended *"with a decisive victory for the forces of freedom—and a single sustainable model for national success:*

*freedom, democracy, and free enterprise."* Consequently, by extension, the American model must be brought to humanity the world over, by force if necessary, even if the history and the circumstances of another nation are diametrically opposed to it.

## Preeminence, supremacy and military dominance

The U.S. government strongly discourages any other country from entering an arms race by declaring impossible—if not straight out illegitimate—any attempt to compete with U.S. military capability, *"Our forces will be strong enough to dissuade potential adversaries from pursuing a military build-up in hopes of surpassing, or equaling, the power of the United States."* The central role of the military is emphasized. *"It is time to reaffirm the essential role of American military strength. We must build and maintain our defenses beyond challenge. Our military's highest priority is to defend the United States. To do so effectively, our military must...dissuade future military competition."* America would be aiming at creating a supremacist world monopoly of military power.

However, the risks of such an enterprise are obvious. If other countries fear the unbridled and unlawful use of America's power, would they not have an overwhelming incentive to wield weapons of terror and mass destruction, in order to deter America's offensive tactics? Violence begets violence, be it be domestic or international. Indeed, an imperial strategy of preventive war through unilateral military build-up is likely to bring about an outcome precisely opposite to any real sense of security and a climate of world peace.

## Moral absolutism and intervention

The Bush Doctrine coated U.S. political interests in a layer of moral absolutism. Nineteenth Century Britain did the same to justify its colonial empire. Arrogant and puritan, it was necessary, they said, to bring civilization to backward and barbarous peoples.

In the words of George W. Bush, American foreign policy is an instrument to promote his religious views of the world. *"Some worry that it is somehow undiplomatic or impolite to speak the language of right and wrong. I disagree. Different circumstances require different methods, but not different moralities. "*

## The international hierarchy of nations

In the eyes of George W. Bush and his advisors, all nations are not equal. First, there are the great powers (Russia, China, India, etc.) which are in a state of transition towards the American model, but whom Washington nevertheless warns, *"We will strongly resist aggression from other great powers—even as we welcome their peaceful pursuit of prosperity, trade, and cultural advancement. "*

Then there is the group of allies and friends, Israel at the top of the list. It is with these countries (Canada, Mexico, Australia, Japan, the European countries, certain Latin American countries such as Chili, Columbia, Brazil, etc.) that the U.S. will establish agreements, such as the expansion of the North Atlantic Treaty Organization (NATO). These countries are under the U.S. military umbrella, and they can count on America's benevolent support, especially if they cooperate in the war against global terrorism.

Farther down the hierarchy, we find Third World countries, too numerous to list, but to whom the U.S. promises to devote more attention and more aid. *"While continuing our present programs, including humanitarian assistance based on need alone, these billions of new dollars will form a new Millennium Challenge Account for projects in countries whose governments rule justly, invest in their people, and encourage economic freedom. "*

At the bottom of the pile, there are what the Bush administration designates as the rogue states (Iraq, Iran, North Korea) who should expect to pay dearly any confrontation with the United States, as Taliban Afghanistan learned at its expense. *"Today our enemies have seen the results of what civilized nations can, and will, do against regimes that harbor, support, and use terrorism to achieve their political goals. "*

## The promotion of American economic interests

For George W. Bush, free trade is not merely an economic policy option among others; it is a kind of moral dogma and a political instrument. To the Bush administration, free trade is the only acceptable commercial policy for any country, no matter what the level of development of the country in question. *"We will actively work to bring the hope of democracy, development, free markets, and free trade to every corner of the world."* And to make sure that the message got through, Bush and his advisors repeated their intention to play an active economic role throughout the world. *"We will promote economic growth and economic freedom beyond America's shores."*

This commitment to free trade as a policy does not necessarily arise from economic considerations, but contains a fair dose of politics. Reversing more than fifty years of attempts to de-politicize international trade relations and to establish non-discriminatory trade practices, such as the most-favored-nation treatment of GATT and the World Trade Organization (WTO), the Bush administration expressed its desire to closely link trade and politics. On May 8, 2003, for example, U.S. Trade Representative Robert Zoellick announced that any country wanting to establish free-trade agreements with the United States would have to agree to *"co-operation or better on foreign policy and security issues."* In other words, nowadays, the United States does not want economic partners but political colonies. Such a threat, if implemented, could unravel the entire movement toward global economic interdependence and economic globalization, with disastrous economic consequences for the entire world.[297]

## Conclusion

The new Bush Doctrine as a guide for U.S. foreign policy proposes all the necessary ideological elements for the establishment of a new international order under American control. In practice, however, the ideas and projects in the document, if they were put into practice, could take the world backwards a half-century or more, possibly many centuries.

This political document contains the seeds of an American imperial hegemony that could overturn the international legal order, laboriously forged since World War II. The Bush Doctrine resussitates an unbridled militarism, unequaled since the tragic days of the 1930's Nazi Germany. The law of guns and bombs threatens to become the means of settling international disputes. It is a return to world domination by brute force.

Indeed, for the supremacist ideologues who promote war and domination—and who are omnipresent in U.S. media—there is nothing wrong in adopting the Hitlerite approach of unprovoked military aggression to pursue one's own interests. In the words of William Kristol and Lawrence Kaplan, for example, "...*what is wrong with dominance, in the service of sound principles and high ideals?*"[298] This echoes the infamous 1964-Republican presidential candidate Barry Goldwater's phrase "*Extremism, in the pursuit of liberty, is no vice, and...moderation, in the pursuit of justice, is no virtue*".

It would seem that this new context was lifted straight from the pages of the Fables of La Fontaine. The United States touted not only its military superiority, but also proclaimed its moral superiority. Armed with these two shields, it announced its readiness to play the role of international prosecutor, judge, and executioner, owing an explanation to no one, except perhaps a unanimous group of American politicians. This project of a new world order seems to be the expression of a unilateral wish to impose American supremacy and hegemony in a borderless empire.

# 12

## U.S. MILITARY POLICY

*"You cannot simultaneously prevent and prepare for war. The very
prevention of war requires more faith, courage and resolution than are
needed to prepare for war."*
Albert EINSTEIN (1879-1955)

*"The United States and Mr. Bush are a danger to the world."*
Nelson MANDELA, 1993 Nobel Peace Prize winner

*"Our country! In her intercourse with foreign nations, may she always be
in the right; but our country, right or wrong."*
Stephen DECATUR, U.S. Naval commander, April 1816.

*"Our country, right or wrong. When right, to be kept right, when wrong,
to put right."*
Senator Carl SCHURZ

*" 'Tis a time—when madmen lead the blind."*
SHAKESPEARE, *King Lear*

The space-based ballistic missile defense system (BMD)

The obsession to protect the American territory against
sudden military attacks from the outside has been constant since
World War II. During the Cold War days, the perceived threats
came from the Soviet Union. That is why, during the fifties and
the sixties, the first answer was to build a system of early warning
radar stations in the Far North. This was the Distant Early
Warning (DEW) Line. In total, about 63 radar bases were built, 42
of them in Canada, the rest in Alaska and in Greenland. Later,
during the eighties and nineties, these radar bases were

supplemented by the massive Ballistic Missile Early Warning System (BMEWS) stations, four in all, located in Alaska, Canada and Greenland.[299] However, with technological advances and with the end of the Cold War, such a purely defensive system has become obsolete and many American planners and politicians have been looking for something else.

This alternative consists in developing a complex multilayered anti-missile system on a global basis, using satellites. In fact, the idea that space can be used militarily surfaced originally in a speech by President Ronald Reagan, on March 23, 1983, in which he announced a plan for a U.S. space-based missile defense system. This was the famous "Strategic Defense Initiative" (SDI) or "Star Wars" system as dubbed by its adversaries. Today, the main promoters of a U.S. military stronghold on space are the same people who are pushing for the United States to transform itself into a world empire—the Richard Perle, Paul Wolfowitz, Lewis "Scooter" Libbys and company.

In September 2000, for example, Deputy Secretary-to-be Paul Wolfowitz and future chief of staff Lewis Libby wrote their famous report entitled *"Rebuilding America's Defenses, A Report of The Project for the New American Century"*, in which they recommended the U.S. take military control of space as an immediate objective of American policy. Policy-makers Wolfowitz and Libby advised, indeed, that the United States should control the new "international commons" of space and "cyberspace," and should create "a new military service—U.S. Space Forces—with the mission of space control".

Such a program goes much further than stopping any transcontinental missile aimed at the territory of the United States, presumably from "rogue" states such as North Korea, but should also allow the U.S. military to place "interceptors" and weapons of mass destruction in space. If this could be achieved, and many scientists, such as Ted Postol of the Massachusetts of Technology (M.I.T.), doubt it, the United States would be in a position to pulverize any military or civilian installation on earth. This would permit it to exercise ultimate political power over the entire world. The U.S. empire would be universal and complete.

It is difficult to accept the idea that the United States needs to spend hundred of billions of dollars to defend itself against a few small and remote so-called "rogue states".[300] Any such country so ill-advised as to plan a missile attack on the United States would surely be committing instant collective suicide. This is not a credible threat. That is why many believe that the main thrust of a U.S. ballistic missile defense system (BMD) is less defensive in nature than it is for offensive purposes.

Many outside the United States feel that the planned deployment of a U.S. ballistic missile defense system (BMD) is part of an offensive weapons system and is an integral part of the Bush Doctrine of world hegemony. Indeed, when George W. Bush squeezed into power in 2000, well before the terrorist attacks of September 11, 2001, one of his first moves was to announce his intentions to unilaterally abrogate the 1972 Anti-Ballistic Missile Treaty (1972 ABM treaty). Bush wanted maximum freedom of action to intervene militarily wherever and whenever he would deem it to be in U.S. interests. Indeed, the development of anti-satellite weapons (ASATs) would have been in direct violation of the 1972 ABM treaty, just as placing weapons in space would be in violation of the 1967 Outer Space Treaty.

As one discerning observer remarked, "*Missile defense isn't really meant to protect America. It's a tool for global dominance.*"[301] Nor are potential U.S. adversaries duped. One of China's top arms control officials observed that "*Once the United States believes it has both a strong spear and a strong shield, it could lead them to conclude that nobody can harm the United States and they can harm anyone else they want anywhere in the world. There could be many more bombings like what happened in Kosovo.*"[302]

The likely consequence of a rush by the United States to invest in a defensive-offensive ballistic missile system would be to undermine decades of arms control agreements and to launch a new weapons race, with many countries attempting to insulate themselves from any future U.S. aggression. It is difficult to imagine that such a super-armed world would be safer than a world submitted to better international arms controls agreements and systems. Moreover, if the United States were to place nuclear weapons in space, which belongs to all mankind, it risks being perceived around the world as a mega-rogue state.

## National sovereignty and the Helsinki Principles of 1975

In their public pronouncements, members of the Bush administration are not far from proclaiming that the only truly "sovereign" nation in the world is the United States of America. In their eyes, the U.S. is the only country endowed with a supreme political authority and the only one that holds monopoly military power, a power that it must project beyond its borders, for the sole reason that it exists.

Through its Bush Doctrine, the second Bush administration attempts to persuade itself and the world—and if need be, coerce other governments into accepting the *fait accompli*—that this country is paramount among nations and should have a special legal status in the international community.

Even though nation-state sovereignty has been the foremost stabilizing principle in the world for three centuries and a half, ever since the Peace of Westphalia of 1648, and was solemnly reiterated with the Helsinki Conference of 1975, the current American administration openly defies and challenges this fundamental concept. It does so under two pretexts: that the U.S. has a special place among nations because it is the major defender of liberty and democracy around the world, and because it is the country that devotes the largest amount of resources to military expenditures. These two considerations are deemed sufficient to serve as a justification for U.S. unilateral behavior around the world.

However, only a little more than a quarter of a century ago, on August 1st, 1975, the international community adopted the ten Helsinki principles, which went further than the United Nations Charter of 1945 in guaranteeing the borders and territorial integrity of all existing states. The Helsinki principles, however, had a *quid pro quo*. For their borders to be respected, sovereign states must respect the human rights of minorities within those borders.

Nevertheless, the Helsinki principles, of which thirty-three European countries plus the United States and Canada are signatories, are of paramount importance because they played a fundamental role in opening up the communist bloc to liberty and freedom. This was confirmed by former President Mikhail Gorbachev who believed that the Helsinki principles ushered in basic reforms within the Soviet Bloc, reforms which would not have taken place otherwise.[303]

The Helsinki accords, besides proclaiming fundamental individual rights and the concomittant principle that these rights cannot be imposed by violating the principle of national sovereignty, stated explicitly that participating states will refrain *"from any intervention, direct or indirect, individual or collective, in the internal or external affairs falling within the domestic jurisdiction of another participating state, regardless of their mutual relations. Countries will accordingly refrain from any form of armed intervention or threat of intervention against another participating state."*

The western powers, and the United States in particular, were very anxious to have the non-interference clause introduced explicitly in international law, hoping such a clause might reduce the chance that the Soviet Union would again intervene in the affairs of Eastern European countries, as it had done in Hungary in 1956, and in Czechoslovakia in 1968.

Indeed, according to the infamous 1968 "Brezhnev Doctrine", the Soviet government, not unlike the Bush government of today, had asserted its "right" to intervene where there could be internal or external forces hostile to Communism. Replace "Communism" with " the United States", and the 1968 "Brezhnev Doctrine" morphs into the 2002 "Bush Doctrine". The Soviet government proclaimed its right to intervene unilaterally against any country that threatened its empire. The Bush government proclaims its right to intervene unilaterally against any country that threatens its security.

But in 2003, the American government under George W. Bush was busy backtracking on what the Republican administration of Gerald Ford had concluded with the Soviet government of Leonid Brezhnev, in 1975. Things have changed and so, it seems, have the principles of international relations that went with them. The Soviet Empire no longer exists and the United States is openly aspiring to become one.

The American government is now challenging the very concept of sovereignty that it supported not long ago, not because it wants America and other nations to delegate more of their sovereignty to multilateral international institutions, such as the United Nations or, in Europe, to the European Union, in order to have a more stable world, but rather because it wants more sovereignty and freedom of action for itself and less for other countries. The Bush administration acts as if it never understood the reasons why the West won against communism. That is, there cannot be basic human rights without peace, and there cannot be a durable peace without respecting the sovereignty of nations.

In the 21st Century, the "American Century" according to certain American ideologues, the United States wants to retain total freedom of action in an interdependent world it aspires to dominate. It is the belief of the Bush administration, for example, that such a uni-polar world would not verge on chaos, but would prosper under a benevolent "Pax Americana" umbrella of political and economic freedom.

These views were clearly expressed by Richard Haass, the director of the State Department's Policy Planning Staff under Colin Powell, in a speech delivered at Georgetown University, on January 14, 2003. Haass and the Bush administration intend to push for a newer concept of sovereignty than the one the world has been accustomed to since 1648, and especially since 1945. What they want to change, above all, is the distinction that international lawyers have traditionally made between a "preemptive" military action against a clear and imminent threat, which is legitimate in international law, and another and more diffuse situation where a "preventive" military action would be taken by one country against another because of a developing and problematic threat. What the U.S. government wants is permission to launch wars "on suspicion" against other sovereign countries, while it alone will decide how serious this "problematic" threat is. The United States revendicates a status of judge and party in regards to international conflicts, without reference to any impartial international authority.

Obviously, the 191 country-world of today cannot accept this "new" concept of national sovereignty. For this is not a "new" concept of sovereignty at all, but the old colonialist and imperialistic concept that prevailed before before the 1648 Peace of Westphalia, and before 1920 when the League of Nations, the ancestor of the U.N., was first created, when the strongest empires routinely intervened in other countries' affairs, trampling the fundamental right of peoples to self-determination.

In this "old" view, national sovereignty for most countries that do not spend much on military gear becomes "conditional" and "circumstantial", and there is no full equality of nations under international law. Nations or empires which do devote a lot of resources to armaments, such as the U.S., acquire *ipso facto* the "right" to meddle in other countries' affairs under the main pretext that they have the means to do so.

### An imperial vision

This was not the first time that Richard Haass expressed the view that the United States should become an imperial power, similar to the Great Britain of the 19th Century. On November 11, 2000, in Atlanta, for example, Haass presented a paper entitled "Imperial America" in which he asserted that the United States should *"re-conceive its role from a traditional nation-state to an imperial power."*

The U.S. role in the world, according to Haass, should resemble the role Great Britain played in the 19th Century. It would extend its control informally, if possible, and formally if necessary. Indeed, authors John Gallagher and Ronald Robinson, writing about Britain a century and a half ago, noted that, *"The British policy followed the principle of extending control informally if possible and formally if necessary."*[304] According to the future State Department's director of policy planning, the same approach could be applied to the American role at the start of the 21st Century.

This implies a militarist and anti-democratic America. For Haass, *"The fundamental question that continues to confront American foreign policy [after the end of the Cold War], is what to do with a surplus of power and the many and considerable advantages this surplus confers on the United States."* In his words, *"Imperial understretch, not overstretch, appears the greater danger of the two."* If it were to be true, it could be said that the disaster of 9/11 unleashed the dormant imperialist and destructive ambitions of the United States. A military power which does not accept any moral constraint is a recipe for disaster and a danger for humanity.

Faced with such a blatant cry of "back to the 19th Century" and of an overt American challenge to international law, the world has no choice but to proclaim that only in legitimate self-defense and only under the legal umbrella of the United Nations can the national sovereignty of a state be violated, and only for clearly defined reasons (threats to international peace or to basic human rights). Proceeding otherwise would be setting the world back three centuries and a half into a more uncivilized past. In the words of Lord Acton (1834-1902), it would be "a retrograde step in history".

# 13

## THE TWO FACES OF AMERICA

*"That there are men in all countries who get their living by war, and by keeping up the quarrels of nations, is as shocking as it is true; but when those who are concerned in the government of a country, make it their study to sow discord, and cultivate prejudices between nations, it becomes the more unpardonable."*
Thomas PAINE, *The Rights of Man*, circa 1792

*"Antipathy toward the U.S. is shaped more by what it does in the international arena than by what it stands for, politically and economically."*
The PEW Research Center For The People & The Press, "What the World Thinks in 2002".

*"Oderint dum metuant" ("Let them hate as long as they fear")*
Favorite motto of the infamous Roman emperor CALIGULA (A.D. 12-41)

America and Americans were popular in Europe after World War II. The U.S. was instrumental in liberating Europe from Hitler's Nazism, then topped that with massive reconstruction aid under the Marshall Plan. The United States was popular in developing countries also, since it took a stand against colonialism and imperialism, two systems that had dominated the world.

In some parts of the world, however, heavy-handed American diplomacy bred resentment. The 1963 film "The Ugly American" featured the less-likable side of American foreign policy. Marlon Brando played an American ambassador who pulled all the strings in order to manage everything in his posted country.

The reality is that the United States presents two faces to the world. It has a Jekyll-and-Hyde set of conflicting personalities—one good and one bad. There is the America that was foremost during the time of John F. Kennedy: idealistic, sincere, mature, urbane, cultivated, sophisticated, balanced, progressive, generous, friendly, democratic, internationalist, law-abiding, understanding, pluralist, multiethnic, tolerant, courageous, confident in itself and in the future, at the vanguard of scientific progress, open-minded and heedful of human rights. It is an attitude that occupies the center of the political spectrum. This is the America that contributed to creating the United Nations on June 26, 1945, and that sent a man to the moon in July of 1969. It has been the pride of humanity. This is the majority.

There is another America, that most exemplified by George W. Bush: materialistic, egocentric, xenophobic, abrasive, acquisitive, condescending, arrogant, lacking education, boastful, simplistic, plutocratic, bathed in religiosity and superstition, isolationist, vengeful, vindictive, bullying, militaristic, belligerent, trigger happy, often crass and petty, projecting a spoiled brat and "instant gratification" mentality, and somewhat paranoiac. Since January 2001, it is this second America, a minority, that George W. Bush embodies and projects around the world, with disastrous results for the international image of the United States. It is an extreme-right America, based mostly in rural parts of the Mid-West and the South.[305]

The prestige of the United States is in a dangerous decline in many parts of the world. Even its natural allies, in Europe and elsewhere, feel a certain sense of exasperation towards the extreme policies of the Bush administration.

In the matter of trade, an Orwellian doublespeak prevails. George W. Bush pursues one of the most protectionist trade policies since the days of the Smoot-Hawley Act in the 1930's, all the while claiming to promote free trade. Whether it be in limiting imports of steel, softwood, clothing, textile, and agricultural products, or in subsidizing exports, the Bush administration offers little resistance to the protectionist aims of Congress and U.S. industry lobbies and is risking damaging international trade wars.

In the area of policy, Bush and his advisors have a simplistic and dangerous worldview. For them, it is uncomplicated—we are good; our enemies are bad. Consequently, we must use our sophisticated armaments to destroy them. This theological and perverse worldview risks putting humanity back where it was before the creation of the United Nations and could even destroy institutions and laws that took centuries to erect.

For George W. Bush, there is *"only one model of human progress left."*[306] It is, of course, his own views of the U.S. model and no other. It's a one-size-fits-all model. Furthermore, it is up to the U.S., by virtue of its overwhelming military strength, to impose this model, unilaterally, wherever it pleases, to the detriment of international rules and laws.

Internationally, this model is not one of freedom and democracy, but resembles more the Law of the Jungle. Imposed democracy is hegemony, not democracy at all. Moreover, the U.S. domestic political model is far from being superior to those of Europe, Canada, or Australia.[307] In fact, because of the exaggerated importance of money in the American political system, the U.S. is much closer to a corrupt plutocracy, based on wealth and property, than a true free democracy based on the power *"of the people, by the people, and for the people"*.[308]

The boomerang effect of American foreign policy

The Pew Research Center for the People & the Press, presided by the former Secretary of State Madeleine K. Albright, conducted a worldwide survey between July and October of 2002. Thirty-eight thousand respondents, in 44 countries, expressed their views and their perceptions of the United States, among other subjects.[309] The results were devastating for George W. Bush. Almost everywhere, except in the countries of the former Soviet Union, the favorable image of the U.S. had deteriorated. It had taken only two years to do so, from 2000 to 2002. In addition, a strong majority of people in Muslim countries—such as Egypt, Pakistan, Jordan, and Turkey—harbor resentment and even hate against the United States.

Even in Europe, Latin America, and Asia, there has been a decline in the number of people who have a positive image of the

United States. Although lower than previously, the positive image of the United States in most European countries and in Canada is still between 60% and 70%; but the positive perception was only 34% in Argentina, 52% in Brazil, and 53 % in South Korea.

Concerning war preparations against Iraq, there was a noticeable difference of opinion between the American public—inflamed by its politicians and the media—and European populations. More than 60% of Americans supported a war against Iraq to overthrow its leaders. In Great Britain, the only real U.S. ally, public opinion was equally divided. In France, and even more so in Germany, a solid majority was against the war. Russian sentiments were negative by 79%. In Turkey, a NATO member and U.S. ally, 83% were opposed to permitting allied planes from using Turkish airbases to launch attacks against Iraq.[310]

American and European perceptions of the motives behind George W. Bush's actions in the Middle East differed also. In the U.S., by a margin of three to one, people thought that the government wanted to depose Saddam Hussein because his regime was a threat to the security of the United States because of his alleged stockpiles of weapons of mass destruction.

In the rest of the world, however, people were convinced that the primary reason the American government wanted a change of regime in Baghdad was tied to its desire to control the oil deposits in Iraq and the region. In France and in Russia, two permanent members of the U.N. Security Council, three quarters of the respondents agreed with that assessment. In Germany, it was five against four, while in Great Britain, the population was again evenly divided on the subject. Obviously, there was a large dose of cynicism in the world about Bush's real intentions, even though the American public seemed to have swallowed the bait hook, line, and sinker.[311]

In 2003, after the War against Iraq, the Pew Research Center repeated the survey on a smaller scale, interviewing 16,000 people in only 20 countries, plus Palestine. In most countries, opinions of the U.S. were markedly lower than they had been a year before.[312] According to the report, *"The war has widened the rift between Americans and Western Europeans, further inflamed the Muslim world, softened support for the war on terrorism, and significantly weakened global public support for the pillars of the post-World War II era–the U.N. and the North Atlantic alliance... The belief that the U.S. pursues a unilateralist foreign policy, which had been extensive last summer (2002), has only grown in the war's aftermath."*

In less than a year, the bottom had fallen out of support for America in most of the Muslim world. In Turkey, a NATO member, unfavorable opinion of the United States stood at 83 percent (from 55 percent in 2002). In Indonesia, while 75 percent of the population had a positive image of the U.S. in 2002, there was a complete reversal of opinion with 83 percent harboring a negative opinion of America. Since 2002, favorable ratings for the U.S. had fallen from 71 percent to 38 percent among Muslims in Nigeria. In Jordan and in Palestine, there was virtual unanimity (99 and 98 percent respectively) about an anti-American stand. Many populations believed that the United States was a military threat to their country. In Nigeria and in Pakistan, 72 percent of the people thought so. In Russia and in Turkey, 71 percent of the population harbored the same fears. Even in allied Kuwait, 53 percent of the population was wary of the U.S.

Europeans had a less negative view of the United States than the Muslim world. However, the Iraq war episode had taught them a lesson about how brutal and unilateral the American imperial will could be. Majorities in five of seven NATO countries surveyed by the Pew Center supported a more independent relationship with the U.S. on diplomatic and security affairs. Fully three-quarters in France (76 percent), and solid majorities in Turkey (62 percent), Spain (62 percent), Italy (61 percent) and Germany (57 percent) believed Western Europe should take a more independent approach than it had in the past toward the United States.[313]

When asked what created a problem with the United States, a majority of people in Brazil, in Canada, and Europeans in Spain, and even in Italy and Great Britain, identified *"George W. Bush as the main culprit"*, as opposed to *"the United States in general."* It seemed that Bush and his imperial doctrine was at the core of anti-Americanism around the world. It was feared around the world that the United States, under George W. Bush, is becoming the bully of the village in a smaller world.

The drop in U.S. prestige and the rise in anti-Americanism do not seem to hinge on American ideology, but rather on what the U.S. government actually does in the world, politically and militarily. American popular culture and technology are still admired and sought after in most countries, with the exception of certain Islamic countries, even though there is much less enthusiasm for American ideas and customs. Therefore, it is not a question of jealousy of U.S. economic success, as some media commentators like to repeat. In fact, there is still much friendship for the United States in the world. It is its foreign policies that people resent.

The source of this wide-spread resentment toward the United States and its government is threefold: U.S. unilateralism in foreign policy, the egocentrism and insensitiveness of American interests towards the interests of other peoples, and the insidious U.S. intervention in the domestic affairs of other countries. U.S. policies make victims in other parts of the world, and that is why they are reproached and denounced.

There is a rift between what the average American thinks about these issues and what his fellow man-in-the-street in other countries thinks. Americans (75 percent of them) are persuaded that the U.S. government is a good world citizen and is respectful of other governments. In most other countries, however, the perception is completely the opposite. A good majority rejects this portrayal of the U.S. government. Among these are 76 percent of Canadians, 76 percent of the French, 58 percent of Italians, and 52 percent of the British.[314]

It is really a case of the U.S. against the world. One country against 190 other countries. This is a most dangerous situation for the United States to find itself in, because the fight against the threat from non-state terrorists requires the international cooperation of numerous governments and a concerted international action. Such an effort cannot be achieved if there is distrust and hostility towards the United States. That is where legitimate preemption lies, in isolating, neutralizing and dismantling terrorist cells wherever they are, not in attacking sovereign states against the principles of international law and without a clear *casus belli*. Doing otherwise risks producing the opposite results, exacerbating world tensions and intensifying the terror threat from non-state actors, resulting in reduced domestic and international security for Americans.[315]

# 14

## WAR AND INTERNATIONAL LAW

*"Paris is well worth a mass."*
HENRI IV, King of France

*"How Bush and his junta succeeded in deflecting America's anger from bin Laden to Saddam Hussein is one of the great public relations conjuring tricks in history."*
John LE CARRÉ, British spy novelist

*"The United States will conquer Mexico, but it will be as the man swallows the arsenic, which brings him down in turn. Mexico will poison us."*
Ralph Waldo EMERSON

*"Better to let them do it imperfectly than to do it perfectly yourself, for it is their country, their way, and your time is short."*
T.E. LAWRENCE

### The geopolitical map of Iraq

Before the U.S.-led invasion, Iraq, the ancient Mesopotamia, was a socialist republic, and Islam was the state religion. In 1920, after the fall of the Ottoman Empire, Great Britain supervised the foundation of modern Iraq, uniting three provinces over which it exercised a protectorate. Today, Iraq is a country of about 25 million inhabitants, but it is still made up of three very distinct populations. In this sense, Iraq is a rather artificial state.

In the mountainous northwest of the country, there are some 5 million Kurds, Sunni by their religion, but of Indo-

European origin. Some 13 million Semitic Arabs, Shiite Muslims, form the majority in the country and occupy the southern Mesopotamian plain. Because of their religion, Arab Shiites are theologically and ideologically aligned with Iran, their non-Arab neighbor. Young Shia clerics follow the guidelines issued by the grand ayatollah in the Iranian holy city of Qum. Indeed, many of them would like to set up a theocracy in Iraq, mirroring that in Iran, including the establishment of Islamic courts. The remaining population is composed mostly of Semitic Arab Sunnis, and is concentrated in the center of the country. It is this group which, under Saddam Hussein's Baath Party, dominated the Iraqi political scene, ran the social and cultural organizations, and controlled the armed forces. There are smaller minorities in Iraq—Turkomans, Assyrians and Yazidis—but they account for less than 5 percent of the population. The capital, Baghdad, has a population of some 5 million inhabitants. It can be said that Iraq is a state, but not a nation, the country being under the control of a minority of the population, the Sunni Arabs.

From a geographical point of view, Iraq is a western Asian country situated between Saudi Arabia, Syria, and Iran. Landlocked, Iraq has only a small opening on the Persian Gulf, with the seaport of Umm Qasr and the terminals of Min al-Bakr. There, cargo is loaded on ships that travel down a waterway to the Persian Gulf. In order to ship its crude oil, besides relying on the Iraqi oil terminals of Min al-Bakr, two pipelines have been constructed to reach Mediterranean ports—the Kirkuk-Ceyhan pipeline through Turkey and the Kirkuk-Banias pipeline through Syria and Lebanon.

In 1958, the British-installed Iraqi monarchy was replaced by an authoritarian government. That regime was overthrown in 1963, by a pan-Arab nationalist and socialist party, the Baath Party, the party of Saddam Hussein. It is an Arab nationalist party, espousing the Arabization and the Baathization of the Iraqi Kurds. Upon gaining power, the new revolutionary regime began expropriating the oil reserves of the Iraq Petroleum Company, which was largely under the control of American and British companies. The nationalism of the Baath Party was strictly Arab and Sunni. Saddam Hussein al-Takriti[316] was the vice president of Iraq from 1968 to 1979. The leader of a minority cabal, Hussein became president in 1979, following a coup d'état. In 1994, he became head of government.[317]

At first, Saddam Hussein was supported by the West, especially the United States and France, because he was considered to be a bulwark against Communism. This sentiment grew after the Islamic revolution in Iran, under the Ayatollah Khomeini. A long conflict raged between Iraq and Iran (1980-1988), during which the Iraqi army used chemical weapons against its opponents.

When the United Nations Security Council, in 1986, condemned Iraq's use of chemical weapons, the United States stood alone as the only nation to vote against censoring its ally, Iraq.[318] Similarly, since it was presumed that the Kurds in the north were under the influence of the Soviet Union, Western countries—the United States and Great Britain in the forefront—closed their eyes when Hussein mounted operations to oppress and even exterminate the Iraqi Kurds. In 1988, Saddam Hussein went so far as to use paralyzing gas against the town of Halabja, an Iraqi city inhabited by Kurds, killing some five thousand people.

A few years later, in January 1990, George H. Bush Sr. signed a presidential proclamation declaring *"it is in the national interest to promote commercial trade with Iraq"*. The United States' benevolent attitude toward Hussein changed in the summer of the same year. On August 2, Saddam Hussein invaded Kuwait. Hussein thought he had received a go-ahead, or at least a message of non-interference, from the American ambassador to Iraq, April Glaspie. His goal was to annex Kuwait to Iraq. The British government had separated the province of Kuwait from Iraq during its protectorate, but Iraq had always desired to take over the ports on the Persian Gulf. And of course, there was the Kuwaiti crude.

The Persian Gulf War (1990-1991) squelched the Iraqi dictator's ambitions. The costs were not only military, but economic. Following a Security Council resolution, Iraq was put under a severe economic embargo, later loosened to permit the importation of foodstuffs and medicine, the "Oil-for-Food" program.

Since 1991, the Kurds have enjoyed a certain level of protection against the Hussein government. The allied countries established a no-fly zone north of the 36th parallel, patrolled by American and British reconnaissance planes, based in Turkey. Since the end of the Gulf War, protected by American and British air power, Iraqi Kurds have enjoyed *de facto* political autonomy. Despite this, the main Kurdish parties—the Kurdish Democratic Pary under M. Massoud Barzani and the Kurdish Patriotic Union under M. Jalal Talabani—have not succeeded in cooperating in the establishment of an effective administration. Only independence, or at the least a federal system, could preserve this autonomy, in the event of the overthrow of the Iraqi regime.

The Kurds speak a language close to Persian, and their religion is Islam. They have been persecuted for a long time, because they refuse to recognize the primacy of the Arabs. In the Muslim world, this submission to Arabs even has a name: Sh'ûbiyya.[319]

During the 20th Century, the Kurds were often the victims of political dealings between Western and Middle East countries. There are around 28 million Kurds, but they have the misfortune to live in a region where four countries meet: Iran, Iraq, Turkey, and Syria. The governments of these four countries are opposed to any attempt to establish an independent Kurdistan. This is why the Kurds are probably the largest people that has been prevented from forming a nation-state.

After the fall of the Ottoman Empire at the end of World War I, there was a possibility that an autonomous Kurdistan become a reality. The Treaty of Sevres, imposed on the Ottoman government by the Allies in 1920, provided for local autonomy for the regions where the Kurds are a majority, to the east of the Euphrates, on Turkish land. Some 15 million Kurds live in Turkey. It was even provided that the population living in the region of Mosul (in Northern Iraq under the British protectorate) could join the future Kurdish state, if they so desired.[320]

Three years later, however, another treaty confirmed the creation of Turkey and relegated the question of Kurdish autonomy to the back burner. The Treaty of Lausanne was signed on July 24, 1923, between Great Britain, France, Italy, Japan,

Greece, Romania, and the Serbo-Croatian-Slovakian state on the one hand, and Turkey on the other. The treaty perpetuated the divisions of the Kurdish national territory. What interested the Western countries was their share of the petroleum resources in the province of Mosul, occupied mainly by Kurds. Before 1914, Kurdistan had been split between Iran and the Ottoman Empire. After political negotiations, the region of Kurdistan was arbitrarily cut up and parceled out among the four strongest political entities in western Asia.

Will the overthrow of Saddam Hussein's regime allow the Kurds of Northern Iraq and the Shiites in the South to obtain either political independence or, more likely, federal-style autonomy?[321] The answer to this question will be found in the details of the conditions that Turkey put before the United States in return for its cooperation in the war to depose the Iraqi dictator.[322] It is said that the Bush administration had accepted that the Turkish government be represented in the new Iraqi government the U.S. military was planning for the post-Saddam era. Indeed, Turkey wanted to be certain that the Kurds of Northern Iraq would not control the oil fields located in their region and would not use the oil revenues to obtain the political autonomy they had sought after for so long.[323]

The strategic importance of Turkey was due not only to its air bases, but principally as a major staging base for American ground troops to rapidly occupy Iraq and secure the vast oil fields in Kurdistan.[324] From there, Baghdad would be caught in a vice by the allied forces pushing up from Kuwait.[325] The U.S. military command was planning a "blitzkrieg" on Baghdad, in order to secure the capital with a lightening attack.

Turkey and Kuwait would thus be the two sides of a pair of pliers used to crush Iraq. This was the contribution from Turkey that George W. Bush sought from Recep Tayyip Erdogan, the Islamic leader of the largest party in Ankara's new governing coalition, when he visited Washington on December 10, 2002. In exchange, the U.S. would allow Turkish troops to follow in the footsteps of American forces and occupy the Kurdish region of Northern Iraq. Turkey would then have a chance to rebuild somewhat the Ottoman Empire that it had lost in 1917.[326]

However, Turkish public opinion was adamantly opposed to having their country get involved in another U.S.-led war with Iraq. It was nevertheless a surprise when the Turkish parliament refused to implement what its government had arduously negotiated with the Bush administration, that is, to let 62,000 American troops use Turkey as a launching pad to invade Northern Iraq. U.S. military plans were dealt a serious blow.[327] This meant that the two dozen American vessels loaded with men and military equipment waiting off the coast of Turkey, near Iskendren, had to be rerouted towards Kuwait and other ports. The Turkish government would not go beyond its treaty obligations to grant only overflight rights to U.S. aircraft.

In 1991, Turkey feared that the fall of Baghdad would ignite Kurdish nationalist sentiments not only in Iraq but also in Turkey. The government of Turkey was gratified when Bush Sr. stopped the war, even though the Iraqi army was beaten and the road to Baghdad was open. Today, the Turks are as much if not more against Kurdish independence than are the Sunni Arabs who used to control Iraq under Saddam Hussein. Will the Western governments—first and foremost the U.S. under George W. Bush—once more abandon the region's 28 million Kurds to their fate and make a long-term deal with the Turks?[328]

Turkey's fears are not imagined. Iraq is an artificial state. With the fall of the Arabo-Sunni regime of Saddam Hussein, the country is in danger of being split into three parts: A Kurdish north[329], an Arabo-Sunni mini-state in the center, and a Shiite south closely tied to Iran. Even if Iraq remains united, democratic elections would likely give power to Shiite Muslims, who represent more than 60 percent of the Iraqi population. What would then be the implications of a Shia-dominated government in Iraq? Would Iran not stand to become the primary power in the Middle East, becoming a direct threat to the Gulf states, Saudi Arabia, Jordan, Syria, Lebanon, and Israel? The other alternative, of course, is a U.S. military occupation, possibly lasting decades.

Indeed, the long-term solution to the dilemma would be for a unified Iraq to become a kind of U.S. military protectorate, under a model not much different from Great Britain's role in that country, after World War I.[330] Such an outcome could still be an improvement for the Kurdish population, and possibly also for the

Shia population of Iraq, who have been kept out of the center of power for so long by Saddam Hussein. This could have consequences similar to a domestic revolution, even though it would be a revolution imposed militarily from the outside. Over time, a federal solution for Iraq is, therefore, the more probable scenario, given the importance of oil in U.S. foreign policy and the need for the petroleum industry to be able to deal with a single center of political control in Iraq.

But a question lingers. Does George W. Bush's America really want to pursue an imperialist and colonialist adventure in the Middle East? If not, his invading armies should quickly be withdrawn from Iraq. But, if Islamic Shiites, who form the majority in Iraq and who are close to Iran, end up being elected in a future Iraqi government, is it in the United States' interest, and the interests of the West, that the theocratic state of Iran, next door, become the dominant power in this explosive region of the world?

Great Britain is well positioned to give imperial advice to the Bush administration. On March 19, 1917, after a quick military victory in Iraq, the newly self-installed Commander of the Army of Occupation, British Lieutenant General, F.S. Maude, issued the following proclamation, "...*Our armies do not come into your cities and lands as conquerors or enemies, but as liberators...It is not the wish of my government to impose upon you alien institutions. It is our wish ...that you should prosper even as in the past, when your lands were fertile, when your ancestors gave to the world literature, science and art and when Baghdad city was one of the wonders of the world.*"

## A diplomatic wrecking crew

The U.N. Security Council Resolution 1441 on November 8, 2002, required its chief weapons inspectors, the Swedish diplomat Hans Blix and the Director General of the International Atomic Energy Agency (IAEA), the Egyptian Mohamed ElBaradei, to submit an interim report on their findings in Iraq on January 27, 2003. It is easy to imagine the trepidation in Washington, since President Bush's annual State of the Union address was scheduled for the next evening, January 28th.[331] In his previous State of the Union address, Bush had announced his plan

171

to overthrow the regime of Saddam Hussein. He grouped Iraq with Iran and North Korea in the infamous *"Axis of Evil"*.

The Blix/El Baradei report, however, was inconclusive. It did not provide the "smoking gun" required for an immediate U.S.-led attack on Iraq, even though it was stressed that Iraq had failed to cooperate fully with the U.N. inspectors. This was most annoying to the Bush administration, which had placed all its hopes on a negative report in order to proceed with its war plans.

Secretary of State Colin Powell had no other choice but to start denigrating the inspectors' work and to say that he had *"lost faith in the inspectors' ability to conduct a definitive search for banned weapons programs"* and to warn that Saddam Hussein had *"not much more time"* to comply.[332] And President Bush, in his 2003 State of the Union message, pledged to *"fight with the full force and might of the United States military"* to *"disarm"* Iraq.

Soon after, following a meeting with British Prime Minister Tony Blair, who was more inclined to wait for an explicit U.N. go-ahead, Bush made it clear that *"Any attempt to drag this process out for months will be resisted by the United States...This issue will come to a head in a matter of weeks."*[333]

Meanwhile, the Bush administration was shamelessly going about the world twisting arms and throwing money around in order to secure an appearance of support from frightened, poor and indebted governments, such as those of the countries from the old Soviet empire and of the poor African countries of Angola, Guinea, Cameroon, etc.[334] It even threatened the Mexican government (Mexico was on the Security Council and is a member of NAFTA, the North American Free Trade Area). And, even though 55 percent of the Japanese people opposed sending troops to Iraq, the Bush administration nevertheless coerced Japan into providing as many as 1,000 troops to Iraq. Such an operation was a precedent that could be in violation of Japan's post-World War II Constitution, which bans the use of force to settle international disputes.[335]

The Administration was saying, *"Any country that doesn't go along with us* (on an ultimatum resolution to Iraq) *will be paying a very heavy price."*[336] The Bush administration was encouraged in its international bullying tactics by a shortsighted local press, whatever the diplomatic or economic consequences.[337]

Incredibly, the president himself attempted to stir up antagonism towards Mexico and Mexican Americans when he said, "...*if Mexico or other countries oppose the United States, there will be a certain sense of discipline*". Colin Powell, the Secretary of State, was undiplomatic enough to issue veiled threats to France if it were to use its veto at the U.N., even though the United States has resorted to their own veto four times more often than France.[338] And taking a cue from the movie "The Ugly American", the U.S. Ambassador to Canada, Paul Cellucci, criticized the Canadian Government for not buying the U.S. line that their war of aggression against Iraq was to defend the territory of the United States. It was, once more, the politics of bullying.

The Bush administration was desperate to obtain from the United Nations a final justification for its war and, in so doing, did not hesitate to behave as an international tough guy. As one observer remarked, this was sheer political stupidity and irresponsibility.[339]

Nevertheless, there was not a single democratic country of importance, besides the United States, with the possible exception of Israel, where a majority of the population supported Bush's plans to invade Iraq militarily. Not in England, not in Italy, not in Spain, not in Poland, not in Japan, not in Australia, all democratic countries whose governments were going against the wishes of their peoples in supporting George W. Bush's military plans. Even in the U.S., notwithstanding a barrage of pro-war propaganda in the media, the population was lukewarm toward a military aggression against Iraq.[340]

And in other great democracies, in France, in Germany or in Canada, the population was three-quarters or more solidly set against Bush's war in the Middle East. In France, the population was 78 percent hostile to Bush's war and was democratically behind President Jacques Chirac's opposition to the war.[341] George W. Bush and his warmongering cohorts were fooling no one, even though the war propaganda in the U.S., in the United Kingdom and in Australia was unremitting and overwhelming.

Nevertheless, many members on the U.N. Security Council (China, Russia, France, Germany and Syria, among others) were not ready to support a war against Iraq and saw rather a need for the inspectors to continue to do their work. For them, the Iraqi crisis was, to a large extent, the result of U.S. fears presented as being universal, which they were not, not even in the states whose territories were geographically adjacent to Iraq.

Even though the Bush administration, prodded by the British, was desperate to obtain some form of fig leaf from the U.N. for its war plans, it was unlikely that nine out of fifteen members of the Security Council, let alone the three other veto-holding powers, were going to acquiesce. This created a serious dilemma for the Bush administration: how to go to war without being seen as undermining the United Nations? Would the world swallow a unilateral American action? Would not the invasion of another sovereign country be against international law?[342] That is why the strategy of the U.S. and the U.K. at the United Nations was to stop the U.N. inspection process in its tracks, at all costs, because it had become a huge embarrassment to them and because it was postponing the military invasion of Iraq that they had planned and wanted for so long.[343]

One important American who was in agreement with the skeptics was Desert Storm hero General Norman Schwarzkopf. The retired four-star Army general told the *Washington Post* that he saw no need to rush to war. "*I think it is very important for us to wait and see what the inspectors come up with, and hopefully they come up with something conclusive*".

The leader of the 1991 Gulf War forces even confessed that the hawks in the Bush administration—particularly Defense Secretary Donald H. Rumsfeld—made him uneasy. "*Candidly, I have gotten somewhat nervous at some of the pronouncements (Donald) Rumsfeld has made; he almost sometimes seems to be enjoying it.*"

For General Schwarzkopf, Mr. Rumsfeld seemed to be acting like a know-it-all, brushing off the advice of Army personnel, "*He gives the perception when he's on TV that he is the guy driving the train and everybody else better fall in line behind him—or else. It's scary, okay?*"

Rumsfeld's recklessness was amply demonstrated when, unbelievably, the 70-year gentleman referred to France and Germany as the "old Europe" and made another comment comparing Germany to Libya and to Cuba. He even insulted Great Britain by musing publicly that that country's role in a war against Iraq was dispensable. In reality, the 2003 Bush administration resembled, as no previous U.S. administration had, the "old Europe" model—interventionist, militarist, colonialist and imperialist along the lines of the British Empire and of the French Empire during the 19th Century and the early part of the 20th Century, and of the Soviet Empire, after 1945. But nobody was pointing that out to the American public at the time.

It seemed the second Bush administration and his super-hawk secretary were not only bent on destroying the United Nations ("an ineffective, irrelevant debating society" in George W. Bush's own demagogic rhetoric)[344] and other international institutions, but also NATO, a 54-year old organization that Arizona Senator John McCain had described as "the greatest political military alliance in the history of mankind."[345] The Bush government's obduracy over its war plans was endangering the entire system of international institutions that the U.S. itself had contributed to build over more than half a century. Perhaps the Bush administration was planning to duplicate the U.N. and NATO with parallel *ad hoc* coalitions that it could control more easily.

Washington was even trying to unhinge the European Union by playing off the new and emerging post-Soviet states, such as Poland, against France and Germany, whose combined GDP is equal to 56% of the total EU gross domestic product. Publicly insulting the two countries that constitute the core of continental Europe was a clear demonstration of an irresponsible gunslinger diplomacy.[346]

And, because the Europeans were resisting attempts by the Bush administration to turn the defensive North Atlantic alliance into an offensive military organization to fit its own world-wide military objectives, the Bush administration and Secretary of State Colin L. Powell even tried to turn the tables on their European allies by declaring that "*the alliance is breaking itself up because it will not meet its responsibilities.*[347] Even the long-term U.S. alliance with some key Asiatic countries, such as South Korea, was strained to the utmost.[348] Unilateralism and the cynical motto of *"divide et impera"*, ("divide and conquer"), were the new tools of U.S. foreign policy.

It was an eerie and unreal spectacle of a militarist government gone amok.[349] At times, the Bush administration gave the appearance of being less and less a government, and more and more a diplomatic wrecking crew. It was an American diplomatic mess all around the world, in Europe, in Russia, in Asia, in Turkey, in Canada and in Mexico. It was a formidable political and diplomatic disaster that no expected quick military victory, alone, could reverse.

Another enlightened American was Ted Turner, the former vice-chairman of AOL Time Warner. He saw a war between the United States and Iraq as hugely imbalanced, sort of a fight between David and Goliath. He saw a country spending $400 billion a year on weapons attacking a country spending only $1.4 billion on armaments. With complete air and ground superiority, the U.S.-led forces' hunt for Iraqi soldiers would be like shooting animals in a zoo.

Turner criticized the plan of a U.S. military attack against Iraq in these terms, *"We got all the bombs and they don't have very much but a few guns. It's the high-tech wealthy Western nation against the Third World country; it's kind of a foregone conclusion that we'll win. It's a question of how many civilians get killed over there—that's what worries me...We're trying to get one man, right? And we're going to kill tens of thousands of people to get him. It seems like a pretty inefficient way to do things."*[350]

Many U.S. religious leaders attempted to dissuade the President from launching an offensive war. In September, 2002, the U.S. Conference of Catholic Bishops wrote to President Bush, *"We respectfully urge you to step back from the brink of war."*

The presiding bishop of the Evangelical Lutheran Church, Mark S. Henson, concluded; *"I do not believe such a war can be justified under the historic principles of 'just war'."* Similarly, James E. Winkler, general secretary of the United Methodist

Church, said, " *It is inconceivable that Jesus Christ, our Lord and Savior and the Prince of Peace, would support this proposed attack.* " The General Secretary of the National Council of Churches, Robert W. Edgar, wrote, *"Pre-emptive military action now being contemplated by the Administration cannot be morally justified."* Incredibly, however, President Bush refused to discuss objections to the war with the head of the National Council of Churches or even the head of his own church, the United Methodist Church.

As a matter of fact, Bush's only moral support for his war of aggression against Iraq came from American born-again televangelists and some neo-conservative Christians.[351] On the matter of moral principles, George W. Bush was virtually alone when he declared, in his 2003 State of the Union message, *"We will fight in a just cause and by just means."* This was reminiscent of a similar declaration made by Adolf Hitler in Mein Kampf, *"I believe that what we want to accomplish is in accordance with the will of the Supreme Creator."*

The foreign ministers of the 114 so-called non-aligned nations, assembled in Kuala Lumpur in Malaysia, proclaimed their support for the United Nations in its efforts to solve the Iraqi crisis and rejected any U.S. unilateral military attack against Iraq.[352] Twenty-two Arab nations, in a summit at Sharm el-Sheik in Egypt, issued a statement expressing *"complete rejection of any aggression on Iraq."*[353] Considering that all of these countries represent more than two-thirds of the U.N. membership, it can safely be said that even if there was not unanimity, the international community seemed to be against George W. Bush's military plans.

But the voices of reason were ignored. With its "damn the torpedoes, full speed ahead" approach, the Bush administration had scheduled a military campaign to begin in March 2003 at the latest, and it was out of the question to let diplomatic pressure, moral considerations or the wishes of more than one hundred countries, or comments such as those of Schwarzkopf, Turner, Mandela or even the Pope, stall the invasion or replace it with a peaceful solution.[354] Even a Canadian plan for compromise, designed to bring back a consensus within the Security Council, was quickly brushed aside by the U.S. The Canadian plan called for giving another month to the U.N. inspectors to complete their work.[355] This was too much to ask the Bush administration. Weather and military considerations were now in command.

Bush himself said that diplomacy would have to give way to a decision on war in "weeks, not months". He seemed to enjoy this tough guy rhetoric, without caring about world opinion. Using his own metaphor, Bush announced that "the game is over". The French Prime minister, Jean-Pierre Raffarin, retorted—in English—*"It's not a game, and it's not over."*

This "brinkmanship" strategy was not without risks. If Bush proceeded too fast and hurried to stage a "preventive" attack against Iraq to topple Saddam Hussein, he would be accused of not waiting for the completion of the weapons inspectors' investigation. He would be charged with disregarding the U.N. Charter, of brushing aside the call for caution by numerous American and world personalities, and of thumbing his nose at most U.S. allies and the rest of the world. On the other hand, the Pentagon could not keep hundreds of thousands of soldiers on high alert for months and months. Something had to give.

The fact is that George W. Bush was obstinate in pursuing his project of military intervention in Iraq, whatever the results of the U.N. inspectors' mission, and whatever the outcome of any deliberations at the Security Council. This is why he was reduced to muttering meaningless phrases such as, *"The Iraqi declaration is disappointing for those who want peace",* as if peace were his true objective. Bush had already deployed 180,000 soldiers to the Middle East, and the force was scheduled to reach 300,000 by the end of March 2003.

Preparations were also being made to mobilize 265,000 additional National Guard troops, as many as for the 1991 Persian Gulf War.[356] As well, he ordered six aircraft carriers (out of twelve) to the Middle East, and nearly 300 combat helicopters and 600 fighting planes to the Persian Gulf. Sadly, the American president, in order to conceal his true intentions, was reduced to uttering George Orwell-type double-speak sentences of the sort, *"We have not made up our mind on military action...[but] I have made up my mind that one way or another Saddam Hussein will be disarmed*"[357] or, again, "*Overthrowing Saddam would encourage Mideast peace.*"[358]

The United States government was wandering and behaving in a very curious manner. Indeed, the Bush administration's avowed objectives in Iraq were changing day by day. One day, the objective was about disarming Iraq, as called for by U.N. resolution 1441. Another day, it was "regime change", an illegal goal under the U.N. Charter. Another day, the stated objective was the exile of the Iraqi dictator. Still another day, the objective had ballooned into one which was to "bring democracy" to the entire Middle East, with bombs and guns. As a last resort and determined to link Saddam Hussein to the September 11 tragedy by all means, George W. Bush made *non sequitur* allegations, "*He (Saddam) has supported 'al Qaeda-type organizations,' or 'al Qaeda types' or 'a terrorist network like al Qaeda'.*"[359]

One was lost trying to identify which was the more genuine pretext. Never, however, was it stated honestly that the ultimate objective, after overthrowing the current Iraqi government, was to secure militarily the entire Middle East in order to better control the region's oil reserves and prevent a future oil crisis.[360]

## A throw of the dice and a rush to war

American multilateral diplomacy had reached a dead-end and was in shambles. The only policy left was brute force and the old-fashioned gunboat diplomacy of unilateral big-power intervention. By embarking on a military build-up before receiving a legal mandate from the United Nations, George W. Bush had clumsily painted himself into a corner. He was checkmated at the United Nations. Having failed to persuade the Security Council to issue a final ultimatum to Iraq, Bush was sorely tempted to go it alone and to give the order to begin the bombings and launch an unprovoked military invasion of Iraq. He needed to save face, and his only ace card was the U.S. military, despite whatever resentment against the United States he would be creating all over the world.

However, casting the dice for such a war of choice, an unprovoked war of aggression, and not a war of necessity, was bound to have long term dire consequences for the United States. It would be an enormous political gamble, sort of an international "coup d'état" against the United Nations and the world legal order.

Nevertheless, in the Spring of 2003, the world witnessed the spectacle of the most advanced and the most militarized country in the world engaging in a war of aggression against a Third World country, not from necessity, but by choice, because it had the means and the occasion to do so, and because it was in its own narrow interests to conquer Iraq. It was a hegemonic war, a retaliatory war, an opportunistic war, and a war for resources. It was a military invasion to the cry of "my country, right or wrong", in order to "stabilize" Iraq and the entire Middle East region, and to secure the all-important oil flows to a thirsty America and a growing world.

There had never be a doubt that, militarily, the United States could crush Iraq and would win such an unbalanced and asymmetrical war. But could it win the peace that would take many years to establish, after the Muslim world was humiliated and shaken to its roots?[361] Could the United States find itself in Iraq in the same quandary as Russia after it invaded Afghanistan, and after the U.S. encouraged young Muslims around the world to come to Iraq to fight the foreign infidel? Similarly, the American occupation of Iraq is bound to prompt young Muslim militants around the world to slip into the country to plan retaliatory attacks and to fight the foreign occupier.[362]

The Bush administration stirred up a hornets' nest and walked into a terrible quagmire with its eyes only half open. George W. Bush was seen pursuing a personal crusade and the United States was in danger of losing its honor and its credibility in the eyes of the world.

It was obvious that a so-called "preventive" Bush-style war was in no way a surprise. It had been a foregone conclusion for a long time. In the spring of 2002, George W. Bush had already decided to "invade Iraq no matter what". Indeed, it was revealed by Richard Haass, the director of the policy-planning staff at the State Department, that George W. Bush had made the decision to invade Iraq well before July 2002. He was told by Condoleezza Rice, Bush's National Security Advisor, during the first week of July 2002, "*not to waste his breath... the decision has been made.*"[363] New information makes it more likely that the decision to attack Iraq was made within days after the September 11th suicide hijackings of 2001, eighteen months before the event.[364] This assessment is reinforced by the fact that Vice President Dick Cheney, in the spring of 2002, told a Senate Republican policy lunch that the question of attacking Iraq was not if, but when.[365]

That is why the hostilities were in full preparation throughout the summer and fall of 2002 and during the early winter months of 2003.[366] An enormous military build-up of troops and equipment was going on in a string of countries around Iraq. Journalists had even been trained to cover the event and were going to be embedded within the military.[367] All this was being done while the U.S. government continued its maneuvres at the United Nations and pretended that disarming Iraq could avoid a war.[368] The president himself said a few days before the start of the war that "*the American people can know that every measure has been taken to avoid war.*"[369]

But by mid- March 2003, the Bush administration thought it necessary to accelerate events.[370] George W. Bush and his strategists were "*losing patience*". They wanted to launch an attack against Iraq before the summer heat and impending sandstorms would make it difficult to conduct a desert war and before the anti-war movement become too widespread. The period around the new moon of April 1st would be an ideal time to launch an offensive, because the U.S. troops were well equipped for battles in the dark.

Even though the vicious dictator met with no sympathy in most countries—with the possible exception of Arab and Muslim countries, where George W. Bush's hostility granted Hussein instant popularity—such an unprovoked attack would be in stark contradiction to international rules.[371] Only defensive measures, and then only when approved by the United Nations, are condoned by international rules.

This idea of a "preventive" unilateral offensive attack is quite problematic, politically, and controversial in international law. How far can such a doctrine take us? Where does it stop? Under a system of laws, preventive arrests are illegal. Preventive, offensive and unprovoked wars are of the same stripe.

Historically, when one country has aggressed another, it was almost always presented as a "preventive" attack in order to increase its own security. This was Hitler's argument when he invaded Czechoslovakia in 1938 and Poland in 1939. It was also Japan's pretext when it made the "preventive" offensive and unprovoked attack against the United States at Pearl Harbor. In many other cases—such as in the invasion of Bulgaria by Greece in 1925,[372]Manchuria by Japan in 1931, Ethiopia by Mussolini's Italy in 1935, Greece by Mussolini again in 1940, or Hungary by the Soviet Union under Khrushchev in 1956, Czechoslovakia by the Soviet Union under Bresznev in 1968 and the Soviet invasion of Afghanistan in 1979—all the invading countries, without exception, claimed to act in the name of their self-defined national interests.[373] Invariably, opposition to such illegal invasions came from outside the aggressing country. Domestic propaganda made sure that any contestation of the government's actions would be subdued.

In 2003, by invoking the same historical pretext, George W. Bush was placing himself in quite unsavory company, since all the above invasions were illegal according to international law. Preventive military actions by one country against another are tolerable only in cases where the necessity of self-defense is clear, immediate and overwhelming, and when the choice of methods and the possibility of negotiations have been completely exhausted. Russian President Vladimir V. Putin reminded George W. Bush of these fundamental facts when he said, *"it would be a grave error to be drawn into a unilateral (military) action...in Iraq, because it would be outside of international law."*[374]

If President John F. Kennedy had acted according to the Bush model during the Cuban missile crisis in 1962, he would have been tempted to order a "preventive" strike without warning to destroy the missiles the Soviet Union had placed in Cuba. The result would surely have been total war. Kennedy rejected that option, preferring to go before the Security Council. Photos in hand, U.S. Ambassador Adlai E. Stevenson persuaded the United Nations to impose a blockade of containment on Cuba until the complete removal of the missiles. The crisis was resolved without bloodshed.

Under the regime of the dictator Saddam Hussein, Iraq was suspected of trying to acquire nuclear weapons. But unlike North Korea, which was actively developing such arms, nothing indicated that Iraq was close to possessing them.[375] The U.N. inspectors were in Iraq to insure that it didn't happen. And even if, in theory, Iraq one day obtained nuclear weapons, this undeveloped country, located 10,000 miles from the United States, was not a credible threat to the U.S. Iraq was a poor country, with no industrial base and few military allies, isolated diplomatically, with an impoverished population caught between a ruthless dictator and devastating economic sanctions imposed by the international community.[376]

The Soviet Union possessed nuclear weapons for more than 50 years and never dared use them, for fear of retaliation. Several other countries, more or less hostile to the United States, such as China, India, and Pakistan have nuclear weapons without the U.S. feeling the need to invade them. According to the Federation of American Scientists, even though only seven countries have confirmed that they possess nuclear weapons (the United States, Russia, Great Britain, France, China, India, and Pakistan), 17 countries either have nuclear weapons or have the means to produce them.[377]

The conclusion is obvious. In the winter of 2003, the United States was in no way immediately threatened by Iraq, especially following the return of the U.N. weapons inspectors. There was no clear and present menace or danger to the United States of America. Therefore, there was no urgency to invade. The real danger for the United States, as amply demonstrated on September 11, 2001, came from Osama bin Laden and his accomplices in the al Qaeda terrorist organization.

And, even in stretching the right of legitimate defense to the limit by claiming that Saddam Hussein encouraged international terrorism and might have had a hand in the September 11 attacks, there was no concrete proof and, in fact, not even a clue supporting such a pretension.[378] It was not at all a case of legitimate defense, but as one expert succinctly put it in the *International Herald Tribune, "Iraq is less a threat* (for the United States and Great Britain) *than an opportunity."*[379]

It was thus mainly for strategic reasons relating to oil supplies and the political situation in the Middle East and within the United States that George W. Bush ordered an armed aggression against a sovereign country. In so doing, this great democratic country took on the uncomfortable role of being the perpetrator of a reverse Pearl Harbor.

Within a span of 62 years—two generations—the United States of Franklin D. Roosevelt has gone from a country victim of the senseless militarism of the Japanese Empire to a country that is itself the assailant. Under the leadership of George W. Bush, a benevolent nation, respectful of international law, has become an aggressive and acquisitive empire. Pursuing its aggressiveness in international affairs, the Bush administration has gone against the United Nations Charter by interfering in the affairs of another sovereign state without the prior acceptance of the U.N., thus violating a U.S. policy that goes back to the days of Woodrow Wilson.[380]

It is undeniable that the Bush administration, by brushing aside the United Nations and previous long-established American policies, has taken a major diplomatic step backwards for the U.S. and for international law. Such a rash step is certainly not a beneficial development for the world at large, nor for the United States. The tandem Bush-bin Laden has contributed to undermining the system of international law, the former not respecting international laws concerning the invasion of another country, and the latter refusing the very existence of such international laws by resorting to Islamist terrorism.

It must be said also that since the attacks of September 11, 2001—perpetrated by 19 young Arabs and resulting in the savage murder of more than 3,000 people—a climate of hate and a thirst for vengeance permeates the U.S. This desire for retaliation gave George W. Bush a political carte blanche to intervene militarily wherever and whenever he wished. But should one injustice be met with another? Should a "Terrorist Pearl Harbor" be met with a

"Pearl Harbor-type war of aggression"? Faced with a bin Laden who dishonored Islam by fomenting murderous terrorist acts against the United States, why did George W. Bush want to commit another injustice by bombing and invading Iraq, making thousands of victims?

A president who is already inclined to chauvinism and to the use of armed aggression to further American interests meets little resistance when he cites the greater national good. It is an extremely unhealthy situation and a very dangerous one for the geopolitical stability of the planet.[381] Some journalists began to wonder out loud if, under George W. Bush, the country was starting to slide down the slope towards becoming a state bordering on fascism and theocracy.[382]

In 2003, Islamist terrorists and American militarists pursued denatured versions of their respective population's fundamental interests. By stooping to the level of his enemies, the president has met injustice with injustice.

The project was, however, already decided. George W. Bush was obsessed with invading Iraq. It was an *idée fixe*. Not since the infamous days of Adolf Hitler and Nazi Germany did a national head of state show such enthusiasm for going to war. Bob Woodward reported that a month into the bombing of Afghanistan, in 2001, when the Taliban stronghold of Mazar-i-Sharif fell, Mr. Bush turned to one of his assistants and asked, *"Well, what next?"*
[383]

There was, thus, a very strong probability that the oilman George W. Bush would look for any pretense to "invade Iraq no matter what" and consolidate American control of the Persian Gulf petroleum reserves, as soon as he could. Exxon-Mobil, Chevron-Texaco, Unocal, Amoco, and Pennzoil were already solidly implanted in the region and they were seeking to control the entire Middle East oil sector, as well as the central Asian region that holds large hydrocarbon reserves.

At the end of 2002, Bush came very close to confirming publicly that economic objectives were high in his own motivations to invade Iraq. He repeated what Vice President Cheney had said and what the editorialists in the *Wall Street*

*Journal* had mentioned several times, that a war against Iraq was necessary in order to protect the U.S. economy.[384]

The president didn't stress the advantage of an assured supply of cheap oil, but rather stressed that it was necessary to prevent a hypothetical attack by Iraq or by a stand-in for Iraq. *"An attack from Saddam Hussein or a surrogate of Saddam Hussein would cripple our economy... This economy cannot afford to stand an attack."*[385] Bush spoke these words at the same time the U.N. Secretary General, Kofi Annan, said that he *"did not see an argument for military action now, because the Iraqi government was co-operating with the U.N. weapons-inspections program."*[386]

Besides the economic considerations, there were two other important factors—political ones—inciting Bush to launch a war against Iraq.[387]

First, and this cannot be dismissed easily, there was the entire political climate in the country. Indeed, following the humiliation of September 11, there was a strong pro-war and pro-revenge sentiment in the U.S against Arabs in general. An example must be made. A lesson must be taught. A statement must be made. Iraq was chosen. The success of the Republican Party in the mid-term elections echoed this bellicose feeling. For the politicians, war was an expedient to turn voters' attention away from the poor state of the economy and the markets, as well as from the financial scandals that touched even the White House.[388]

Second, there was strong pressure from the Sharon government, and also from the powerful Perle-Wolfowitz-led lobby within the U.S., to get rid of Saddam Hussein, a supporter of the Palestinians presented as an enemy of Israel, and, by extension, of the United States.[389] Political support from this pressure group was crucial to the Republican Party.[390] And conversely, there was a need for the neo-conservatives to ally themselves with, and possibly take over, the Republican Party. Neo-conservative "godfather" Irving Kristol unabashedly put it this way about the neo-conservatives' plan to invest the Republican Party: *"The historical task and political purpose of neoconservatism would seem to be this: To convert the Republican party, and American conservatism in general, against their respective wills, into a new kind of conservative politics suitable to governing a modern democracy.*"[391]

All these factors came together to persuade George W. Bush that war preparations and war itself would not hurt him politically, so he thought, even if his country risked alienating the rest of the world and becoming isolated and reviled internationally.[392]

U.S. Army (Ret.) General William E. Odom, former director of the National Security Agency (NSA), cogently summarized the corrosive influence that the U.S. far right and the pro-Israel neo-conservative lobby had on George W. Bush's military plans in Iraq. In his eyes, there was an obvious lack of planning in the war against Iraq. It seemed to him that a small group of neo-conservative people, connected to the Israeli Likud and the U.S. Religious Right, wanted a war to transform the Middle-East and, so they believed, to protect Israel. Now that it was a mess, they couldn't care less. The only thing that mattered to them was to see the Arabs weakened.[393]

It could be said that the Bush administration has succeeded in its plan to transform the war against terrorism into a triple opportunity—a strategic opportunity to secure access to Iraq's enormous oil reserves by force; a Republican opportunity to stir up patriotism at home and thus outflank the Democrats, in order to elect Republican candidates to Congress and to re-elect George W. Bush in 2004; and, not the least, an opportunity to consolidate the State of Israel in the Middle East through some sort of "Pax Americana".[394]

In conclusion, as it has been amply documented throughout this book, we can say that the above end result is the consequence of the determining influence of three powerful lobbies on American foreign policy: the pro-Israel neo-conservative lobby, which is the strongest (the long standing Wolfowitz-Perle cabal); —the oil lobby, which plays a crucial role in any policy related to the Middle East (resulting in the 2000 election of oilmen Bush and Cheney to the White House); and the Religious Right and Christian conservative lobby, which gives a general conservative and anti-Arab bent to U.S. foreign policy (for example, the anti-Islamic fervor after September 11 and the need to eliminate Islamist terrorism around the world). The 2003 War against Iraq is the consequence of the convergence of interests of these three important overlapping groups, and their strong political affinity with the character and personality of George W. Bush.

## Great Britain and the war

The support of British Prime Minister Tony Blair for an American military operation in Iraq was no surprise, even though he seemed to be torn between his desire to preserve U.N. authority and his wish not to displease President Bush. It should be remembered that Great Britain played a key role in Middle East politics after the fall of the Ottoman Empire, since it exercised a protectorate in Iraq. It was Great Britain that bit off a piece of Iraq to create the state of Kuwait, as well as presiding over the establishment of a Jewish state in Palestine.

Nevertheless, it is somewhat ironic that Great Britain was practically the only true U.S. ally when it came to military preparations against Iraq, even though the strong arm-twisting tactics of the Administration had persuaded a number of smaller countries—especially some East European NATO aspirants—to acquiesce to U.S. military plans.[395] In fact, London (some experts call it "Londonistan") is the western capital of anti-American Islamic groups.

There is no better recruitment center for Islamist terrorists than the London mosques, one of them can house 10,000 disciples. Radical Islamic clerics, publicly and with impunity, incite their followers to murder and to *jihad*, under the relatively helpless eyes of British justice.[396] Just as for some churches in the U.S. South, London mosques are places of political gatherings and meetings, and sermons often center on current political themes. The London police is well aware that Osama bin Laden's al Qaeda network has a "substantial presence" in Britain.[397]

The Islamic Liberation Party (Hizb-ut-tharir) is based in London. This anti-democratic party fights against secular governments in the Middle East and seeks to install religious dictatorships. There are some 2.5 million Muslims in Great Britain. The leader of the English section of Hizb-ut-tharir, Imran Waheed, has proposed establishing a caliphate where Islamic law would be practiced.[398] Tony Blair's Labour government initially closed its eyes to these subversive activities and open calls for terrorism. Only after encountering international bewilderment did it finally accept to act.

Tony Blair's unconditional support for George W. Bush's war in Iraq was therefore somewhat suspicious. Even though a propaganda argument could be raised in the United States linking the events of September 11 and Iraq's Saddam Hussein, no such argument could be made in Great Britain. Iraq could not be considered, by any stretch of the imagination, a threat to the United Kingdom. Perhaps Prime Minister Blair was less interested in fighting international terrorism than in assuring Great Britain its share of Middle East oil. There is no doubt that British companies, British Petroleum and Ramco in the forefront, would get their quotas in the new distribution of Iraqi oil that would inevitably follow Bush's new political order in the Middle East. The same would be true for the important access to hydrocarbon reserves in the Caspian Sea region. Even before the hostilities began, it was whispered that British Petroleum, which had been expelled from Iraq in the 1960's, was updating its old geological maps.[399]

Russia was much more reticent to give its assent to an American invasion of Iraq, even though the latter had cancelled a contract with the Russian company OAO Lukoil to exploit the West Qurna-2 oil field, in southern Iraq.[400] Russia looked with jaundiced eyes on Washington's efforts to jeopardize its long-standing economic interests in Iraq. In 1972, indeed, Russia had signed a treaty of friendship with Iraq that paved the way for large-scale arms sales to the Middle East country. In 2003, however, the U.S. government was assuring Russia that its economic interests in Iraq would be maintained, if only Russia were to support the U.S.-led operation to topple Saddam Hussein.[401] Nevertheless, the Russians were not naive. They knew that one of George W. Bush's objectives was to flood the world with Iraqi oil, lower oil prices and, in the process, destroy OPEC. Russia, like Canada, produces expensive oil and these two countries were expected to suffer economically from a U.S. take-over of Iraq.

But the question lingers. Why was the Bush administration using Iraqi oil as a bargaining chip, even before invading Iraq, to persuade Russian President Vladimir Putin to support the resolution/ultimatum the U.S. and Great Britain presented to the Security Council?[402] The control of Middle East oil was truly at the heart of oilmen Bush and Cheney's foreign policy.

Even Jacques Chirac's France tried to stifle its reprobation as much as possible. The French government couldn't risk seeing the main French oil companies, among them Total SA, completely excluded, by a vengeful and vindictive George W. Bush, from the restructuration budgets and the new distribution of oil rights that were sure to follow the overthrow of Saddam Hussein. When the Americans took control of Iraq and the entire Near East, there was a risk that they would declare the French contracts obsolete, even if it meant legal entanglements for years to come.

Nevertheless, France was in the thick of the action. In January 2003, it acceded to the presidency of the Security Council, following the rotation in alphabetical order.[403] But the French government was tired of defending international law and U.N. prerogatives, and it was more or less resigned to a U.S. intervention in Iraq.

Even though the French Prime Minister had remarked that *"war, that is what is left when we have tried everything else, and we want to try everything to avoid war"*, all the French government wished for was that no military action be taken by the U.S. before March 7, when the Security Council would receive the third interim report from the U.N. inspectors on Iraqi disarmament. On February 14, the chief arms inspectors had reported some progress in their inspection work in Iraq. They cited measures Iraq had taken to allow surveillance flights. The Iraqi government had provided new documents and had opened investigations of past arms stocks as indications that its cooperation had improved, even if such efforts fell somewhat short of being unconditional, as required by the previous relevant U.N. resolutions.

With the support of Germany, France made a daring proposal that the U.N. inspection team be reinforced, even tripled, and allowed to continue its work, while increasing the aerial surveillance of Iraqi territory. This was an indication of France's strong preference for a continuance of the containment of Saddam

Hussein's Iraq, as an alternative to a bloody military conflict. Eleven out of the fifteen members of the Security Council wanted the U.N. inspectors to continue their work in Iraq.[404]

The Bush government was truly isolated at the United Nations. In desperation, it even tried to put pressure on Hans Blix *"to come down hard on Iraq"* in his crucial February 14 report.[405] Indeed, the Bush administration hoped that the February 14 inspectors' second report would confirm that Iraq was not cooperating in getting rid of the prohibited chemical, biological, and possibly nuclear weapons that could harm its neighbors or the far-away United States. This would have been helpful for the Bush administration in its plans to "liberate" Iraq. Later, Hans Blix would confirm that *"the [Bush] administration leaned on us"* to use more damning language in the inspectors' reports in order to swing votes on the UN Security Council.[406]

But the chief inspectors refused to play the administration's game. And, incredibly, the Bush administration abased itself by peddling faked documents in order to show that Iraq had purchased uranium from Niger.[407] Chief inspector El Baradei told the U.N. Security Council that such documents were forgeries and not authentic.[408]

As a last attempt to avoid a war and the thousands of deaths that would inevitably result, France and Germany, joined by Vladimir Putin's Russia and Jiang Zemin's China, forming a bloc of more than 1.5 billion people, even advanced a plan to deploy thousands of United Nations peacekeepers in Iraq, in order to assist an enlarged contingent of weapons inspectors. The plan was presented as a sensible and credible substitute to a costly and senseless military conflict. But to no avail.

The Bush administration did not support the plan for a U.N. peacekeeping force in Iraq, just as it did not support such a force in Palestine. An internationally sanctioned police mission didn't provide what it was after—complete U.S. sway over the Baghdad government.[409]

Disarmament was a façade to dissimulate the real objective, no matter how costly it would be in human lives and no matter if it destroyed the credibility and usefulness of the United

Nations for decades to come. At the U.N., French Foreign Minister Dominique de Villepin defended the case for peace in eloquent terms, *"In this temple of the United Nations, we are the guardians of an ideal, the guardians of conscience. This onerous responsibility and immense honor we have must lead us to give priority to disarmament through peace."* He was applauded by the delegates of countries not in the Security Council—an unheard of event.

But for many French deputies it seemed that the French government had not succeeded in its attempt to make the final decision about war and peace a matter for the international community and the United Nations, and not solely that of the U.S. and of George W. Bush.[410] Alas! in the French president's words, the war could be imposed upon him and upon the rest of the world.[411]

All the secret deals being made between the U.S. government and a host of other countries began to look like a comprehensive attempt to justify a war at any cost. Any justification would do. It also had the appearance of a complicated plot, or a global chess-game, to divvy up Iraqi oil, as a first step, and then possibly the oil of other Middle East countries, such as Saudi Arabia and Iran, as a second one. It was the beginning of a new form of colonialism, debuting with a new Yalta for oil.[412]

# 15

## A HEGEMONIC WAR UNDER FALSE PRETENSES

*"What difference does it make to the dead, the orphans and the homeless, whether the mad destruction is wrought under the name of totalitarianism or the holy name of liberty or democracy?"*
Mohandas GANDHI (1869-1948)

*"The democratic processes...are subverted when intelligence is manipulated to affect decisions by elected officials and the public."*
The TOWER Commission, November 1987

*"A democracy cannot and should not go to war under false or incorrect premises."*
*Samuel R. BERGER, President Clinton's national security advisor*

[The War against Iraq]: *"One of (the United States') periods of historical madness."*
John LE CARRÉ

Unable to obtain an explicit authorization from the U.N. Security Council for his war of aggression against Iraq, and forced to withdraw the resolution that he and Tony Blair had deposited at the Security Council, George W. Bush chose St. Patrick's Day of March 17, 2003, to proclaim his disassociation from the United Nations and international law by giving a 48-hour ultimatum to the head of another sovereign state to get out of his own capital before American troops started bombing and invading his country.[413]

Even though the U.S. constitution clearly states that only Congress can declare war, Congress never issued a formal declaration of war against Iraq. George W. Bush didn't bother with such technicalities. He felt that the October 11, 2002

Congressional resolution had given him carte blanche to wage war.[414] He announced that his armies would invade Iraq, after a 48-hour ultimatum, at a moment of his "choosing".[415] The grand drama would begin to unfold and a new colonialism could begin.[416]

## The war of March 20, 2003

George W. Bush made his choice on March 20, 2003, an ominous day for Iraq and for the United States. The president declared war and ordered the bombing of territories and cities in Iraq, insensitive to the possibility of causing thousands of deaths among the civilian Iraqi population. Indeed, though certain of a military victory, without a legal mandate from the United Nations, the Bush-led military troops in Iraq were in the position of a foreign army of occupation, operating with no legitimacy and in an international legal vacuum. This is bound to have serious consequences in the years ahead.[417]

During the 1945-46 Nuremberg trial, the chief British prosecutor, Sir Hartley William Shawcross, insisted upon the fact that the Nazis had grossly disregarded international treaties and that their intention was worldwide conquest. "*They ... made it possible for the German Reich to tear up existing treaties, to enter into new ones and to flout them, to reduce international negotiations and diplomacy to a hollow mockery, to destroy all respect for and effect in international law and, finally, to march against the peoples of the world to secure that domination in which, as arrogant members of their self-styled master race, they professed to believe.*"

The chief prosecutor also quoted Adolf Hitler, who had said, "*I shall give a propagandist cause for starting the war, never mind whether it be true or not. The victor shall not be asked later on whether he told the truth or not.*" [418] Was George W. Bush, believing that "*history is written by the victors*", willing to adopt the same tactics? His principal political advisor, Karl Rove, thought so. He told *Washington Post* journalist Bob Woodward, "*Everything will be measured by results. The victor is always right. History ascribes to the victor qualities that may or may not actually have been there. And similarly to the defeated.*" It is truly amazing that mid-Twentieth Century Germany and early Twenty-

First Century America had political leaders on the same wave lengths.

Three weeks later, on April 10, 2003, the U.S. military conquest of Baghdad had, for all practical purposes, been accomplished. However, days of mayhem, chaos, anarchy in the streets, disorder and killings ensued.[419] The Bush administration made the terrible mistake of dissolving the 400,000 strong Iraqi army, and proceeded to the lustration of 50,000 members of the Baath Party, forcing dangerously-armed people into unemployment.[420] A foreseeable tumult followed. Buildings, including hospitals, schools, libraries and museums, were looted, ransacked, pillaged and gutted.[421] In fact, virtually all public buildings in Baghdad were systematically looted and destroyed, with the notable exception of the Iraqi Oil Ministry. In museums, the history of a 7,000-year-old civilization went up in smoke or disappeared. It looked as if Iraq had been invaded by the Mongols, even though the pillage was being done by Iraqis under the watchful eyes of American G.I.s. By invading a Muslim country, the United States made itself the No. 1 enemy of the Muslim world and plunged itself into a war of occupation it could never win.

Stunned by the engulfing chaos, Defense Secretary Donald Rumsfeld attempted to sound approbative when he said, *"Freedom's untidy. And free people are free to commit mistakes, and to commit crimes"*.[422] But under international law and the Fourth Geneva Convention, occupying forces have a clear obligation to protect civilians and maintain law and order. Mayhem and "crimes" are not part of freedom.[423]

The country with the most sophisticated weapons had defeated a country that spent nearly 300 times less on defense, but it had forgotten to plan for the need to establish law and order after the hostilities. The world witnessed the most sophisticated modern army defeat a much smaller and less well-armed foe. The military outcome of the war against Iraq had never been in doubt, but the lawless aftermath was a surprise. Having chosen force over law, the Bush administration and the U.S.-led forces were ill-prepared to rule the country they had destroyed and conquered.

## The empty shell of "weapons of mass destruction"

The Bush administration's chief justification for launching an unprovoked war against Iraq had all along been to get rid of Iraq's stores of chemical and biological agents and to dismantle its effort to produce a nuclear bomb. These weapons were said to be a threat not only to Iraq's neighbors, but also to the United States, because of the alleged links that the Iraqi government could have had with international terrorist organizations.[424] George W. Bush asserted that Iraq posed an imminent threat to the United States and indicated that his administration knew the exact location of the weapons and, what is more, that these dangerous weapons were ready to be deployed at a moment's notice. That was the *casus belli.*

On September 18, 2002, for instance, testifying before the House Armed Services Committee, Defense Secretary Donald Rumsfeld was categorical. *" We do know that the Iraqi regime has chemical and biological weapons. [It] has amassed large, clandestine stockpiles of chemical weapons—including VX nerve gas, sarin, cyclosarin and mustard gas. "*[425]

On October 7, 2002 in Cincinnati, President George W. Bush himself, in a speech entitled "Denial and Deception", asserted that *"It [Iraq] possesses and produces chemical and biological weapons. It is seeking nuclear weapons... And surveillance photos reveal that the regime is rebuilding facilities that it had used to produce chemical and biological weapons."* And, as late as March 17, 2003, a few days before the U.S.-led invasion of Iraq, the President had repeated, in his Address to the Nation, that *"Intelligence gathered by this and other governments leaves no doubt that the Iraq regime continues to possess and conceal some of the most lethal weapons ever devised."* It was a foregone conclusion: the U.S. must invade Iraq in order to remove the threat of dangerous weapons of mass destruction.

The United Nations' inspection team, however, insisted such weapons had been destroyed. In fact, the work of the United Nations weapons inspectors had left Iraq virtually defenseless, with no air force, making it a tempting prey for an aggressive invading army. Nevertheless, the Bush administration persisted in saying that such weapons still existed.

Even after Iraq presented its weapons declaration, on December 7, 2002, stating publicly it had no more prohibited weapons, the Bush administration removed over 8,000 pages out of the 12,200-page document while attempting to discredit the report and presenting it as incomplete.[426] From the outset, indeed, President Bush had insisted that it was not for the United States or the U.N. weapons inspectors to prove whether or not Iraq had prohibited weapons, but for the Iraqi government to show it did not. He made this point, one day after Iraq's weapons declaration, in his Saturday weekly radio address, December 8, 2002. *"The responsibility of inspectors is simply to confirm evidence of voluntary and total disarmament. Saddam Hussein has the responsibility to provide that evidence as directed and in full"*. It was the old trick of asking somebody the self-incriminating question, *"Since when have you stopped beating your wife"*, with the accused being logically unable ever to provide a definitive proof that he did not beat his wife.

Nevertheless, Bush attempted to persuade the American people that war was being *"forced upon"* him. On February 26, 2003, less than one month before the invasion, in a speech before the American Enterprise Institute, a pro-war think-tank, the President repeated the coded phase he had so often used during the previous months, *"If war is forced upon us by Iraq's refusal to disarm, we will meet an enemy who... is capable of any crime."*

Later, however, during the 2003 U.S.-led military operations, U.N. chief weapons inspector Hans Blix observed that finding weapons of mass destruction did not seem to be high on the list of U.S. war objectives. *"I think the Americans started the war thinking there were some [prohibited weapons]. I think they now believe less in that possibility."*[427]

If, faced with its very survival, the Hussein regime did not use such weapons of mass destruction, it was most likely because they did not exist, or at the very least, because they had been destroyed in 1991, just as Scott Ritter and the U.N. inspectors had reported. In their March 7, 2003 report to the Security Council two weeks before the onset of the war, chief U.N. inspectors Hans Blix and Mohammed ElBaradei were very clear. *"No evidence of proscribed activities has so far been found....No underground facilities for chemical or biological production or storage were found so far... After three months of intrusive inspections, we have ... found no evidence or plausible indication of the revival of a nuclear weapons program in Iraq."[128]*

There was indeed a strong suspicion that the Bush administration had "cooked the books" on Iraqi intelligence, just as it had fudged the numbers for its projections of future government deficits, in order to strengthen its case for huge tax cuts, and just as some corporate crooks had cooked their financial books in the private sector.[429] It was a clear case of the victory of propaganda over truth.[430]

Then, after the war, instead of asking for the return to Iraq of Hans Blix and his trained inspectors, in order to establish once and for all if there were still weapons of mass destruction in the country, now that the country was under military occupation, the Bush administration chose instead to dispatch a contingent of 1,400 American, British and Australian experts to uncover the famous "weapons of mass destruction". In Blix's eyes and in the eyes of the world, it was obvious that somebody who works for an occupying power cannot have the same credibility as an independent inspector. But to no avail.[431] Even though the production of chemical and biological weapons requires large industrial plants and a substantial work force, which are not easy to conceal, and after investigating 350 Iraqi sites, no weapons of mass destruction were discovered in Iraq.[432] It seemed that the Bush administration had made a decision to pump up the case against Iraq and make it look more dangerous than it was, in order to persuade the American public to support a war of aggression in a remote land.

Indeed, when Lt. Gen. James Conway, commander of the 1st Marine Expeditionary Force, was asked why his Marines failed to encounter or uncover any of the weapons of mass destruction that the U.S. administration had warned them about, his honest answer put the Bush White House to shame. *"We were simply wrong,"* Conway said. *"It was a surprise to me then, it remains a surprise to me now, that we have not uncovered (nuclear, chemical or biological) weapons"* in Iraq. And, he added, *"believe me, it's not for lack of trying. We've been to virtually every ammunition supply point between the Kuwait border and Baghdad, but they're simply not there.* "[433]

## A lack of credibility

Now that the military invasion of Iraq had been accomplished, and that U.S. forces were unable to find the so-called unconventional weapons, where did this leave the Bush administration's credibility in the world? This lack of credibility was reinforced by the Bush administration's adamant refusal to let the U.N. inspectors return to Iraq to verify the presence of the so-called weapons of mass destruction.[434] Indeed, if the main rationale for invading Iraq—the imminent threat that Iraq allegedly posed to the United States—turned out to be false and had rather all the appearances of a fabrication or a gross exaggeration, what then was the true motive for invading and destroying the country?

On May 1st 2003, after a grandiose landing on the deck of the carrier Abraham Lincoln in a Viking jet, George W. Bush celebrated his victory in Iraq before a military crowd and declared that the major combat operations *"have ended"*. On the same occasion, he was forced to admit that his principle official reason for an all out war against Iraq—to eliminate weapons of mass destruction, which were supposedly spread all over the country—had not been warranted. No weapon of mass destruction had been found, a full six weeks after the beginning of the bombings.[435] Similarly, no credible link had been established between al Qaeda and Iraq, so that his second official reason to invade Iraq did not hold any water either. The official arguments to invade Iraq had been empty. Nevertheless, all the electronic media were present for the celebration, including PBS. U.S. media were in a complete swoon over the recent demonstration of American military might.[436]

The partisan political fall-outs were overwhelming. The Republicans' political advantage over the Democrats on national security had never been greater. The "news" of the end of the war came conveniently the very same day that eleven former Enron executives were indicted. It would appear that the news would serve to obscure the torrent of scandals that originated from corporate and financial America.[437] Americans were applauding a president who had lied to them. As Senator Bob Graham of Florida pointed out, the Bush administration had manipulated intelligence data on the questions of Iraq's nuclear program and its connections with al Qaeda *"to sell the decision to go to war"*, a war which the president had already decided to wage a full year before.[438] Why should they be surprised that the world looked upon the entire operation with deep cynicism and dismay?

Many Americans, either from blind patriotism or out of a lack of concrete information and objective analysis, had accepted the idea that the thrust of the Bush administration's operations in Iraq was about disarming that country and that Saddam Hussein posed an imminent military threat to America. A good example of these sentiments can be found in a December 2002 memorandum issued by the Council on Foreign Relations and the James A. Baker III Institute for Public Policy at Rice University. It stated that *"If Saddam Hussein fully complies with UN Security Council Resolution (UNSCR) 1441 and disarms Iraq's weapons of mass destruction (WMD) program, military action would not be necessary."* Nothing could have been further from the truth.

A Bush administration official candidly told ABC News, in reference to the real threat that Saddam Hussein posed to the United States, *"We were not lying; it was just a matter of emphasis."* As ABC speculated, the Bush administration supposedly went to war because it *"wanted to make a statement, ...and Saddam Hussein was the perfect target."*

The Bush administration, after September 11, 2001, wanted to make a demonstrative statement to the world about the military supremacy of the United States. The take-over of Afghanistan had not been sufficiently flamboyant, Osama bin Laden and the al Qaeda terrorist network not having been destroyed. Iraq was a more tempting prize. It was a country most hostile to Israel, it was a country with huge oil reserves, and it was a country that had been taunting the Bush government, since Saddam Hussein was still in power after the 1991 Persian Gulf War. It was a win-win-win situation not to be missed.

Revenge and retribution against Arabs allowed George W. Bush to redirect American anger against Osama bin Laden and al Qaeda toward Saddam Hussein and Iraq. However, by doing so, the Bush administration was enlarging the war against terrorism by bridging the gap between al Qaeda and Iraq and by putting American soldiers in harm's way as terrorists' targets. But, as Bush himself told U.S. military personnel, *"You have shown the world the skill and might of the American Armed Forces...the terrorists and their supporters declared war on the United States. And war is what they got."* [439]

Once the main reason to go to war was proven to be inexistent, the other pretexts chosen didn't matter. The Bush administration ignored all the intelligence assessments that said Iraq was not a threat to the United States. Indeed, on September 7, 2002, George W. Bush said that Saddam was *"only months from having nuclear weapons"*, citing an International Atomic Energy Agency report. *"I don't know what more evidence we need."* In fact, the AEA had never said such a thing for the obvious reason that it had never issued such a report. It was later learned that, in order to make it seem as if there was an imminent threat to the United States, America's own experts on chemical and biological weapons had been pressured by senior Bush administration officials to write reports that they believed overstated evidence that Iraq had illegal weapons programs and terrorist links.[440] In truth, the U.S. public was misled into going to war by its leaders and by its media, most of them owned and controlled by large corporate interests.[441]

Indeed, when former Supreme Allied Commander of NATO General Wesley K. Clark, on a June 15, 2003, edition of NBC's "Meet the Press" with anchorman Tim Russert, declared that, *"There was a concerted effort during the fall of 2001, starting immediately after 9/11, to pin 9/11 and the terrorism problem on Saddam Hussein,"* the other U.S. media remained silent. It seems that U.S. media were strangely reluctant to pursue firsthand information suggesting that the flawed intelligence on Iraq— and therefore the war— may have been the result of deliberate deception, rather than incompetence, on the part of the Bush administration.

However, it was Deputy Defense Secretary Paul D. Wolfowitz's candor that closed the debate. In an interview to the magazine *Vanity Fair*, the chief architect of the war couldn't help from gloating aloud on the Bush administration's strategy. In order to make an illegal war look legal and in order to rally maximum support, Wolfowitz, at least tacitly, acknowledged that the charge of Iraqi chemical and biological weapons was a pretext, *"for reasons that have a lot to do with the US government bureaucracy, we settled on the one issue that everyone could agree on, which was weapons of mass destruction as the core reason."*[442] Official lies had to be invented regarding the alleged links between Iraq and al Qaeda and about the alleged Iraqi stockpiles of weapons of mass destruction in order to persuade a reluctant American public to support an invasion and to obtain a minimum of support from the United Nations.

The cry about "weapons of mass destruction" was a rallying bureaucratic and "politically convenient" strategy, both for domestic and foreign consumption, and had little or nothing to do with facts.[443] Essentially, the only weapons of mass destruction in post-war Iraq were those maintained on Iraqi bases by U.S. forces.[444] On July 9, 2003, testifying before the Senate Armed Services Committee, Wolfowitz's boss, Defense Secretary Donald Rumsfeld, was obliged to confirm that the entire "weapons of mass destruction" was a ploy and a smokescreen to conceal a hidden agenda, *"[We] did not act in Iraq because we had discovered dramatic new evidence of Iraq's pursuit of weapons of mass destruction. We acted because we saw the evidence in a dramatic new light—through the prism of our experience on 9-11* [September 11].*"*[445] The decision to invade Iraq had been made a year and a half before the fact and, from then on, the "case" against Iraq had to be made, by any means, including, as outlined by the editorial writer of the *New York Times*, "dishonesty and delusion", the manipulation of information and the abuse of intelligence.[446] There was a predetermination to go to war against Iraq no matter what the evidence was and whatever happened at the United Nations. All efforts to avert a war in Iraq were crushed, and all offers to establish that Iraq no longer had weapons of mass destruction, and that it offered to allow American troops and experts to conduct a search to that effect, were brushed aside. [447]The cost to U.S. democracy will be felt for years to come.

Everybody had been hoodwinked.[448] The whole thing was a machination from the outset.[449] War against Iraq was a preexisting policy of the Bush administration. Revenge and retribution, with a background of pro-Israel cabal and of oil fumes, were at the center of the oilmen Bush & Cheney's Middle East war plans.[450] The *"weapons of mass destruction"* pretext was a massive historical scam, maybe one of the most blatant ever.[451] As the House Intelligence Committee stated it, the Bush administration *"mischaracterized the available intelligence"* to justify a war against Iraq— intelligence which was *"fragmentary and sporadic"* at best— and jumped on *"the absence of proof that chemical and biological weapons and their related development programs had been destroyed as proof that they continued to exist."*[452] As it was emphasized, at the very least there seemed to be an unseemly eagerness to believe any information which would portray the Iraqi threat as being extremely grave and imminent.

But the goal had been attained. The official lies had convinced most Americans that Saddam had nuclear arms and was in bed with Osama bin Laden, and, therefore, posed a direct threat to the United States.[453] For instance, in June 2003, 71 percent of Americans thought the administration had implied, to justify its war, that Saddam Hussein had been involved in the Sept. 11 attacks.[454] However, six months after the invasion of Iraq, George W. Bush admitted there was "no evidence" that Saddam Hussein was involved in the terrorist attacks on the USA.[455]

Nevertheless, an illegal war could be launched, and Americans could put their hands on Iraqi oil riches, just as the British had gotten hold of South Africa's riches in gold and diamonds at the end of the 19th Century.[456] Many people had been fooled.[457]

Indeed, shortly after his inauguration, George W. Bush had joked to a crowd of Washington insiders about his political philosophy, *"You can fool some of the people all of the time, and those are the ones you need to concentrate on."* To paraphrase Winston Churchill, the American people will some day stumble upon the truth, but, by then, it will be too late.[458] U.S. soldiers had no right to occupy a sovereign nation, outside of international law, and doubly so because it was done under false pretenses.[459] Those who raised objections against this first imperialistic preemptive war of the 21st Century, launched without solid or lawful foundations, with faked, deceptive and fraudulent pretexts, were on the right side of history.[460]

Even so, the Republican-dominated Congress staunchly refused to investigate whether there had been an abuse or a violation of the public trust. However, when former Vice President Gore accused the Bush Presidency of "*a systematic effort to manipulate facts in service to a totalistic ideology*", in a speech delivered in New York City on August 7, 2003, the campaign to establish an independent commission to investigate the falsehoods and the distortions of evidence on Iraq received a boost. There was hope that enough representatives and senators would rise above partisan politics to erase one of the greatest blemishes on American democracy.

### The economic risks of war

In 1991, the Persian Gulf War had cost the U.S. practically nothing. The U.S. government had indeed spent $61 billion, but the allied countries of the Middle East, Europe, and Japan contributed some $54 billion to the American effort.[461]

With sixteen of the U.S. Army's thirty-three combat brigades in Iraq, and with crucial allies having been rebuked, U.S taxpayers were left to foot most of the bill for the 2003 invasion and reconstruction of Iraq. Indeed, not one single allied country volunteered to subsidize the U.S. Treasury, even though Great Britain did contribute directly to the war. Before the war, it was estimated that a new Gulf War could cost from $50 to $140 billion in direct expenses, depending on the duration of the hostilities.[462]

Lawrence Lindsey, the Administration's economic advisor, committed the "blunder" of stating publicly that the projected war against Iraq could cost "*up to $200 billion*". On the other hand, he considered that a regime change in Baghdad could profit the U.S. economy by increasing the world supply of crude oil by some 3 to 5 million barrels a day.[463] Lindsey was forced to resign in December of 2002, and was quickly replaced by a New York investment banker, Stephen Friedman. When a government is going to war, it is better that the citizens know as little as possible about the motives, the consequences and the costs.[464]

However, there was the huge prize of Iraqi oil. The Bush administration was openly counting on Iraqi oil to finance the U.S. war effort and the reconstruction of the devastated country. It was hoped the 2003 war against Iraq would cost the U.S. Treasury even less than the 1991 Gulf War. To attain this goal, the Pentagon planned for a boost in Iraqi oil production in order to generate the funds that would be transferred to its coffers. The only debate within the Administration was whether Iraq's oil sector would be managed publicly, as proposed by the U.S. State Department and its allies at the Treasury and Justice Departments, or whether it would be privatized, as proposed by Rumsfeld's Department of Defense and the White House. What was agreed upon was that U.S. oil companies, assisted by British companies, would dominate Iraq's oil sector, while leaving consolation prizes to the Russians and, if possible, leaving close to nothing to the other European firms.[465]

Secondly, a U.S.-led attack on Iraq held enormous risks for the country's macroeconomic stability, and in fact for the entire world economy. In a study titled "War with Iraq: Costs, Consequences and Alternatives", the American Academy of Arts and Sciences concluded that the total costs of a new Iraqi war would be a minimum of $99 billion and a maximum of $1.9 trillion ($1.9 thousand billion).[466]

The U.S. economy was in a slump, shaken by accounting and financial scandals and by a strong movement towards debt deflation. A spike in the price of oil would be the equivalent of taxing consumers' budgets, not only of Americans, but throughout the world. Consumer spending, the motor of two-thirds of the economy, could fall. A back to back recession was not out of the realm of possiblity, even if its odds were low before the invasion of Iraq.[467]

In fact, the National Bureau of Economic Research, the organization that declared that a recession had begun in March 2001, waited until July of 2003 to conclude that the recession had ended in the fall of 2001, after the GDP started growing in the last part of 2001. The main reason for the delay in calling an end to the recession was the anemic state of the job market which, far from improving, was worsening. There were fewer people working in 2003 than were employed in 2002.

This is all to say that perhaps the Bush administration was combatting the economic slowdown by borrowing from the future at a ferocious rate. The months and years to come would confirm or infirm the fears, depending on the length of the conflict, if it spills over into other countries and if it rekindles Islamist terrorism and becomes a guerrilla war of attrition. Incredibly, the Bush administration and its security czar, Tom Ridge, were telling Americans to stock up on duct tape so they could seal off their habitat, in order to protect themselves against potential terrorist attacks.[468] One can say with certitude that an extended and protracted conflict in Iraq cannot be good for international peace, for the stability of the international oil market, for the stock market, for the U.S. economy nor for the world economy.[469]

For the U.S., on the other hand, there was a rainbow at the end of the storm. The study conducted by the American Academy of Arts and Sciences concluded that the control of the enormous crude oil reserves in Iraq would insure the U.S. supply of imported oil, at the present levels and at favorable prices, for almost a century, procuring benefits to the American economy of some $40 billion!

This figure seems widely underestimated. According to more realistic calculations, the expected gains to the American economy of taking over Iraq should be multiplied by twenty-five, at the minimum, and possibly by one hundred.[470] And this does not take into account the increased profits of American oil companies in Iraq, nor the juicy contracts allocated to U.S. engineering firms (Halliburton, Bechtel, Fluor, etc.) for the reconstruction of the devastated country.

The American seizure of the Iraqi government and of the Iraqi oil reserves would be a very good deal for the U.S., economically speaking, provided a military occupation of the country could be accomplished at a low cost. To emphasize the point, it was reported that American oil-men in conquered Iraq were treated like royalty. *"They travel like foreign dignitaries, their SUVs escorted by two US Army Humvees and a security detail led by a master sergeant. No Iraqi official is too busy to meet them and when it comes to Iraq's most precious resource, oil, they are granted total and instant access."[471]* The American invasion of Iraq to gain control over its vast oil reserves could go down in history as the biggest planned heist of the 21st Century.[472] The U.S. went into Iraq, not because the Iraqis wanted them, but because the Bush administration figured out that acquiring an oil colony in the Middle East would be good for the United States.

## Other costs?

Other important costs had not been considered. First, with the dramatic drop of goodwill towards the United States all over the world, this antagonism is bound to negatively affect U.S. businesses abroad. One is not viewed in the same manner when one represents a law-abiding democratic state or a colonial power. Second, the collapse of an international institution is also bound to create international insecurity and uncertainty, possibly many years of international conflicts, with disastrous economic consequences. Third, the value of all the innocent lives bound to be sacrificed on the altar of war should also have been taken into account. As to the alleged benefits of reduced terrorism after a military incursion into Iraq, the cost-benefit equation is very hard to establish. One could argue either way. Nevertheless, a genuine cost-benefit analysis of the situation would have considered the total social costs and the total social benefits, both private and public, resulting from the war and not just the accounting financial flows.[473]

Clearly, the Bush administration was convinced, and behaved as if it believed, that the perceived benefits of a unilateral war of aggression in the Middle East (oil benefits for decades to come, a more secure Israel, political benefits of a more dominant role for the United States in the world, political benefits at home for the Republicans over the Democrats, etc.) exceeded the perceived costs of such provocative actions (budgetary costs, costs of international uncertainty, costs of increased terrorist activities, costs of a disruption of world trade and travel, costs due to a reversal of economic globalization for international investments, costs of possible world economic stagnation, etc.).

## The human costs of war

All wars are disastrous in human terms, especially for civilian populations and, in particular, for children. They bring devastation to countries, leaving behind unexploded mines and radioactive residues that linger in the environment for decades. The human costs of war are not only borne by civilians, but also, long after, by military personnel and their families. For example, the "Gulf War Syndrome"—a generic term for the strange illnesses developed by veterans of the 1991 war in Iraq, as well as unusually high rates of birth deformities among children fathered by war veterans—has been traced to depleted uranium weapons.

On August 16, 2002, a vote was held at the annual U.N. Human Rights Commission to ban the use of such weapons, pending the results of thorough medical studies. Only two countries voted against the motion—one old colonial power, Great Britain, and one new super-power, the United States.[474]

Because of the unpredictable nature of armed conflicts, it is difficult to calculate in advance the loss of life that bombs and armored tanks might cause. During the Persian Gulf War of 1990-1991, 3,500 civilians and some 56,000 Iraqi soldiers were killed, and around 110,000 Iraqi civilians died later from the harmful effects of the war on their health. Based on this experience, an organization of doctors against the war (Medact) made an estimate of the cost in human life of a military invasion of Iraq, both for the civilian population and the combatants themselves.[475]

For the 2003 war against Iraq, where well-equipped U.S. military troops, like in a shooting gallery, faced a grossly under-equipped army, the least pessimistic prediction of Medact was around 50,000 total deaths, but they feared that the number could go much higher. When he was asked about the Medact's scenario for the loss of lives, Karl Rove, Bush's chief political strategist answered that he felt more preoccupied *"by the 3,000 people who died on September 11th"* than by the possibility of thousands of deaths in Iraq.[476]

The greatest worry was the open admission by the Bush administration that it planned to use maximum terror against the Iraqi population. The Pentagon's plans called for *"unleashing 3,000 precision-guided bombs and missiles in the first 48 hours of the campaign"*. As for General Richard B. Myers, chairman of the Joint Chiefs of Staff, he warned that an American attack against Iraq would result in Iraqi civilian casualties, *"But we can't forget that war is inherently violent,"* he said. *"People are going to die. As hard as we try to limit civilian casualties, it will occur. We need to condition people that that is war. People get the idea this is going to be antiseptic. Well, it's not going to be."*[477] In a single day, on April 6, 2003, for instance, the U.S. central command (CentCom) even claimed that between 2000 and 3000 Iraqi soldiers, possibly more, had been killed.[478]

The horror of these bombings and killings will remain a stain on the international reputation of the United States for years to come. Gone are the days when America was perceived as a force for peace and democracy. American brute force, selfishness and cruelty will be engraved forever in the minds of hundreds of millions. With what consequences? In such a context, it can be understood, if not condoned, why the Bush administration was so adamantly hostile to the establishment of the International Criminal Court.

Indeed what country possesses the largest stock of weapons of mass destruction? By far, it is the United States of America. The U.S. has numerous nuclear arms laboratories, tens of thousands of atom bombs and all the accompanying sophisticated gear enabling it to kill and maim.[479] The U.S. therefore has a moral obligation to take the lead in establishing an international legal framework for peace and not to satisfy itself with the barbaric illusion of unilateral armed peace. The greatest loss to the United States, after launching an unprovoked aggressive war, will not be the loss of lives or the loss of economic opportunities, but its lost honor. For years to come, the United States will be regarded with suspicion by progressive public opinion around the world and will cease being viewed as a benevolent and disinterested power committed to peace and democracy.

More generally, and considering the cruelties imposed on civilian populations as a result of the destructive capabilities of modern weapons, we can ask if war still has a place in a truly civilized world.[480] The more one reflects, the more one comes to the conclusion that modern war is unworthy of a civilized world and should be outlawed. Submitting civilian populations to terrible suffering in the hopes of influencing their government is a remnant of a primitive past. In the 20th Century, war was unacceptable; in the 21st Century, it is a scandal for humanity.

In order to take Baghdad, the U.S.-led military coalition (in fact, American forces) had to bomb many small villages surrounding the city and many buildings within the city, often using "cluster" bombs that are responsible for numerous civilian deaths?[481] The Iraqi people were not welcoming their heavily armed "liberators" by dancing in the streets, as some misguided American ideologues had predicted. Vice President Dick Cheney himself had assured the American people on NBC's "Meet The Press", on March 16, 2003, that he was sure the Iraqi people would welcome American troops as "liberators" and not as "conquerors". But contrary to assurances, Iraqis were protesting in the streets against the arrival of the new invader-colonialists. And, in turn, American troops were firing on civilians.[482]

Therefore, if it were one day established that the U.S. not only initiated an illegal war of aggression but used weapons in Iraq that can be considered against the laws of war, such as cluster bombs,[483] the targeting of civilian morale and the use of excessive lethal force in urban areas, the 2003 War against Iraq could have long term legal ramifications.[484,485]

The U.S. government claimed that the war would bring a "provisional administration" of Iraq, and not a permanent occupation. This is what the British said in 1917 after invading Iraq. They remained there forty-one years! It was a dangerous illusion to think that, in the 21st Century, the hostile and illegal occupation of a foreign country would be easy.[486] As in all colonial and imperialistic "preemptive" wars, the troubles start after victory, especially if the occupying power faces a protracted, ideologically motivated guerrilla resistance.[487,488] Imperialism and colonialism bring about their own action-reaction dynamics. Indeed, just as Osama bin Laden was inspired to attack the United States partly because of his hatred of the American military presence in Saudi Arabia, thousands of young Muslims, enraged about the American military presence in Iraq and Afghanistan, began flocking to Iraq to participate in a jihad, or holy war, against the American invader.

General Eric Shinseki, the Army Chief of Staff, said that the military occupation of Iraq would require "*several hundred thousand soldiers*", but he was rebuked by the Panglossian Bush administration, which had fantasized that a military adventure in Iraq would be short and sweet, and economically rewarding. Civilian Under Secretary of Defense Paul Wolfowitz, for example, told Congress on February 27, 2003, that Shinseki's number was *"wildly off the mark,"* and that *"It's hard to conceive that it would take more forces to provide stability in post-Saddam Iraq than it would take to conduct the war itself and secure the surrender of Saddam's security force and his army."*[489] Not enough competent thinking had been given to planning the transition from a military mission to the unavoidable political mission afterwards.

## The United Nations in post-war Iraq

Because of its relative brevity however, the financial costs of the 2003 Iraq war were initially lower than for the 1991 Persian Gulf War, which had cost about $61 billion. For a full year in Iraq, the Pentagon estimated outlays totaling some $50 billion.[490] This did not include, however, the costs of post-war reconstruction of the devastated country, costs which were expected to run into the tens of billions, possibly hundreds of billions of dollars.[491]

The Bush administration also faced the crucial problem of legalizing the international sales of Iraqi oil, because that is where it planned to recoup most of the costs of the war, of the occupation and of the reconstruction. Oil, oil, oil was at the top of priorities and the urgency of urgencies. In a first step, it made sure the Iraqi Oil Ministry would escape being looted and ransacked, as was the case for most of the other government buildings in Baghdad. In a second step, it named an American, Philip Carroll, a former executive at Royal Dutch/Shell Group, to direct a U.S.-installed team of Iraqi oil managers. As one oil ministry employee said, *"It is certainly clear now that they are after Iraqi oil."*[492] Clear to everyone around the world, except to U.S. media and to a gullible American public who still did not want to admit that their government, comprised of oilmen, could be interested in Iraqi oil.

But now that Iraq was conquered militarily, the Bush administration was anxious to have the Security Council abrogate the more than 12-year-old economic sanctions, imposed by the United Nations on Iraq through many U.N. resolutions, and let Iraqi oil flow on international markets. The first one, resolution 660, dated from as far back as August 6, 1990. The sanctions had been imposed against the nation of Iraq, not against any particular government, so they could be lifted before a new temporary government could be created.

However, with the U.N. sanctions gone, the United Nations would have no more legal authority in Iraq, other than what the Bush administration condescended to give it. The $3.2 billion in escrow bank accounts would no longer be under United Nations control, and oil sales and other imports of food and medications could proceed through the network of 44,000 distribution centers throughout the country, without United Nations supervision. The American government, or its surrogate, would be in total control of Iraq. U.S. Deputy Defense Secretary Paul Wolfowitz also flatly told a Senate panel that the United Nations "can't be in charge."

Other governments that had debts owed by Iraq or which had national companies holding development contracts in Iraq were not as anxious as the Bush administration to see the United Nations pushed aside from the ruling and the reconstruction of Iraq. Conditions would have to be attached to the removal of the series of resolutions which had paved the way for a U.S.-led invasion of that country.

### A legal vacuum

Because the U.S.-led invasion had not been conducted in accordance with the United Nations Charter, the interim administration of Iraq could not be transferred to the United Nations, as was the case in East Timor from October 1999 to May 2002, after an Australian-led international coalition occupied the country and removed it from an illegal Indonesian control, and before a local government took the reins of power. Such had also be the case in Kosovo and in Afghanistan. But for Condoleezza Rice, Iraq is unique, in this mimicking a declaration by Donald Rumsfeld who had said *"Iraq is different, it has oil"* [493494] Iraq was unique in another way. Paul D. Wolfowitz, Deputy Secretary of Defense, became the real U.S. Secretary of State regarding Iraq, not Colin Powell, by selecting the post-war Iraqi interim government.[495]

212

There were consequences derived from this legal void. Indeed, because the war was waged in defiance of the United Nations, complications arose regarding the entire legal and diplomatic process of removing the old Security Council resolutions regarding Iraq, sixteen in all, and adopting a new resolution to establish an American-led government.

Even the process of the international sale of Iraqi oil, which was under the authority of the United Nations, was in doubt and could be mired in legal complications. The proceeds from such sales are derived from the U.N.'s "Oil-for-Food" program and are used to finance the Iraqi population's humanitarian needs. Since 1991, the United Nations is effectively the trustee of Iraqi oil assets, including the $3.2 billion in oil money which was in United Nations-controlled escrow bank funds and the eight million to nine million barrels of oil filling the storage tanks at Ceyhan, a Turkish port on the Mediterranean. Without the United Nations' formal approval, the international sale of Iraqi oil is illegal.[496]This did not stop Vice President Dick Cheney from predicting that Iraq would be pumping between 2.5 and 3.0 million barrels a day before the end of 2003.[497] As a matter of fact, Halliburton, Vice President Dick Cheney's former oil servicing company, received the most enticing oil reconstruction contracts in post-war Iraq.[498] In 2003, Halliburton's contracts in Iraq amounted to the huge amount of more than $2 billion, most of them awarded without bids.[499]

For the Bush administration, the management of the Iraqi oil sector was a crucial issue. Thus, it lost no time presenting a resolution to the U.N. Security Council, on May 9, 2003, to have the U.N. sanctions removed and to have the U.N. transfer its oil authority and accumulated Iraqi oil revenues to a new Iraqi Assistance Fund to be *"disbursed at the direction of"* the United States and Britain and to be administered by the Iraqi Central Bank, run by an American, Peter McPherson, a former assistant secretary in the U.S. Treasury.

The U.S. proposal unblushingy began with the following surreal sentence, *"Reaffirming the commitment of all Member States to the sovereignty and territorial integrity of Iraq"*, a sovereignty which had just been blatantly violated by the U.S.-led invasion. The "occupying powers" (the United States of America and the United Kingdom) had taken over Iraq's sovereignty.

Initially, the only role reserved for the United Nations was to sit, along with the International Monetary Fund, the World Bank and some "regional institutions", on a toothless advisory board whose only responsibility would have been to appoint auditors to examine the accounts of the newly created Assistance fund. The U.N. could also have a special co-ordinator in Iraq, but his role would be nebulous and symbolic, being most likely limited to channeling U.N. foreign assistance.[500] After much wrangling, and in order to appease somewhat the permanent members of the U.N. Security Council, it was accepted that the U.N. would name a special co-ordinator who would help organize a transitional Iraqi government and would be involved in selecting some of its members. For all practical purposes, however, no one doubted that the United Nations had been pushed aside and replaced in Iraq by a new international master, the United States, and its junior ally, the U.K.

After minor concessions to France, Russia and China, the Resolution 1483 to transfer to the United States and Britain, as occupying powers, the control of Iraq and of its oil wealth was adopted on May 22, 2003, by 14 members of the Security Council out of 15, Syria not participating in the vote.

The punitive economic sanctions against Iraq were lifted without the U.N. weapons inspectors officially declaring the country free of the weapons of mass destruction that the Bush administration and Tony Blair had alleged existed to justify their military invasion.

The new U.N. resolution extended for one year the existence of the United Nations weapons inspection team but did not mandate it to go back to Iraq, in order to ensure that the very reasons the sanctions had been imposed to begin with, did not exist anymore (or, had perhaps never existed). In the end, the Security Council bowed to the United States and approved something it had disapproved a few months before, that is, the invasion and occupation of a sovereign nation by the United States and the U.K. George W. Bush's bluff at the United Nations had totally succeeded. France, Russia and China, the permanent members, had been intimidated and were falling into line. The U.S. and its accommodating ally, Great Britain, could tap Iraqi oil under their command.

Indeed, the geopolitics of oil was paramount in post-war Iraq, a country with oil reserves potentially larger than those of Saudi Arabia. There was an estimated three trillon dollar bonanza (three thousand billion dollars) in profits and royalties waiting to be tapped by the government and oil companies following the removal of the United Nations' economic sanctions. In 1998, the chief executive officer of Chevron-Texaco, Kenneth Derr, admitted, *"Iraq possesses huge reserves of oil and gas—reserves I'd love Chevron to have access to."*[501]

If an American could govern Iraq as a viceroy, these wishes would become reality, provided the U.N. economic sanctions were lifted. If not, and if the oil contracts held by other companies were not respected, a legal mess could result. Iraqi oil tankers could be seized and future oil contracts could be in limbo.[502]

Indeed, if Iraq were to become an American military protectorate, governed *de facto* during many years by an American viceroy, without a clear United Nations' mandate, what would be the legal basis for such an occupation? This had been the model retained after World War II in Germany and Japan, but that was before the creation of the United Nations and after formal declarations of war had been issued against the two countries that had provoked the war to begin with.[503] This would be a model similar to the protectorate that Great Britain exercised in Iraq from 1917 to 1958, but in this latter case, the League of Nations had given its authorization. Some international cover could be provided by involving NATO. Indeed, in order to legitimize *a posteriori* its invasion of Iraq, the U.S. government much preferred relying on NATO, an organization it controls, than on the United Nations, the supreme international organization it only partly controls.[504]

No matter what, the Bush administration was determined to keep Iraq under U.S. control. L. Paul Bremer III, chairman of the U.S. National Commission on Terrorism, was designated as the U.S. special envoy in Iraq. He quickly replaced Jay Garner, a retired lieutenant general and a former CEO of SY Technology, as acting U.S. administrator of Iraq. It seemed that Garner was too willing to adopt the Department of State's plan for reconstructing Iraq, and not enough enamored with the Pentagon's rosy scenario for post-war Iraq.[505] In an important symbolic gesture, Bush made sure that Bremer was to report directly to the Pentagon and not to the civilian Department of State under Colin Powell.

The Bush administration divided Iraq into three smaller administrative units, in order to reflect the divergence of interests of the three main ethnic groups living in Iraq: the Kurds in the north, the Sunni Muslims in the center and the Shia Muslims in the south. Three American officials were appointed to administer the Iraqi regions. Central Iraq was initially placed under former U.S. Ambassador (Yemen) Barbara Bodine, and two retired generals were appointed to administer the northern and the southern districts.[506]

In order to make sure that that fallouts derived from the military occupation of Iraq would profit American companies, in its version of a $79 billion spending bill for the reconstruction of Iraq, the House of Representatives even went so far as to stipulate that France, Russia, Germany and Syria were to be specifically excluded from the reconstruction contracts.[507] In the minds of many members of Congress, the United States had just acquired a new colony in the Middle East.[508]

The Bush administration had a larger agenda. Indeed, according to the Bush Doctrine, its designs extended to the world at large, not just the Middle East, and certainly not only to Iraq. In its October 2002 resolution to Congress, it had asked for an authorization to establish international peace and security in the "Persian Gulf region" and not just in Iraq. It was only at the insistence of the Democrats that the word "region" had been replaced by "Iraq".

And to make sure that it will be so and that Iraq will serve in the future as a permanent regional military launching pad for the United States, the Pentagon planned a long-term control of four Iraqi military bases, one at the international airport just outside Baghdad, another at Tallil, near Nasiriya in the south, the third at an isolated airstrip called H-1 in the western desert, along the old oil pipeline that runs to Jordan, and the last at the Bashur air field in the Kurdish north.[509] Armed with these permanent bases, the U.S. military could place the entire Middle East, and even most of Asia, under its surveillance.[510]

With Bush's approval, Secretary of Defense Donald Rumsfeld lost no time in turning around and threatening Syria and Iran.[511] In so doing, however, the United States violates other peoples' fundamental right to political self-determination and undermines international law.

### The U.N. as a cover

Initially, not willing to share responsibilities and benefits alike in newly conquered Iraq, the Bush administration was adamant in not admitting U.N. peacekeepers into the devastated country, instead pressing easily influenced individual countries to commit troops to Iraq. However, most countries would not participate in this strategy of circumventing the United Nations and politely declined the invitation.

As the mess it created in Iraq became more and more untractable, it became increasingly obvious that the military occupation of Iraq would not be the benign and self-financing enterprise that the White House hawks had mistakenly envisaged. Indeed, Deputy Defense Secretary Paul D. Wolfowitz told Congress during the war that "*we are dealing with a country that can really finance its own reconstruction, and relatively soon.*" This was despite a voluminous report from a secret task force, the Energy Infrastructure Planning Group, based at the Pentagon as part of the planning for the war, which had warned the Bush administration that Iraq's oil system, as a result of trade embargoes, was in bad shape and would not deliver the riches that the war sponsors were claiming. Reconstruction money would have to come out of the U.S. taxpayers' pockets.[512]

With daily acts of sabotage on oil pipelines, initiated by the Iraqi and Islamist guerrilla, it was becoming obvious to Bush's neocon planners that Iraqi oil exports would be running well below their prewar levels for some time to come, and that oil revenues would not come anywhere close to covering the direct military cost of the occupation (more than $4 billion a month), let alone the tens of billions that rebuilding and running Iraq will cost in the years ahead. As with other pretenses, the Bush administration exaggerated public estimates of Iraq's oil revenues in order to sell its plans to attack Iraq.[513]

Moreover, the Bush administration also began to dread the fact that each day one or two young American soldiers were killed in a foreign land and were being brought back to America in body bags or in in flag-draped caskets.[514] The war, it seems, opened up a new front for international terrorism and al Qaeda operatives were filtering into Iraq to fight the "infidels". All this was happening against the background of a politico-religious civil war that the U.S.-led invasion had ignited between Sunni and Shiite Muslims, resulting in numerous losses of Iraqi lives.

Both from a political and an economic point of view, occupied Iraq was becoming a burden to the Bush administration. The "Q" word began to be used more and more frequently to describe the quagmire the United States waded into in Iraq, and the word "lie" appeared more and more often in the titles of books and articles.[515] Indeed, things were not going as well as expected in conquered Iraq, and the harsh realities of military colonialism in the 21st Century, by a democratic country, seemed to be forcing a review of a policy that had been ill-considered, unlawful and badly-planned from the very beginning.[516]

That is why, when U.N. Secretary General Kofi Annan opened the door to the possibility of having U.N. troops in Iraq under the command of a U.S. general, the Bush administration saw a window of opportunity to share the burden of military occupation, without basically relinquishing the bounties. Even though the U.S. Defense Department was completely in charge in Iraq, not only for military affairs but also for civil matters, it was the State Department Deputy Secretary who declared that the Bush administration was ready to allow a multinational force in Iraq to operate under the sponsorship of the U.N., as long as it was commanded by an American.[517]

In so doing, the U.S. government could obtain what it wanted, the merging of the occupation armies into a U.N.-sponsored multinational force, under U.S. command. This was perceived, above all, as a new attempt to obtain some sort of legitimacy and endorsement by the Security Council for the American-led occupation of the country, after the fact, and as a way to attract more foreign troops and more international funds to Iraq.

Having snubbed the United Nations and invaded a sovereign nation in violation of the United Nations Charter and having underestimated the practical consequences of such an unlawful action, the Bush administration was now apparently anxious to have the United Nations rely on its credibility and legitimacy to help clean up the mess in the Middle East.

It was insisting, however, that while the U.N. would serve as a cover and as a potential convenient scapegoat for the inextricable Iraqi situation, the United States Central Command would maintain full military authority, and that the real civil authority in Iraq would continue to rest with the U.S. viceroy, L. Paul Bremer III, reporting directly to the Pentagon. In the words of French President Jacques Chirac, Iraq had the unhealthy privilege of having a governor who was "*Christian and foreign*" administering an Arab and Muslim country.

Having openly violated the principles contained in the U.N. Charter, George W. Bush was now relying, not without some impudence, on the "*fundamental principles and objectives*" of the United Nations to appeal for unity, just as the United Nations Secretary General Kofi Annan was stingingly denouncing exactly such a preemptive approach that could lead to "*a proliferation of the unilateral and lawless use of force*".[518]

Obviously, the United Nations had a role to play in George W. Bush's game plan, even though he had no intention whatsoever of meeting other countries half-way. The president wanted to "have his cake and eat it too." But, even without the U.N.'s caution, generous U.S. packages of military and economic inducements were able to entice some countries, such as Poland and Turkey, to consider sending thousands of troops into Iraq and possibly orient the situation to their own advantage, even though the American-appointed Iraqi Governing Council unanimously opposed the deployment of troops from neighboring countries, especially from Turkey, because of the fear of a return of the Ottoman Empire in Iraq.[519] However, other countries could not be bought so easily and a formal U.N. backing was required to persuade some of them to send troops and contribute money.[520] The central objective was to allow George W. Bush to distance himself somewhat from the Iraqi predicament and continue to run for the 2004 presidential elections, while claiming a "victory" in Iraq.[521]

However, many countries were hesitant to have the United Nations serve as a cover for the occupation of Iraq, but did not wish to defy openly a vengeful Bush administration.[522] When Kofi Annan disclosed his own reservations, saying that the fig-leaf subordinate role the Bush administration had reserved the United Nations in unstable Iraq did not justify putting U.N. workers' lives at risk, it became clear that it would be difficult to harness the nine votes required for a resolution to pass, even if no veto were cast. After making symbolic concessions and after tremendous diplomatic pressure by Washington was applied on non-veto African and Latin American members, the Security Council members, holding their noses and *"in the interest of unity"*, finally gave a mostly symbolic, non convincing, but unanimous approval to a resolution containing no specific timetable for transferring political control in Iraq to Iraqis. The U.S.-dominated occupying powers could remain the government in Iraq for the foreseeable future.[523] However, President George W. Bush had obtained a permit to go around the world begging for money to help finance his colonial adventure in Iraq.[524]

Even a half-hearted U.N. resolution would be enough, however, to satisfy the British ally and impress upon an increasingly skeptical Congress the need to vote the necessary credits for the continuation of the Iraqi operations. Indeed, even a lukewarm U.N. endorsement would help in persuading the American public and Congress to cough up some $87 billion more to cover the immediate costs of the U.S. presence in Iraq and Afghanistan, on top of a previously voted sum of $79 billion, at the same time as the total U.S. budget deficit was expected to push way above $500 billion. This was supposed to tide the Bush administration over until the 2004 presidential elections.

The dubious foreign policy and the questionable fiscal policies are a reflection of George W. Bush's seeking of "quick gratification" and immature character. As a *New York Times'* editorial put it:

*"Mr. Bush is a man who was reared in privilege, who succeeded in both business and politics because of his family connections...[Many] wrong turns were chosen because of a fundamental flaw in the character of this White House. Despite his tough talk, Mr. Bush seems incapable of choosing a genuinely tough path, of risking his political popularity with the same aggression that he risks the country's economic stability and international credibility...But at the moment when we need strong leadership most, he is still a politician who is incapable of asking the people to make hard choices. And we are paying the price."*[525]

Regarding Iraq, George Bush Jr. would have been better advised to take counsel with his father. Indeed, President George H. Bush, a man with more experience, endowed with a better judgment, and able to surround himself with competent people (Baker, Scowcroft, etc.), ruled out a military campaign against Iraq, in 1991, in these terms, *"I firmly believed we should not march into Baghdad....To occupy Iraq would instantly shatter our coalition, turning the whole Arab world against us and make a broken tyrant into a latter-day Arab hero....assigning young soldiers to a fruitless hunt for a securely entrenched dictator and condemning them to fight in what would be an unwinnable urban guerrilla war....Had we gone the invasion route, the United States could conceivably still be an occupying power in a bitterly hostile land."*[526] Hundreds of young Americans and many thousands of Iraqis would be alive today if this judicious advise had been heeded.

An oil colony and a religious colony?

For many in America, the war in the Middle East had strong religious overtones. For U.S. Lieutenant General William Boykin, for instance, an Evangelical Christian and a Bush-nominated deputy undersecretary of defense for intelligence, the international war on terrorism was a religious war, a sort of conflict between Judeo-Christian values, Islam and Satan. The general confessed that when he captured a Muslim Somali warlord, he knew [that his own] God was bigger than his. *"I knew that my God was a real God and his was an idol"*, dangerously giving the impression to the Muslim world that the American war on terror was really a war on Islam. And, the general added, "(George W. Bush) *is in the White House because God put him there.*"[527]

Indeed, it is difficult not to conclude that the Bush administration is pursuing a policy which is contrary to the Helsinki accords approach (see chap. 12). By removing the external threat, the Helsinki accords encouraged pro-West sentiment within the Soviet Bloc and ultimately led to the opening of these countries to liberty and freedom. An aggressive anti-Islam approach has the reverse effect. It has the consequence of stifling modernization movements within Muslim countries and retarding secularization and democratic reforms. In the Muslim world, Bush is doing the Islamists' work. The lessons of the seventies have not been learned.

Similarly, for American proselytizing Christians, there was hope that the war against Iraq would open new territories for evangelization. Indeed, as if to prove the close links that exist in America between religion and politics, the Southern Baptist Convention (16 million members), an organization founded by Billy Graham, announced that it believes the Iraqi people were in need of "spiritual" deliverance. Their goal: to convert the country's Muslims to Christianity. Consequently, the Convention planned to descend on a postwar Iraq with "25,000 trained evangelists".[528]

The status of women in "religious" post-war Iraq was also suffering at the hands of religious zealots. Women have never been so excluded from the Iraqi society. Shopkeepers put up signs such as "Sister, cover your hair" and increase pressure for women to wear the hijab head covering. Women can no longer safely go out, walk on the streets or drive their car around Baghdad. It is even dangerous for them to go to the market.[529]

Religious zealots even attempted to have universities separate male and female students. Some movie theaters have been closed or forced to remove "immoral movies", that is, any movie showing a woman's body. Observers feared that religious censorship and repression are on their way to re-establishing themselves in "liberated" Iraq.[530] The external threat and the American-led invasion of Iraq had the consequence of giveivg added importance to reactionary mullahs and imams, not only in Iraqi politics but in all Muslim countries.[531]

It should have been known in Washington that a democracy which does not protect its minorities is not a democracy, but a mob-ruled populist and intolerant dictatorship. Therefore, it would be the supreme irony if the end result of the U.S.-led invasion of Iraq were to be the establishment of a *de facto* Muslim theocracy and the installation of Sharia laws in that country.

## Germany in the 20th Century and the United States in the 21st Century

At the beginning of the 20th Century, Germany was the most advanced country in science, industry, and the military. It was among the world's dominant countries, just as the United States is in the beginning of the 21st Century, except that the United States is larger and more powerful than 20th Century Germany. It was also a proud but humiliated country; its people believed that they didn't receive their due in world affairs, and they embraced the supremacist ideology. Within the space of 40 years, after two disastrous wars, and after falling into the hands of a madman, Adolph Hitler, who was first elected in 1933, Germany had succeeded in destroying itself. Is the United States condemned to the same fate?

The United States has already suffered from a disastrous discretionary war, the Vietnam War (1962-1973). By plunging head first into a second discretionary petro-religious war in the Middle East, forty years after the first fiasco, it again risks getting bogged down in the kind of conflict and military occupation that destroys countries and forces a retreat of civilization.

In Germany, under the boot of leaders crying "Deutchland! Deutchland!", the country went to the slaughter. Today, the language is somewhat different in the U.S.—except there is that cry, "Homeland! Homeland!" In Germany in the first half of the 20th Century, or the United States in the beginning of the 21st Century, when the steamroller of patriotism calls, rare are the enlightened minds who dare to object.The new imperialism is too intoxicating.[532] In Nazi Germany, they had public rallies to burn books critical of the regime.[533] In the Bush-era United States, there are rallies to destroy records and CDs of artists who criticize the government's war policies.[534]

The same simplistic populism, the same anti-intellectualism, the same aggressive isolationism, the same xenophobia, the same militarism, and the same scorn for international laws and institutions are found in some U.S. Republican leaders today. The United States is perhaps in greater danger than many think. If this unsettling tendency continues, in the vein of the impracticable Bush Doctrine, the United States could be on a path to auto-destruction. The greatest success of the Islamist al Qaeda terrorists on September 11, 2001, will not have been the killing of 3,000 innocent people, but rather the transformation of a great democratic republic into a neo-conservative and neo-fascist society.[535]

Economic globalization has been achieved during the last half century, in great part because of an enlightened U.S. leadership. This was accomplished under the principles of opening up, of freedom and of respect for peoples and nations. But now, there is a clear risk that the United States could become a militarized country, in disregard of international laws. In such circumstances, there could be a retrenchment, if not an outright reversal, of the economic globalization process. If so, at what cost?

Indeed, if the world were to regress to the old 19th Century principles of imperialism and colonialism, under a misplaced American will to power and a new hubris, the gains that the United States could reap in the short run, under the form of spoils of war, would pale in regards to the economic and political losses they would suffer in the long run.

Many global firms are American. If the United States were to become despised throughout the world, and if, because of the nearsightedness of its leaders, it were to undermine the legitimacy and the authority of international institutions such as the United Nations, the International Monetary Fund, or the World Trade Organization, it would spell the end of the globalization of the economy. The United States would have traded multilateral and international security for imperial security. American citizens and

American firms would be the first to lose, even though the reversal would be felt in all parts of the globe. The step backwards for civilization would be universal.

# 16

## GREATNESS AND DECADENCE OF THE WEST

*"Promiscuity and degradation thrived.*
*Roman morals had long become impure,*
*but never was there so favorable an environment*
*for debauchery as among this filthy crowd.*
*Even in good surroundings people find it hard to behave well.*
*Here every form of immorality competed for attention,*
*and no chastity, modesty, or vestige of decency could survive."*
TACITUS (c. 55-120), Annals, 14:15.

*"...if a state overextends itself strategically—by, say, the conquest of*
*extensive territories or the waging of costly wars—it runs the risk that*
*the potential benefits from external expansion may be outweighed by the*
*great expense of it all..."*
Paul KENNEDY, *The Rise and Fall of the Great Powers*[536]

*"Each civilization has the garbage it deserves."*
Georges DUHAMEL (1884-1966)

Numerous ancient empires and civilizations have appeared, only to vanish into the night of time. One of course thinks of the Roman Empire, but there have been many others.

Empires, and the civilizations that sustain them, have a limited life. They follow a long megacycle of several centuries, going through phases of implantation, ascension, and expansion until their summit of grandeur, only to mark time during a period of consolidation, followed by a more or less rapid decline ending in their final disintegration. Civilizations, like empires, are not eternal. They are complex, and therefore fragile, and at the mercy of all sorts of disruptions. The more complex they are, the more fragile and vulnerable. Due to the vicissitudes of major shocks, catastrophic events, or the harmful influence of incompetent and corrupted leaders, they can follow the wrong path, hastening their decline and final eclipse.[537]

## The 600-year megacycle

From a cyclical standpoint, it is interesting to observe that, in the past, certain empires seem to have followed a 600-year cycle. Let us look at three of the most notable ones.

The Roman Empire. In supposing that Ancient Rome's hegemony really began after the destruction of its rival, Carthage, in 146 B.C., the Roman Empire's period of expansion and subsequent decline lasted approximately 622 years. Its expansionist period lasted from the reign of Agustus Caesar (r. 27 B.C.- 14 A.D.) until that of Diocletian (284 A.D.) For two more centuries, internal struggles and barbarian attacks caused its decline, until its ultimate fall at the hands of the Barbarians, in 476 A.D.[538]

The Muslim Empire. From the death of Mohammed in 632, the Muslim Empire expanded rapidly under the dynasty of the caliphate of the Umayyaads. By 750, the empire extended from Spain to India. After 945, however, under the caliphate of the Abbasids, the Muslim Empire lost its cohesion and began a long decline. Its final disintegration came in 1258, at the hands of the Mongols. It had lasted 626 years.

The Ottoman (Turkish) Empire. From its foundation by Osmon I in 1290, the Ottoman Empire expanded geographically until the conquest of Constantinople, in 1453, which was transformed into the imperial capital of Istanbul under the direction of Sultan Mehemet II. The empire continued its expansion until the reign of Sultan Soleiman II the Magnificent (1520-1566), who conquered Hungary. At its peak, this empire extended from Hungary in the north to Rhodes in the west, to Persia in the east and to Arabia in the South. After Soleiman II was stopped at the gates of Vienna, in 1532, the Ottoman Empire began a long retrenchment, until it fell to the Allied Forces in

1917, having sided with Germany in 1914.[539] From birth to death: 627 years.

Is there an unwritten law that determines that the length of time an empire can grow and withstand the weight of endogenous and exogenous forces is approximately six centuries? Without making it an inevitability, it seems that there is a megacycle concerning civilizations and empires that lasts for about 600 years.[540]

As for the global explanations for these declines, the thesis of Paul Kennedy is of particular interest. Great powers, and by extension, great civilizations, are usually condemned to follow an internal dynamic which brings them, by the arrogance or the recklessness of their leaders, to overexpand and to overextend their reach.[541] The nation that extends itself into other territories is in a permanent state of weakness and of constant danger. Sooner or later, the marginal costs of this excessive expansion exceed the marginal benefits, and the empire ceases to get richer, begins to get poorer and then breaks apart.

The question is pertinent. Has the West, and especially the United States, become over-extended under the double umbrella of economic globalization and planetary military hegemony? Will the revolt of populations in the countries that have been left behind generate more costs, in upheavals of all kinds, than the gains procured by this domination? Can the West preserve its values and fundamental principles?

### The values of Western civilization

Many people believe that religion was the corner stone of Western civilization. They see religion as the vehicule for the development of spiritual and moral values, beginning with the biblical Ten Commandments of Moses, and resulting in the blossoming of Western civilization.[542] It is true that Judeo-Christian values were the source of certain great principles of civilization, among them:

1- the idea that every individual posesses intrinsic value, and consequently must assume a personal moral responsibility;
1- the principle of the superiority of reason over superstition;

229

2-  the subordination of nature to human progress;
3-  the concept of private property and the motivation to economize scarce resources, as well as the incentive to improve conditions and to accumulate productive capital.

Without diminishing the importance of the civilizing influence of the Judeo-Christian tradition, nor underestimating the contribution of the great religions concerning individual spirituality and morality, one can advance that, historically, Western civilization really began to flower when the civil society freed itself from the political-religious institutions that had controlled Western populations for centuries.[543]

In fact, compared to other civilizations of the time in Asia and Africa, the rise of Western civilization really began in the 15th and 16th Centuries, when a series of shocks, events, and fundamental transformations opened the way for the establishment of political and economic freedoms. The totalitarian tradition of religious and royal power that had dominated Europe for more than a millennium ruptured and weakened, and this period marked the slow development of liberal democracy.

Beginning in the 15th and 16th Centuries, and especially by the 18th Century, the century of the Enlightenment, a revolutionary idea gained hold. It was the idea that the individual had an absolute sovereignty and that political power did not come from abstract deities, as all religions had previously taught, but from the people itself. Therefore, republican and democratic principles went much further than the religious idea of individual self-worth.[544] They reinforced and completed Judeo-Christian ideas about the organization of public life by rendering possible the rise of liberal democracy as a political system.

While it is true that the Judeo-Christian religious traditions of emphasizing individuality had prepared the philosophical terrain for the establishment of democracy, it was necessary for the idea that political power comes from the people and not from a remote god to take hold, before power could be transferred from religiously appointed kings and princes to elected representative governments. It must be said, therefore, that the conception of the lofty democratic ideal is essentially of a European and secular origin. This ideal proposes that:

1- individual liberty is a natural human endowment;
2- all men are born equal, are capable of self-government, and political power derives from the people and not from abstract deities;
3- government should be secular and not religious;
4- philosophical or religious fatalism should be rejected in favor of the idea of progress through science and knowledge;
5- property should be distributed and not centralized;
6- trade can be free while being regulated by means of laws and contracts.[545]

Just as in some Islamic countries today that are at the same stage as Europe four centuries ago—that is, ruled by political and economic systems based on a poisonous combination of politics and religion—Europe's development was paralyzed during more than a thousand years by the domination that religions held over the lay population.[546]

One cannot really speak of Western civilization during the Middle Ages. Even less can one consider the darkest part of the Middle Ages as representing Western civilization. The terrorist regime of the religious Inquisition subsisted in Europe from its first justification by the Council of Verona in 1184, and its official creation by Pope Gregory IX in 1233, until its final abolition in 1820.

Fundamental reasons for the West's success

How did the Western Empire get to its present form in the 21st Century? First of all, the relative success of Western civilization did not happen in a vacuum. It was built on solid political, economic, and military foundations.

Historically, the greatest achievement of the Western world was at the same time political and economic. The West succeeded in reconciling, both in its principles and its institutions, the demands of individual freedom and the requirements for economic prosperity. It was this combination of political and economic liberty that made possible the investments and the initiatives which in turn produced increased revenue and wealth.

Seven factors are found at the heart of the rise of the Western world, or what can be called the Democratic Western Empire, beginning in the middle of the 15th Century: new ideas, new territories, new communication and production technologies, new political organizations, a new decentralized economic system based on property rights and on free markets, social stability through social progress and military superiority in order to defend freedom.

New ideas favoring political and religious freedom and the decentralization of political power in Europe in the 15th, 16th, 17th, and 18th Centuries;

The discovery of the Americas at the end of the 15th Century, opening up new territories to colonization and immigration, which relieved the demographic pressure on European populations and strengthened the European countries that exploited the New World's natural resources;

The invention of new communications technnologies in the 15th Century and the Industrial Revolution in the middle of the 18th Century led to increased investments and a rise in workers' productivity, while preventing the decreasing returns of labor on farmlands.

At the end of the 18th Century, the advent of democracy and the establishment of the nation-states ushered in new political and economic organizations. The resulting deconcentration of power in Europe brought an end to the stagnation imposed by totalitarian powers, both religious and aristocratic.

The advent of a decentralized capitalist economic system turned out to be a wealth-creating machine parallel to no other and it has been the envy of the rest of the world ever since. An example of a new type of organization in the economic sphere is the limited responsibility corporation. This institution promotes economic development by encouraging risk-taking and investments, while limiting the financial risk of shareholders to their initial capital investment.[547]

The West's democratic and social philosophy of using the State as a mechanism for wealth distribution, was not only a contributor to domestic political stability, but has been copied all over the world, creating a climate favorable to economic growth.

Finally, because of their economic and military superiority, western countries could more easily resist any destabilizing attempts of subjugation from the outside and could remain free to develop and progress.

Economically, indeed, the new system of ideas, values, and norms based on personal liberty and free enterprise resulted in the extension of property rights—previously concentrated in the hands of the aristocracy and the clergy—to private individuals. The concentration of property and the heavy taxes levied on the people to maintain extensive royal and ecclesiastic institutions kept resources from being devoted to more productive use, and were thus a source of economic stagnation. Entrepreneurial freedom, the freedom to invest and innovate, the rise of commercial and industrial capitalism, and the creation of free markets constituted an enormous progress in Europe. These cultural, political, and social innovations liberated energy and creativity in a way that no centralized system based on the concentration of property could have done.

Well before the Industrial Revolution in the 1750's, technology played an important role in the diffusion of humanist ideas of political and economic freedom. In 1423, the discovery of wood engraving and, in 1452, of metal engraving, and especially of course, in 1450, the invention of printing with movable type by the German Johann Gutenberg, enabled new works and knowledge to spread rapidly. Gone were the days when only a few learned ecclesiastics wrote theological books in Latin, inaccessible to the public. Humanists quickly began to use the vernacular language to communicate with the public at large.

The renewed interest in nature encouraged the development of the sciences. The objectivity and precision of the scientific method supplanted the vagueness and confusion of the scolastics.[548] Universities were established—Venice, Bale, Paris, Louvain, and others—to investigate the new areas of study. In medecine, it was the study of the human body. In astronomy, the precise study of the sun and planets' place in the solar system. The Renaissance was the true beginning of the modern era.

## Totalitarian versus democratic values

Western history is indeed a long battle between totalitarian and democratic values. Thanks to the intellectual and scientific renewal during the Renaissance, the universal values of freedom and democracy triumphed over totalitarian theocratic and aristocratic values. Today, we enjoy the fruits of the victory of democracy over totalitarianism.

The West has been perfecting its 10 founding principles over more than five centuries:

1- equality, dignity, and liberty of all people, guaranteed by inherent and constitutional rights
2- tolerance among all peoples and individuals
3- social solidarity
4- the secularization of the state
5- universal and secular education
6- the equality of the sexes
7- political democracy
8- free enterprise
9- confidence in progress through science and knowledge
10-the right of all individuals to seek happiness.

These are the values that can be contrasted with the totalitarian principles that other, less advanced, civilizations and philosophies offer the world.

## The rise of the Western Empire

The interdependent Western nations that have contributed in building Western civilization have constituted over time a *de facto* empire, not because they were subjected to a single political authority, but precisely because of the absence of such a supreme, centralized government.

All the while sharing the same humanist values, and sharing the same experience of geographic expansion and technological and economic development, the European and American nation-states stimulated each other in a competition that was sometimes creative, sometimes destructive, but, in the long run, very positive. Because European and American nations shared a common Western civilization, it is realistic to qualify this group of countries as the Democratic Western Empire, even though this empire has several centers and contains several sub-empires that rival each other.

It is a super-empire that began its true ascension after the fateful date of 1453, when Constantinople and the Byzantine Empire fell at the hands of the Muslims. This event shows how a short term set-back can be a blessing in the long run. The date is doubly important. First, the "accident" of the discovery of the Americas by the Europeans, in 1492, is the direct result of the closing of the spice road to the Far East. Naval technology for the construction of ships capable of sailing the high seas did the rest.

Second, it was also around the year 1450, that military technology using gunpowder became operational. The French were the first to perfect the new artillery weapons. Economist Leonard Dudley has well documented this point in his book *The Word and the Sword:*

*In 1450 and 1453, "the French artillery played an important role in the victories that drove the English from French soil...By the 1490's, the French artillery was the best in the world. It is no coincidence that the French monarchy was also the most powerful in Europe."* [549]

The Chinese had discovered gunpowder, but they hadn't mastered the techniques of molding cast iron shot and cast-metal artillery pieces. It was the Europeans, and especially the French, who transformed the Chinese discovery into a devastating military innovation. Artillery became the key element for the efficiency of European armies on the battlefield.

Navies gained also from the new techniques. When England mounted canons on the bridge of its seagoing ships, the small island became the ruler of the seas and extended an empire upon which "the sun never set". Leonard Dudley aserts that Western civilization and its fundamental values would not have emerged without the protective umbrella of military superiority over the other world powers of the times.

The leadership of the Democratic Western Empire changed several times. In the beginning, a few monarchies shared the hegemony—France under François I (1494-1547), Austria and Spain under Charles V (1500-1558), and the Austrian Habsburg family until 1659 (the Treaty of the Pyrenees). Thus, at the outset, there were embryos of European power. Later, France became the dominant power in central Europe in the 17th and 18th Centuries, first under Louis XIV (1638-1715), then under Napoleon Bonaparte (1769-1821), until the Battle of Waterloo in 1815.

From 1815 to 1914, Great Britain spearheaded the advance of Western civilization throughout the world. It was England that was first to profit from the Industrial Revolution that began around 1750. The arrival of industrial machinery in Great Britain, and later also in Germany and France, revolutionized the traditional economy—based upon agriculture and trade—and ushered in the great developments of industrialization and urbanization.

The shock of World War I (1914-1918) and the even more devastating shock of World War II (1939-1945), considerably weakened the traditional European powers. These two ruinous wars were exhausting fratricidal adventures, opposing Germany and Italy, on one side, and France and Great Britain on the other.

The cost of the two debilitating wars to the European pole of Western civilization was the economic, military, and political ascendance of the American pole, represented by the United States. Without these two crippling wars, the nerve center of the Democratic Western Empire might never have crossed the Atlantic. During World War I, the outputs of Germany and France dropped over 10 percent and 25 percent respectively, while those of Great Britain and the United States continued to grow. During World War II, the same thing happened and the outputs of Germany and France dropped by over 50 percent in both cases, while the United Kingdom kept growing, and the United States grew even more rapidly.[550]

Since 1914, and certainly since 1945, the West's leadership torch has been passed to the United States of America, essentially because of its relative economic ascendancy. Today, the Democratic Western Empire comprises the nations of the

North Atlantic Treaty Organization (NATO), less Turkey. It is incontestably the greatest military power in the world. It is also an empire in expansion, since ten Eastern Europe countries joined the European Union in May of 2004, both reinforcing and consolidating it.

When the balance sheet is in, the apogee of the Democratic Western Empire under American leadership may be set at the 1989-91 period, at the fall of communism and the demise of the Union of Soviet Socialist Republics (USSR). The only credible rival of the Democratic Western Empire for worldwide hegemony has disappeared. For those who control the greatest military force, that is the United States, this absence of competition could remove all restraints and open the door to the worst follies. Perhaps in the future, the determining factor in the eventual decline of the Democratic Western Empire will be seen to be this dangerous concentration of power in a single dominant pole, based upon military force, apart from all other nation states.

Over the long term, the political, economic, and military tensions that exist between the American and European poles of the Super Empire are certainly a threat to sustaining the dominant position of Western civilization in the world. Indeed, the United States fears a united Europe that could one day challenge its political and economic dominance. For instance, the euro has the potential to overcome the U.S. dollar as the international medium of exchange of choice for trade and financial transactions. In a context of internationalism and of secured peace, Europe could more easily prosper and extend its influence and could supplant the U.S. as the main world political pole. Conversely, a reversal to international tensions and to wars would play to American military strength and would keep Europe divided and subdued.

The 2003 U.S.-initiated war against Iraq in order to control the Middle East oil spigot can be seen as part of a larger U.S. strategy to influence European economic and political development, the EU being even more dependent than America on imported oil. Indeed, with Europe and Japan being most dependent on oil supplies from the Persian Gulf, it is obvious that whoever controls this region militarily will maintain leverage over oil supplies to the rest of the world for decades to come.

This creates a major dilemma for Europe. Even if its size and advanced development make it strong economically, it remains relatively weak politically and militarily. Indeed, with the United States flexing its hegemonic muscles all over the world, it may be dangerous for Europe to remain indefinitely mired in a state of political and military impotence that prevents it from playing a leadership role in world affairs. It remains that Europe is at the center of Western Civilization and is a model of economic and political integration for all the nation states of the world, in contrast to a monolithic and imperial America.

Therefore, which view of the world—the European multilateral approach or the American unilateral approach—will prevail is bound to profoundly influence the acceptability and the legitimacy of western values and influence in the world. If Paul Kennedy's thesis is founded—that empires regress when they become over-extended and heavily indebted—the unilateral and arrogant actions of the American pole, in accordance with the "Bush Doctrine", are more likely to elicit antagonism in the rest of the world than the European attitude of internationalism, of collaboration and of openness to other civilizations.

At the beginning of the 21st Century, the United States has become an empire on its own, with a military presence in 120 countries. It is the country with the world's largest military force, but also with the world's largest debt. Historically, there is no precedent for a country to be both politically dominant and heavily in debt.

Indeed, the cost of American intervention in world affairs is starting to weigh on the U.S. With a foreign trade deficit surpassing $450 billion, and an external current account deficit of $430 billion, in 2002, the United States takes more out of the world economy than it contributes. The current account deficit, in particular, is the reflexion of the net foreign borrowing that the U.S. does each year internationally. These borrowings represent about 5% of the U.S. gross domestic product (GDP). This is not far from the pivotal 6%, the threshold that has triggered financial crises for other nations. As a consequence, the U.S. has become a heavy net international debtor.

At the end of 2001, the net international debt of the United States, that is, the difference between the value of U.S.-owned assets abroad and foreign-owned assets in the U.S. (including stocks, bonds and direct investments), amounted to $2.3 trillion. And this may have to increase in the future, as the U.S., armed with the myth of empire building, needs an ever expanding army in order to achieve security through imperial expansion and through worldwide imperial involvements.[551]

At the same time, the Republican administration of George W. Bush has been insistent in pressing its objective of reducing taxes for the wealthy, and in the face of growing public expenditures, letting the domestic fiscal deficit explode. The twin U.S. deficits, fiscal and external, are a direct consequence of the fiscal choices made by the Bush administration. It is a recipe for disaster, for it means relying on foreign savings to finance the enormous U.S. military expenditures. In 2002, these amounted to $343.2 billion, or 43 percent of all military expenditures carried by all the world's countries. U.S. military expenditures represent 80 percent of the yearly current account deficit that it registers with the rest of the world. [552]

In 2003, things got even worse. The Bush administration was truly on a militarist-spending binge. At the 2003 projected level of $400 billion of expenditures for the Pentagon, the United States, with less than 5 percent of the world population, is spending nearly as much on defense as all the rest of the world combined.[553] When those investors start selling, especially those from the second largest economy (Japan) and from the third largest (Germany), their sales will drive the U.S. dollar down, and the same can be said of American financial markets (stocks and bonds).

The main victims will be the U.S. dollar and the U.S. economy, when consumers retreat and taxes have to be increased substantially to forestall a debt explosion, at the same time that interest rates will have to rise in order to stop the outflow of capital. The twin deficit is a weakness that will come back to haunt the United States in the future. In 2003, the Bush administration did not suspect the long-term damage it was doing to the U.S. economy and by extension, to the world economy.

Under the contested leadership of the United States, how long will the Democratic Western Empire maintain its dominant world position in the face of other rapidly expanding economies, such as China? As pure speculation, if, as previously noted, the average duration of past empires is 625 years, when applied to the Democratic Western Empire, its decline or its decadence would already be well advanced by 2078.

Of course there is no determinism in this conjecturing. There are always so many unexpected shocks and future events, it is impossible to predict. In fact, in 1918, the German historian Oswald Spengler wrote of the decadence of the West.[554] If the 625-year megacycle of empires holds true, Spengler will have erred by more than a century and a half!

## A uni-polar, bi-polar or tri-polar world in 2050?

If it were only a matter of economic strength, the uni-polar hegemony of the United States at the beginning of the 21st Century is probably temporary. Indeed, there are two candidates on the horizon who will seriously compete with the U.S.

Within the Democratic Western camp, the demographic and economic force of the European Union is undeniable. Even with only the 15 member nations in 2002-2003, this European block of 377 million people is a world economic giant. After May 1, 2004, with the addition of ten new countries, the European 25 will be a formidable unit of 452 million inhabitants. In 2007, its GDP will reach $14.9 trillion U.S., compared with 18.0 trillion for the United States (see Table below). However, when the European block expands, it will lose in political cohesion what it gains in economic power. For this reason, the eventual arrival of Russia in the EU, which is not inconceivable, will be problematic.

The other mega-state of the 21st Century will be continental China, along with Hong Kong and Taiwan. With a population of 1.27 billion people, of whom two-thirds live in rural areas, its population is ten times larger than Japan's. Although it is an authoritarian state and not a democracy, it is strongly oriented towards export-led economic growth. Around 1979-80, China took a capitalist turn, opening itself to foreign investment, allowing the establishment of mixed foreign and domestic corporations, and creating four special economic zones.

The re-integration of Hong Kong in 1997 gave another boost to Chinese capitalism, stimulating other large economic centers such as Shanghai. Since December 11, 2001, China is officially a member of the all-important World Trade Organization (WTO). In joining the WTO, in order to comply with the rules of the trade body, it had to amend more than 2,300 of its laws and regulations and to abolish 830 of them. This move should give China a big impetus in its integration into the world economy. In 2008, China will host the Olympic Games. It should then be able to show the world the profound reforms and transformations it has undertaken during the last quarter century.[555]

At its present rate—that is with economic growth two times greater than the United States and three times greater than Europe—Greater China may match the economy of the European Union of 25 countries by 2007, not in terms of standard of living, but in terms of total GDP. China already produces more steel than the United States and Japan combined.

The Chinese are using the new communications technology to break out of their isolation—first linguistic, then economic. China is in fact benefiting from two big transformations in modern life. New technologies of communication that standardize methods and unify peoples, and the globalization of the economy that creates opportunities for specialization and enrichment, and brings economic growth through exports. In 2002, Chinese exports amounted to a staggering $325.6 billion.[556]

Due to its low labor costs and undervalued currency, continental China maintains huge foreign trade surpluses, especially vis-à-vis the United States. In 2002, China had a $100-billion trade surplus with the United States. However, the Chinese government staunchly refused to revalue its currency, the Renminbi yuan, pegged to the U.S. dollar at 8.28 yuans for a dollar, since 1994. As a result, China has accumulated large international reserves. Indeed, China's official reserves reached $316 billion in 2003, while Hong Kong and Taiwan had reserves of their own, totaling $116 and $175 billion respectively. If China's currency were freely convertible to other currencies, it would be expected to appreciate by as much as 40 percent, and possibly by 100 percent. This would mean that Chinese wages could rise from about 60 cents an hour to $1.20 an hour. This would have two results: China's external trade imbalances would contract, and deflationary forces in the world economy would be somewhat weakened.

However, even if it were to revalue its currency, China could still rely on an inexhaustible pool of cheap labor, enabling domestic and foreign firms alike to produce ever more sophisticated products with relatively low labor costs. It will take decades, indeed, before the average wage in China catches up with those in developed countries. Continental China has good universities, so much so that many young people from Taiwan prefer to study there rather than in the United States. This is enough to draw many foreign companies to China. In 2002, for example, foreign direct investments in China amounted to $50 billion.

Just as the Turkish leader Atatürk (Mustapha Kemal), in 1928, improved the usefulness and the prestige of the Turkish language by latinizing its alphabet, Chinese leaders understood— as far back as 1956—that modern electronic means could facilitate the simplification of their national language (putonghua or mandarin) by using a more standardized alphabet, the pinyin (pin: spell, yin: sound). Also, as Japan did in the 1950's and 1960's, China imported up-to-date foreign technology to strengthen its economy. This openness to capital, to technology and to trade should propel China to new heights in the 21st Century.

The Greater China economic block could equal, and possibly surpass, the GDP of the United States in 2012. These extrapolations, although quite tentative, show that Greater China could substantially outdistance the U.S. in 2017, with a GDP of some $31.3 trillion US, compared to $23.8 trillion US for the United States and $18.2 trillion US for the European Union of 25 countries. At that time, Greater China could be more than four times more important economically than its Asian competitor, Japan. Of course, unexpected tragedy, for example the spread of new diseases, such as the severe acute respiratory syndrome or SARS, could throw a curve to any country's economic future and stifle its growth. In the case of China, it is also vulnerable to any conflict that could arise with the United States regarding the status of Taiwan. Such a military conflict would devastate the Chinese economy and stop short its drive to catch up with industrialized countries.

Nevertheless, there is a good chance that the three main economic powers of the 21st Century will be the United States, the European Union, and Greater China. Indeed, history teaches us that such concentrations of demographic and economic powers are sooner or later accompanied by concentrations of political and military power. It would be surprising if the period of U.S. unipolar hegemony that exists in the first part of the 21st Century continues for several more decades. By the middle of the century, at the latest, from an economic and geopolitical standpoint, we will most probably live in a tri-polar world.

Will George Orwell's predictions of a tri-polar world in his novel *1984* be realized, almost one century later?[557]

# 17

## CONCLUSION

*"Since the creation of the United Nations [in 1945], there has not been a world war. Therefore for anybody, especially the leader of a superstate, to act outside the United Nations is something that must be condemned by everybody who wants peace."*
Nelson MANDELA, 1993 Nobel Peace Prize winner

*"A Party member lives from birth to death under the eye of the Thought Police. Even when he is alone he can never be sure that he is alone. ...At the apex of the pyramid comes Big Brother. Big Brother is infallible and all-powerful. Every success, every achievement, every victory, every scientific discovery, all knowledge, all wisdom, all happiness, all virtue, are held to issue directly from his leadership and inspiration."*
George ORWELL, *1984*

*"Despise reason and science,*
*humanity's greatest attributes,*
*indulge in illusions and magical practices*
*that reinforce your self-deception,*
*and you will be irremediably lost."*
Johann Wolfgang von GOETHE, *Faust*

There are dates in history that resound like gun shots: June 28, 1914 (the assassination of Archduke Franz Ferdinand, igniting World War I), September 1, 1939 (the invasion of Poland by Hitler's Germany, touching off World War II), December 7, 1941 (the Japanese attack on Pearl Harbor), August 6, 1945 (the dropping of the first atomic bomb on Hiroshima), September 11, 2001 (the al Qaeda terrorist attacks in New York and Washington), and March 20, 2003, (when George W. Bush ordered the bombing of Baghdad and the military invasion of

Iraq). These dates heralded the beginnings of new eras and of profound changes for the world.

Each time, some people thought they were able to take inconsiderate risks by attacking another country or by staging a spectacular assault. Uncountable victims suffered from the atrocities and the consequences that these events set in motion. In the end, however, it was always the people who were responsible and their countries that were the most severely punished. For this reason, leaders who are tempted to wage wars of blind terrorism or wars of aggression should think twice. The strikes that they aim at others risk one day being turned back against themselves and their countrymen.

In the 21st Century, even more so than during the past centuries, resorting to terrorist tactics and using war as a political instrument constitutes a step backwards for civilization. Today, technologies of destruction make both modern warfare and politico-religious terrorism immoral. Killing thousands of innocent people or bombing human populations from 30,000 feet—and having the gall to claim it is in the name of an abstract diety—is the epitome of savagery and cowardice. Those that do so must one day answer to history.

There is no doubt that the democratic world will succeed in overcoming the scourge of Islamist terrorism, as it prevailed over totalitarian communism. Human beings cannot forever be kept in shackles and in prisons. Although vigilance is always necessary, the determining factors in the victory of humanism over totalitarianism will be found in the fundamental, universal values that Western civilization brings to humanity.

However, the role played by the United States in the building of a better and more prosperous world is still uncertain. Indeed, since 1945, there is no other country in the world which has promoted more enthusiastically and benefited more from the globalization of the economy. As a consequence, American corporations, financial institutions and brand names are all over the world, and international trade has grown three times faster than all other economic activities.[558]

The U.S. government, under Roosevelt, Truman, Eisenhower, Kennedy, etc., has been at the forefront of the development of the legal and political international framework to support this globalization of the economy, with the establishment of the United Nations, the General Agreement on Tariffs and Trade (GATT), the World Trade Organization (WTO), the International Monerary Fund (IMF), the World Bank and the North Atlantic Treaty Organization (NATO), to name only the most important multilateral international institutions. Without outright American support, such a beneficial development would not have been possible.

But, paradoxically, at the beginning of the 21st Century, the U.S. government, under George W. Bush, has adopted go-it-alone supremacist policies that threaten to unravel what took half a century to build. By withdrawing from international treaties, by snubbing the other 190 countries of the United Nations and by waging war unilaterally, the Bush administration has undertaken to dismantle piece by piece the international legal and political system that has been the foundation of the post-war era of peace and prosperity.

To support such a fundamental about turn, it uses the pretexts, primo, that the collapse of the Soviet Union has left the U.S. with a "surplus of military power" that it feels justified to use, not to promote a safer world for everybody, but to promote its own selfish and narrow national interests whenever and wherever it wishes; secundo, that the U.S. is the main target of militant international Islamist terrorism and has to take extraordinary measures to protect its borders; and tertio, that international organizations have become too confining, too cumbersome and too inefficient to face up to the new problems. As a consequence, the Bush administration adopted, in 2002, a doctrine of "imperial supremacy" that is a repudiation of what the United States has stood for during the last half century and which puts this country at odds with the rest of the world. This doctrine has made America look more isolationist, more unilateralist, more militarist, more supremacist, more interventionist, less democratic and less supportive of a more open and interdependent world. Historically, when militarism and military conquest showed their ugly heads, it also meant economic exploitation.

In the end, we can ask if the United States, as a democratic republic, can be a world leader in promoting interdependence, democracy and freedom without bullying other countries and other populations. The answer depends to a large extent on how the domestic political climate in the United States evolves in the coming years and if the United States can shake off the self-destructive attitude it has recently adopted. Two political philosophies are presently at odds in the U.S.: hegemonism and multilateralism. Hegemonism is a go-it-alone supremacist strategy that is froth with isolationism, interventionism, and the idea of preeminence. Multilateralism is about respecting people and diffusing and sharing power among nations with equal rights, within international democratic institutions. Which approach is more congenial with the ideals of democracy and peace? Which political philosophy is more likely to advance both international and American long-run interests? These are the questions that will have to be answered in the coming years.

Since Republican George W. Bush was inaugurated, in January 2001, the world has become a more dangerous place for Americans, and the United States has become a somewhat more dangerous country to the world. Terrorism has ceased being a merely local political phenomenon and has emerged as a worldwide threat and, since 9/11, an even more menacing threat to the United States and to American interests around the world.

At the center of these developments is the election of President George W. Bush, on November 7, 2000. During the first three years of its administration, George W. Bush has blurred the separation between Church and State, embarked upon two wars of his own choosing in Afghanistan and in Iraq, withdrawn from a string of international agreements and international institutions that he considered too confining, adopted a provocative with-us-or-against-us rhetorical style, declared an end to the policies of deterrence and of a balance of power as a way to preserve international peace, and has challenged other nations as a policy goal not to attempt to rival American military superiority, thus running the risk of rekindling the arms race.

Many people around the world have been shocked and offended by such a frightening shift in U.S. policies. They perceive the Bush administration as less internationally-minded than previous administrations and as too anxious to abandon many of the ideals that inspired the American dream—dreams of individual equality, of individual freedom, of equality of opportunity, of human rights, of democracy and of respect for human life, not just for Americans but for all citizens of the world. They are afraid that an exaggerated reliance on sheer military power will undermine world peace and a genuine security for the United States.

The United States and the world took the wrong turn in 2001, and it is not too late to bring back democracy and due process in international institutions, in order to insure peace in the world and prove wrong British Astronomer Martin Rees, who says that this century could be humanity's last.[559] But who will take on the indispensable leadership to avoid regressing and to create the necessary mechanisms for a more civilized, a more peaceful, and consequently, a more prosperous world?

Just as in 1945, after the disaster of World War II, the United States is still the key-nation that can advance democracy and rules-based multilateralism in world institutions. It is a responsibility that it cannot recuse without risking the destabilization of the entire planet. Above all, it must behave as a democracy and not as a tyrant, and it should believe in self-limitation of its power for the sake of world peace. This is a small price to pay for creating a better world for all. Current U.S. politicians should meditate about what President Harry S. Truman had to say at the 1945 San Francisco conference that gave birth to the United Nations:
*"We all have to recognize—no matter how great our strength— that we must deny ourselves the license to do always as we please."*

It remains to be seen, however, if the present-day U.S. political system can generate the types of individuals and braintrusts capable of looking beyond the partisan electoral horizon and devoted to building a better world for future generations. For that, America must follow policies true to its original ideals. It should not fear to embrace Benjamin Franklin's seven "great virtues" in public affairs—aversion to tyranny, support for a free press, a sense of humor, humility, idealism in foreign policy, tolerance and respect for compromise.

# NOTES

[1]  An adaptation of this chapter has been published in the review Freethought Today, in its March 2003 issue.
See Rodrigue Tremblay, "The Manichaeism of Osama bin Laden and George W. Bush", *Freethought Today*, March 2003.

[2]  Douglas Martin, "Carl McIntire, Evangelist and Hawkish patriot", *The New York Times*, March 22, 2002, p. C13.

[3]  Stephanie Nolen, "Bin Laden quoted as admitting to attacks", *The Globe & Mail*, Nov. 12, 2001, p.A4.

[4]  "You will be killed just as you kill", Excerpts of statement attributed to Osama bin Laden, as translated by BBC Monitoring, *USA Today*, Nov. 14, 2002, p. 4A.

[5]  "Therefore, I, George W. Bush, Governor of Texas, do hereby proclaim June 10, 2000, Jesus Day in Texas and urge the appropriate recognition whereof,
In official recognition whereof,
I hereby affix my signature this
17th day of April, 2000."
George W. Bush, "Jesus Day 2000" Proclamation.

[6]  During the 2000 election campaign, even the Democratic presidential candidate, Al Gore, felt obliged to proclaim his religiosity. Gore stated that he makes important decisions by asking himself: WWJD? — *What would Jesus do?*

[7] Tomás de Torquemada was the Grand Spanish Inquisitor (1483-1497). By virtue of the "Patriot Act", adopted in 2001, and which Republican Senator Arlen Specter (PA) compared to "a big black hole", the Attorney General authorizes the FBI to use wiretaps and other forms of electronic surveillance on citizens, even when they are not suspected of a crime.
See John Markoff, "Pentagon Plans a Computer System That Would Peek at Personal Data of Americans", *The New York Times*, Nov. 9, 2002.
Under the Patriot Act, a concentration camp was established in Guantanamo, a U.S. military base on the island of Cuba, where 600 prisoners were kept indefinitely, without the protection of the Geneva Convention and without the protection of the U.S. Constitution.
See Mimi Hall, "Deal set on homeland department", *USA Today*, Nov. 13, 2002.
The Justice Department is relying with increasing frequency on secret warrants that allow its officials to go to a secret court to get approval for surveillance and bugging warrants in terrorism and espionage investigations, without notifying the targeted person. In 2002, the Justice Department used secret warrants a record 1,228 times.
Eric Lichtblau and James Risen, "Broad Domestic Role Asked for C.I.A. and the Pentagon", *The New York Times*, May 2, 2003.
In fact, the Patriot Act suspends the right of Habeas Corpus.

[8] Jonathan E. Smaby, "American Ramadan", *The New York Times*, Nov. 18, 2001, p.WK13.

[9] Paul Koring, "Bush pledges to conquer 'evil' ", *The Globe & Mail*, Nov. 12, 2001, p.A4.

[10] Bush was not the only one to put the United States on a pedestal of absolute moral purity. Rudolph Giuliani, the mayor of New York, echoed the words of the president, after September 11th, *"On the one hand, you have democracy, the rule of law and the respect for human life; on the other, tyranny, arbitrary executions, and mass assassinations. We are Good; they are Evil. It's as simple as that."* The New York Times, October 1, 2001.

[11] It is not only George W. Bush but also many other American politicians who ask God to intervene against their enemies. On March 27, 2003, for example, the Republican majority in Congress passed a resolution recommending "fasting" and "praying" in order to receive

divine protection against terrorism and victory in war.
Agence France-Presse, "La guerre en Irak - Quand Bush et Hussein font appel à Dieu", *Le Devoir*, March 31, 2003.

[12] Jooneed Khan, "Les États-Unis reculent sur l'Irak", *La Presse*, October 18, 2002, p.A1.

[13] John F. Burns, "Iraq Arms Quest Uncovers a Zest for Drink", *The New York Times*, Dec. 7, 2002.

[14] David Waters, "Bush can't Begin to Judge Religion", Scripps Howard News Service, Dec. 8, 2002.
Maureen Dowd, "Butch, Butch Bush!", *The New York Times*, August 3, 2003.

[15] Manichaeism was a religion founded by Mani (c. 216-276), a Persian who thought the the universe was simultaneously under the control of Good and Evil, but that one day these forces would be separated, each one in its own domain. This religion disappeared in the West in the 6th Century, but survived in the Orient until the 14th Century.

[16] Statement attributed to Osama bin Laden. Associated Press, Salah Nasrawi, "Arab station airs tape with bin Laden reportedly naming all 9-11 hijackers", Sept.11, 2002.

[17] During a meeting with Palestinian Prime Minister Mahmoud Abbas, President Bush is reported to have said, *"God told me to strike at al Qaeda and I struck them; and then he instructed me to strike Saddam [Hussein], which I did; and now I am determined to solve the problem in the Middle East. If you help me I will act, and if not, the elections [of 2004] will come and I will have to focus on them."*
*Ha'aretz Magazine*, June 24, 2003 and *Freethought Today*, August 2003.

[18] During the same period, Samuel de Champlain founded the city of Quebec (1608) and New France. Jacques Cartier had discovered Canada in 1534.

[19] French Huguenot settlers first established a camp in 1562 at Charlesfort, on present-day Parris Island near Beaufort, South Carolina. It failed within a year. Two years later, in 1564, a second French expedition built a camp at Fort Caroline on the St.Johns River near present-day Jacksonville and 38 miles north of St. Augustine, Florida. On September 1565, Spanish soldiers killed most of a contingent of shipwrecked French soldiers and most of the inhabitants of Fort Caroline. A Spanish fort was established in St. Augustine, Florida, in August 1565.

[20] A survey of 44 countries by the Pew Global Attitudes Project, in 2002, found that six of ten Americans said religion plays a "very important" role in their lives. This made them twice as religious as Canadians, and considerably more so than people in Japan or Europe.
Kelley Patrick, "U.S. day of prayer observed across nation", *The Globe and Mail,* May 2, 2003, p. A12.

[21] A world-wide public opinion survey conducted by the Pew Research Center in 2002 (see chapter 13) showed that among industrialized countries, it is in the United States that religious leaders have the highest approval rating (62%). This contrasts with Canada (54%), France (58%), Great-Britain (52%), Italy (39%), Germany (39%), and Japan, only (13%)) It is also in the U.S. that the military is the most admired (87%).

TABLE : Rating of Institutions
(Percent saying a "good influence" in their country)

| | Military | National gov't | News media | Religious leaders |
|---|---|---|---|---|
| **North America** | | | | |
| United States | 87 | 64 | 65 | 62 |
| Canada | 72 | 63 | 69 | 54 |
| **Western Europe** | | | | |
| Great Britain | 74 | 66 | 70 | 52 |
| France | 80 | 61 | 55 | 58 |
| Italy | 58 | 40 | 60 | 45 |
| Germany | 70 | 51 | 77 | 39 |
| **Asia** | | | | |
| Japan | 69 | 22 | 48 | 13 |

Source: The Pew Research Center For The People & The Press, "What the World Thinks in 2002", December 4, 2002.

²² Martin E. Marty and R. Scott Appleby, editors, *The Fundamentalism Project, 1991-2002,* University of Chicago Press, Chicago, 2002,

²³ Doug Saunders, "Making the world safe for...theocracy?", *The Globe and Mail,* August 30, 2003.

²⁴ Frank S. Mead (revised by Samuel S. Hill), *Handbook of Denominations in the United States,* 9th Edition, Abington Press, Nashville, Tennessee, 1990.

²⁵ Dateline *NBC,* "Where Does World-Famous Televangelist's Money Go?", Dec. 27, 2002.

²⁶ Books have been published to explain the best techniques for getting the most money from the "faithful". See Norman Shawchuck and P. Kotler, B. Wren and G. Rath, *Marketing for Congregations,* Abingdon Books, Nashville, Tennessee, 1992, 424 p.

²⁷ In terms of membership, it is the Roman Catholic Church that is the largest. There are over 63 million Catholics in the U.S., divided among 19,000 parishes. They constitute 23% of the total population. One third of Catholics are Hispanics, a group increasing through immigration, both legal and illegal. Only 5% of American Catholics are Black.

²⁸ If our world is not destroyed by human means beforehand, there will be, in a far distant future, an end of the world. Indeed, it is estimated that our sun has a physical life of about 10 billion years, before exploding and turning into a gaseous red giant. It is now about 5 billion years old. Therefore, the Earth and the rest of the solar system will undergo a fundamental transformation in about 5 billion years. This is, course, if the predicted gigantic collision of our galaxy, the Milky Way, with the Andromeda galaxy, merging each other's black holes, does not happen before. In the latter case, forecasted to occur in three billion years, our solar system will vaporize in the ensuing chaos and be recycled into a new giant elliptical galaxy. Presently, the two galaxies are rushing toward each other at the speed of 500, 000 kilometers per hour, or 310,000 miles per hour, and could start merging in about three billion years.

NPACI On Line, "Astrophysicists Run Largest Galactic Collision Simulations Ever on NPACI's Blue Horizon", May 3, 2000.

Closer at home, it is estimated that humanity came very near to becoming extinct about 74,000 years ago when the supervolcano Toba, on the Island of Sumatra, erupted and left only some 10,000 persons alive on earth. It is feared that the eruption of a supervolcano, such as the one believed to be present in Yellowstone Park, which sooner or later is expected to erupt, could so contaminate the earth's atmosphere that it could destroy agriculture and provoke widespread famine. Scientists have revealed that the Yellowstone supervocano has been on a regular eruption cycle of 600,000 years. The last eruption was 640,000 years ago... so the next is overdue.

Supervolcanoes, *BBC Horizon*, February 2000.

[29] Extreme right evangelical religious radio stations in the United States use all kinds of tactics, more or less on the up and up, to take the place of pluralistic and polyvalent stations, such as National Public Radio (NPR).
Bill Roberts, "Don't Tune out Diversity", *The Globe & Mail*, Oct.24, 2002, p. A21.

[30] In 1979, in Jonestown Guyana, the Reverend Jim Jones drew 900 people into a collective suicide by inciting them to drink poisoned Kool Aid. In February of 1993, a religious sect, led by David Koresh, barricaded themselves in their enclosure in Waco, Texas. After a siege of 51 days, a confrontation with federal police ended in a fire that killed 76 people, including women and children.

[31] According to a test conducted by UNICEF, among the 24 richest countries, the United States is classed 18th for the quality of its system of secondary education. The five top countries are South Korea, Japan, Finland, Canada, and Australia.
"U.S. education trails other rich nations", *USA Today*, Nov. 25, 2002.

[32] Scientific data establish the Earth's age at around 4.5 billion years. The first life forms date from 3.1 billion years ago, when micro-organisms such as algae and bacteria appeared. The process of evolution produced all the different life forms on the Earth. The earliest traces of man date from 7 million years ago.
The Earth and our solar system are part of the Milky Way Galaxy which was formed almost 15 billion years ago, after the intergalactic explosions scientists call the Big Bang. However, there are other types of galaxies

that were formed in different ways and at different times. The universe is composed of enormous empty spaces and swarms of galaxies, forming the centers of gigantic networks, connected by threads of matter.
Carl Zimmer, "How old is the Universe?", *National Geographic*, September 2001.


[33] See the Catholic Inquisition in southern France against the Cathars and in Spain against the Jews.


[34] Nicholas D. Kristof, "Believe it, or Not", *The New York Times*, August 15, 2003.


[35] In 2003, Chief Justice Roy Moore of Alabama, an elected judge, defied the U.S. Supreme Court order to remove a 5,280-pound monument of the biblical Ten Commandments that he had secretly and illegally installed one night in the lobby of the State Supreme Court. Even though the monument was subsequently removed, the incident illustrates how superstition and idolatry seep in U.S. public life.
Jeffrey Gettleman, "Alabama Judge Defiant on Commandments' Display", *The New York Times*, August 21, 2003.


[36] George W. Bush is the first president to lose the popular vote and still be elected by the Electoral College since Benjamin Harrison, in 1888. In the November 2000 elections, Al Gore won 48.3% of the popular vote, against 48.1% for George W. Bush, with a difference of some 537,000 votes. Independant candidate Ralph Nader won 2.6% of the popular vote. It is very possible that without Nader, Al Gore would have been elected, with more than 50% of the vote and more than the 270 electoral votes needed to be declared the winner.
The greatest contributing factor to the Democrats loss was the political-sex scandal of Bill Clinton. Without the "Monika Lewinsky Affair", it can be argued that the Democrats would have stayed in the White House.


[37] Almost two-thirds of all the tax savings, in George W. Bush's 2001 and 2003 tax cuts, will go to the wealthiest 10 percent of taxpayers, and the richest 1 percent will get an average tax reduction of nearly $100,000 a year.
See David E. Rosenbaum, "Bush May Have Exaggerated, but Did He Lie?", *The New York Times*, June 22, 2003.

[38] As soon as he took power, George W. Bush established the Office of Community Initiatives (called "faith–based initiatives"), in order to grant public monies to the churches that had favored his election.
Andrew Cohen, "Bush has radical plan for church and state", *The Globe and Mail*, Jan. 30, 2001, p. A9.

[39] One adult out of four, i.e. 50 million people, would thus be religious fundamentalists in the United States.
See, Grace Halsell, *Forcing God's Hand*, Crossroads International Publishing, Washington DC, 1999.

[40] Elisabeth Bumiller, "Evangelicals Sway White House on Human Rights Issues Abroad", *The New York Times*, October 26, 2003.

[41] Republican congressman Walter B. Jones Jr. (N.C.) is sponsoring a bill "The Houses of Worship Political Speech Protection Act" (H.R. 2357), which would neutralize Senator Johnson's 1954 resolution. As of February, 2002, the bill was supported in the House by 108 Republicans and 4 Democrats.
Laurie Goodstein, "Churches on Right Seek Right to Back Candidates", *The New York Times*, Feb. 3, 2002.

[42] Doug Saunders, "U.S. got what it deserves, Falwell says", *The Globe & Mail*, Sept. 15, 2001, p. A2.

[43] Abraham Lincoln, in his Thanksgiving proclamation on October 3, 1863, spoke in a similar vein, "...the awful calamity of civil war which now desolates the land may be a punishment inflicted upon us for our presumptuous sins."

[44] The word Armageddon comes from a deformation of the name of the town of Meggido, in Israel.

[45] "Apocalypse Now", *Time Magazine*, July 1, 2002, pp.31-38.

[46] The series of children's novels "Harry Potter", by British author J.K. Rowling, is the story of a boy, the son of witches, at the Hogwarts School

of Witchcraft and Wizardry, where the students learn magic. The books are aimed at children from 10 to 14, that is, the age at which young people begin to ask themselves questions about their place in the world and about their individual strengths and talents, but also an age at which children know the difference between real life and fantasy.

[47] American fundamentalist groups spread the idea that the reunification of Europe is an indication of the return of the Roman Empire and the emergence of the Antichrist.

[48] For Jews, these books of religious fiction and political propaganda are a two-edged sword. The story says that after the last battle, in Jerusalem, with the Antechrist, two thirds of the Jews will accept Jesus as the true Messiah, but the others will be killed or will be forever damned. It would be the end of Judaism.

[49] Islamic Muslims and Evangelist Protestants have one thing in common: they interpret the contents of the Koran and of the Bible textually, considering everything they find to be true. Catholics, for example, tend to interpret the Bible in a metaphoric fashion, its fables and myths not to be taken litterally.

[50] The German title is *Der Wille zur Macht. Versuch einer Umwerthung aller Werte.*

[51] In this beginning of the 21st Century, religion is involved in numerous armed conflicts: the Israeli-Palestinian conflict between Jews and Muslims, the conflict between Protestants and Catholics in Northern Ireland, the conflict between Muslims and Christians in Kosovo, the conflict between Muslims and Christians in Nigeria, the conflict between the Islamic al Qaeda movement and the United States, etc.

[52] It is estimated that there are 250 million guns in circulation in the United States, or more than one gun for each adult. The Department of Justice forbids the FBI to check lists of gun buyers in order to identify criminals who might have bought a gun to commit a crime. Known criminals can thus buy hundreds of combat weapons without being investigated. The current Attorney General, John Ashcroft, is himself a member of the National Rifle Association, the organization which blocks

any effective control of the sale of arms.

[53] A book by Gore Vidal carries this very title: Gore Vidal, *Perpetual War for Perpetual Peace*, Avalon Publishing Group, New York, 2002. The expression "perpetual war for perpetual peace" comes from historian Charles A. Beard.

[54] These three countries do not form an axis at all. They are not allies, and they have no common objectives. Bush's vocabulary is one of disinformation. These countries are perhaps the enemies of civilization, but they do not, objectively, form a political "axis".

[55] The six U.S. allies named by bin Laden were Great Britain, France, Germany, Italy, Canada, and Australia.
Jack Kelley, "Officials: Voice on tape is bin Laden", *USA Today*, Nov. 13, 2002.

[56] The Islamist terrorists had already struck within the United States. On February 26, 1993, four Islamic terrorists planted a bomb in the World Trade Center underground parking, killing six Americans and wounding over a thousand people.

[57] Michael Elliot, "They had a Plan", *Time,* August 12, 2002.

[58] One who thinks there was more than negligence on the part of the Bush-Cheney administration is Gore Vidal. See Gore Vidal, "The Enemy Within", *The Observer*, October 27, 2002. Also, Gore Vidal, *Dreaming War: Blood for Oil and the Cheney-Bush Junta*, 2003, 108 p.

[59] Ever since Saudi Arabia helped finance the Mujaheddin in the holy Islamic war that expelled the Soviets from Afghanistan in the nineties, many have argued that Saudi Arabia's money was also behind the al Qaeda international terrorist network and played an important role in American politics.
See Robert Baer, *See No Evil: The True Story of a Ground Soldier in the C.I.A.'s War on Terrorism*, 2002.

<sup>60</sup> The proclamation, which was signed by the town's secretary and bore the municipal seal, read, *"Be it known from this day forward that Satan, ruler of darkness, giver of evil, destroyer of what is good and just, is not now, nor ever again will be, a part of this town of Inglis. Satan is hereby declared powerless, no longer ruling over, nor influencing, our citizens. In the past, Satan has caused division, animosity, hate, confusion, ungodly acts on our youth, and discord among our friends and loved ones. No longer!"*

<sup>61</sup> Rick Bragg, "Florida Town Finds Satan an Offense Unto It", *The New York Times*, March 14, 2002, p.A1

<sup>62</sup> On June 26, 2002, the Ninth District Court, which is responsible for nine western states, decreed that the words "under God" that schoolchildren must recite each morning, violates the First Amendment, which stipulates that *"Congress shall make no law respecting an establishment of religion."* Unbelievably, discarding the principle of separation of the legislative and of the judiciary, the House of Representatives, on March 20, 2003, passed a nonbinding Resolution 400-7 with 15 abstentions, denouncing the federal appeals court's ruling that the phrase "one nation under God" in the Pledge of Allegiance, is unconstitutional.

In its judgment, the Court found that the phrase sent a message to non-believers that they were put aside and not full members of society, while sending a message to believers that they were favored members of society. Saying that "A profession that we are a nation 'under God' is identical...to a profession that we are a nation 'under Jesus', a nation 'under Vishnu', a nation 'under Zeus' or a nation 'under no god,' because none of these professions can be neutral with respect to religion," (Circuit Judge Alfred Goodwin).

Since this judgment will surely be brought before the Supreme Court, it will be very interesting to follow the deliberations, since the Court itself begins each session with the declaration *"God save the United States and this honorable court."*

Following the judgment, George W. Bush remarked through his spokesman, Ari Fleischer, that "this ruling is ridiculous".

John Ibbitson, "U.S. Court Bans Pledge of Allegiance in Schools", *The Globe & Mail*, June 27, 2002, p. A1.

The same man who obtained the judgment declaring the words "under God" to be unconstitutional, the Californian Dr. Michael Newdow, has also gone to court contesting the fact that Congress hires chaplains, at a

salary of up to $148,500, to recite opening prayers at each session of the House and the Senate. Following the principle of the separation of Church and State, he claims that it is unconstitutional for chaplains, paid from public funds, to conduct public prayers in the houses of Congress. In 2000, the Supreme Court judged unconstitutional public prayers at high school football games.
Agence France-Presse, "Un Athée réclame le départ des aumôniers", *Le Devoir*, August 31, 2002, p. A2.

[63] *Freethought Today*, October, 2003.

[64] The sculptor is William Hunter, from the upscale suburb of Scottsdale, Arizona.

[65] For a list of the numerous occasions when George W. Bush has had difficulty expressing himself, see the Web site: dubyaspeak.com.

[66] Jimmy Carter, a peanut farmer and a Sunday preacher was elected in 1976, but compared to George W. Bush, he was relatively reserved in making religious declarations in public. Bush Jr. is a born-again Christian who professes to read each morning from a book of short, evangelical sermons titled "My Utmost for His Highest", and credits his relationship with God for his 1986 decision to stop drinking.

[67] George W. Bush's chief speechwriter is Michael Gerson, an evangelical Christian who studied theology at Wheaton College.
Radio speech by George W. Bush, on March 30, 2002.
Elizabeth Bumiller, "Bush Strikes Religious Note in an Address for Holidays", *The New York Times*, March 31, 2002, p. 21.

[68] See Rodrigue Tremblay, "The Manichaeism of Osama bin Laden and George W. Bush", *Freethought Today*, March 2003, pp 6-7.

[69] Jack Beatty, "In the Name of God", *The Atlantic Monthly*, March 5, 2003.

[70] Tim Collie, "Shuttle Breaks up", *South Florida Sun-Sentinel*, February

2, 2003, p. 21 A.

[71] An exception could be Ariel Sharon, the Prime Minister of Israel. In his end-of-the-year message in 2001, he declared, *"From Jerusalem, the eternal, undivided capital of the Jewish people for the last 3004 years and forever, I send you my warmest greetings for a happy, healthy and prosperous New Year...Israel is the only place in the world where Jews have the right, the capability and the duty to defend themselves by themselves. For this we must thank God every day...At this New Year, I fervently pray we will be blessed with security, peace and joy for all of us."*

[72] In Utah, there is a *de facto* state religion, the Mormon Church.
Michael Janofsky, "Plaza Dispute in Salt Lake Roils Citizens Over Religion", *The New York Times*, Nov. 16, 2002.

[73] Jean-Pierre Stroobants, "Le primat de Belgique en a assez du 'God Bless America'"[ "The first bishop of Belgium has had enough of 'God Bless America'"], *Le Monde*, Dec.24, 2002.

[74] Bob Woodward and Dan Balz, "At Camp David, Advise and Dissent; Bush, Aides Grapple With War Plan", *The Washington Post*, Jan. 31, 2002, p. A01.

[75] Bob Woodward, Op.cit.

[76] Bill Keller, "God and George W. Bush", *The New York Times*, May 17, 2003.

[77] As Mr. Bush's former speechwriter David Frum put it, "Attendance at Bible study was, if not compulsory, not quite uncompulsory."
David Frum, *The right man: The Surprise Presidency of George W. Bush*, Random House, 2003.

[78] See Edward Hull, *The Wall Chart of World History, From Earliest Times to the Present*, DAG Publications Ltd., London, 1999.

[79] The First Amendment reads, *"Congress shall make no law respecting an establishment of religion, or prohibiting the free exercise thereof"*

[80] Jacques Isnard, "Le Pentagone veut expérimenter et produire des mini-bombes nucléaires'", [The Pentagon wants to test and produce mini atomic bombs"], *Le Monde,* March 8, 2003.

[81] Nicholas D. Kristof, "Secret, Scary Plans", *The New York Times,* February 28, 2003.

[82] In Truman's defense, one must say that during the summer of 1945, the Japanese military and political hierarchy refused to surrender. The U.S. had few atomic bombs, and a land invasion of Japan by the army would have cost the lives of several thousand G.I.s. Would a demonstration of nuclear force in an unpopulated area have changed the position of the Japanese government? We will never know.

[83] Christopher Reed, "Searching for a Hollywood Ending", *The Globe and Mail,* Dec. 31, 2002.

[84] Fox News Channel, "Fox and Friends", Dec. 11, 2002,
David E. Sanger, "Bush Warns Foes Not to Use Weapons of Mass Destruction on U.S. Troops", *The New York Times,* Dec. 11, 2002.

[85] In the 1650's, an Irish bishop, James Ussher, calculated the age of the Earth by adding the ages of Adam and his descendants, as written in the Bible. He arrived at the conclusion that God created the Earth on October 22, 4004 B.C. For two hundred years, this date was referred to in religious circles as the day God created the universe.

[86] On September 26, 2002, the Cobb County School Commission, in a suburb of Atlanta, voted an amendment permitting schools to teach that "God created the Earth in six days".
The Economist, "A suburban school board declares that evolution is just another theory", Oct. 3, 2002.

[87]   In 1987, the Supreme Court ruled that the teaching of "creation science" violated the constitutional separation of Church and State.

[88]   The evidence seems to indicate that matter and energy in the Universe are constantly changing form in a long, eternally repeated, cycle, going from "Big Bang" to "Big Bang". The last "Big Bang", when numerous galaxies collided, happened less than 15 billion years ago. This theory of the Universe was first proposed in 1955, by the astronomer Lyman Spitzer, and confirmed in 1999, by specialists at NASA working with the orbital space observatory FUSE.
Astrophysicians are now trying to evaluate when the previous "Big Bang" happened.
Paul Steinhardt and Neil Turok, "The Endless Universe: a Brief Introduction to the Cyclic Universe", *Science on line*, April 25, 2002, and *Science Magazine*, May 24, 2002.
Fred Hoyle, Geoffrey Burbidge, and Jayant Vishnu Narlikar, *A Different Approach to Cosmology: From a Static Universe Through the Big Bang Towards Reality*, Cambridge University Press, 2000, 357 pp.

[89]   Joe Stephens and David B. Ottaway, "From U.S., the ABC's of Jihad Violent Soviet-Era Textbooks Complicate Afghan Education Efforts", *The Washington Post*, March 23, 2002, p. A01.

[90]   In 1995, Congress voted $300 million in aid to the Moujahdin fighters against the Soviet Union. The aid was sent through Pakistan, which received F-16 military jets for their cooperation.

[91]   Martin Schram, "Can this be the enemy? How American texts schooled terrorists", Scripps Howard News Service, March 28, 2002.

[92]   The Office works in cooperation with the independent United States Commission on International Religious Freedom. The latter was also created by the International Religious Freedom Act of 1998, as a separate and independent source of policy recommendations on religious freedom for the president, secretary of state and the Congress. The Commission issues its own report, but has only advisory and monitoring authority, unlike the Office in the State Department that has the authority to act.

The United Nations also has an organization devoted to religious freedom. In 1986, the U.N. Commission on Human Rights established the office of the Special Rapporteur on Religious Intolerance, now the Special Rapporteur on Freedom of Religion or Belief. The U.N. Commission issues reports on a variety of countries, regarding religious freedom.

[93] In May 1999, Robert A. Seiple was sworn in as the first Ambassador-at-Large. Tom Farr is the director of the Office of International Religious Freedom at the Department of State and is responsible for preparing its annual report.

[94] There exists in the United States a Freedom From Religion Foundation (FFRF). It publishes the magazine Freethought Today. It is located in Madison, Wisconsin: P.O. Box 750, Madison WI 53701 (www.ffrf.org).
Another U.S. publication devoted to freedom from religion is The Humanist,
P.O. Box 1188, Amherst, N.Y. 14226-7188 (thehumanist@juno.com).
For anti-war sites see: http://www.moveon.org/ or http://www.nowarforisrael.com

[95] The German government has concluded that the Church of Scientology is not a religion but a commercial enterprise, and should be regulated as such. French authorities also view the Church of Scientology with suspicion and don't recognize it as a religion. They consider it to be a totalitarian organization, opposed to democracy, and an economic enterprise that sells services for money, and which, therefore, should pay taxes. The cult was also denounced in Greece because, although it had obtained a license to operate as a non-profit, public interest organization, it was seen instead as an organization devoted to making money, besides putting people's mental and physical health at risk by practicing a variety of mind-control techniques.

[96] The U.S. military manages such a concentration camp in Guantanamo, a U.S. military base on the island of Cuba, where prisoners are kept indefinitely, without the protection of the Geneva Convention and without the protection of the U.S. Constitution.
Philip Shenon, "Report on USA Patriot Act Alleges Civil Rights Violations", *The New York Times*, July 21, 2003.

[97] The European Union showed its leadership by announcing that it

would compensate the loss of U.S. funds by donating an additional 32 million euros to the United Nations Population Fund.

[98] Doug Saunders, "Birth control no solution for AIDS, U.S. argues", *The Globe and Mail*, May 8, 2002, p.A7.

[99] George W. Bush, *A Charge to Keep*, Morrow, New York, 1999. In this book, written in collaboration with his director of communications, Karen Hughes, the words "oil" and "religion", two of Bush's principal preoccupations, do not even appear in the index.

[100] Prior to 1954, this lobby went under the more descriptive name of "American Zionist Council of Public Affairs". AIPAC is a large pro-Israel umbrella organization. It is extremely powerful, since it gives millions of dollars to selected electoral campaigns.
Robert S. Greenberger and Jeanne Cummings, "Faith, Trust and War Keep Bush Firmly in Israel's Corner", *The Wall Street Journal*, April 3, 2002, p. A24.
To see how AIPAC operates in the U.S., see Hedrick Smith, *The Power Game, How Washington Works*, Ballantine Books, New York, 1988, pp 216-31.

[101] See Helen Caldicott, *The New Nuclear Danger*, The New Press, New York, 2002, p. XVII.

[102] Maureen Dowd, "Perle's Plunder Blunder", *The New York Times*, March 23, 2003.

[103] See Seymour M. Hersh, "Annals of National Security, Lunch with the Chairman", *The New Yorker*, March 17, 2003, pp. 76-81.

[104] Seymour M. Hersh, "The Iraq Hawks" *The New Yorker*, Dec. 24 and 31, 2001, pp.58-64.

[105] The participants in the Study Group on "A New Israeli Strategy Toward 2000" were:
Richard Perle, American Enterprise Institute, Study Group Leader,

James Colbert, Jewish Institute for National Security Affairs,
Charles Fairbanks, Jr., Johns Hopkins University/SAIS,
Douglas Feith, Feith and Zell Associates (future aide to Donald H.Rumsfeld)
Robert Loewenberg, President, Institute for Advanced Strategic and Political Studies,
Jonathan Torop, The Washington Institute for Near East Policy,
David Wurmser, Institute for Advanced Strategic and Political Studies, and future policy planner at the State Department, and
Meyrav Wurmser, Johns Hopkins University and director of the Center for Middle East Policy at the Hudson Institute in Washington.

Source: "A Clean Break: A New Strategy for Securing the Realm," report prepared by the Study Group on a New Israeli Strategy Toward 2000, at the Institute for Advanced Strategic and Political Studies, 1996.

[106] Maureen Dowd, "Bush Ex Machina", *The New York Times*, March 2, 2003.

[107] The total report can be read by visiting the following site:
http://www.israeleconomy.org/strat1.htm

[108] David Stout, "White House Seeks to Minimize Iraq Differences With Rumsfeld", *The New York Times*, October 8, 2003.

[109] Charles Krauthammer, "Coming Ashore", *Time*, Februaray 17, 2003, p. 37.

[110] The Spectator, 1899.

[111] This narrow circle of defense policy intellectuals would be at the forefront of a determined advocacy campaign to have the U.S. directly involved in a Middle East war against Iraq. Their principal leaders were: Paul D. Wolfowitz, Deputy Defense Secretary in George W. Bush's administration, Richard Perle, a former Reagan administration defense official who heads the Defense Policy Board, the Pentagon's advisory panel, and William Kristol, who was previouslly chief of staff to Vice President Dan Quayle and is now the editor of the ultra-conservative *Weekly Standard* magazine. This group promotes two central supremacist

ideas: 1- that no new superpower should be allowed to rise to rival the United States' enlightened domination of the world; 2- that American foreign policy should rely, independently if necessary, on pre-emptive military attacks to achieve this objective, even if it meant acting outside of international law.

[112] Josuah Micah Marshall, "Bomb Saddam", *The Washington Monthly*, June 2002.

[113] A U.S. Congressman, Jim Moran (D. VA), who attempted to denounce the corrosive influence of the cabal on American foreign policy was chastized and stripped of his regional leadership post within the Democratic Party.
See, "US politician who accused American Jews of goading US into war with Iraq resigns", *The Jerusalem Post*, March 15, 2003.

[114] It was also an opportunity to profit from some $400 billion annually in "unproductive" military expenditures.

[115] Jeremy Rifkin, *L'Économie hydrogène après la fin du pétrole, la nouvelle révolution économique*, Éditions La Découverte, Paris, 2002.

[116] Among his supporters, Joe Lieberman is considered a 'Jewish Jew'.
Agence France-Presse, "La classe politique américaine en ébullition", *Le Devoir*, August 5, 2002.

[117] The FBI, which operates under the Justice Department and Attorney General John Ashcroft, investigated Scott Ritter three times after his public intervention. This speaks volumes on the decline of democracy in the U.S.
Nadani Ditmars, "Ex-weapons inspector prefers patriot label", *The Globe and Mail*, Oct. 7, 2002, p. A15.

[118] "End the Iraq War", *The Seattle Times*, May 14, 2001.
Also Scott Ritter, *Endgame: Solving the Iraq Problem, Once and For All*, Simon & Schuster, New York, 1999.

[119] Under United Nations Resolution 661, there was a total economic embargo placed upon Iraq from 1990 to 1995. The only exemptions were pharmaceuticals and humanitarian aid. From May 1996, under the United Nations Resolution 986 called "Oil for Food", Iraq signed an agreement authorizing the sale of oil, subject to the control of a UN sanctions committee, with the sums being deposited in New York banks and used only for accepted purchases. In May of 2000, under Resolution 1284, the program was removed from the sanctions committee, and placed under an international commission, but still uniquely for the purchase of foreign goods considered to be essential.

[120] The Secretary of Defense, Donald Rumsfeld, indirectly confirmed this when he declared indignantly that, over two weeks, Iraq had fired 67 times on English and American planes that were patrolling the no-fly zones over Iraq, without hitting a single one.
Alan Freeman, "U.S. Struggles to Win Support of Key Players on Iraq Plan", *The Globe and Mail*, Oct. 1, 2002, p. A10.

[121] Scott Ritter interview in the *National Post*.
See Jan Cienski, "Iraqi arms capability played down", *The National Post*, Aug. 7, 2002, p. A11.

[122] Associated Press, "Bush Warns of Iraqi Nukes", Aug. 8, 2002.

[123] Even the CIA stated that it was improbable that Iraq launch an attack against the U.S. in the foreseeable future, although they said it might try if provoked.
Patrick Worsnip, "CIA warns that Iraq will retaliate", *The Globe and Mail*, Oct. 10, 2002, p.A15.

[124] Joe Lauria, "UN finds no evidence of link between Al-Qa'ida and Iraq", Southam News, *The Gazette*, Dec. 18, 2002, p. A28.

[125] Eric Lichtblau, "On Terror, Doubts Anew After a Scathing Report", *The New York Times*, July 25, 2003.

[126] In June 2003, George W. Bush gave a sort of ultimatum to Iran, regarding the development of nuclear weapons.

David E. Sanger, "Bush Says U.S. Will Not Tolerate Building of Nuclear Arms by Iran", *The New York Times*, June 19, 2003.

[127] Another of Strauss' neo-conservative disciples was Abram Shulsky, Director of the Pentagon's Office of Special Plans.

[128] American neo-conservatives are not "conservative" at all and are more revolutionaries, in the sense that they want to rearrange the entire Middle East in the interests of Israel and, domestically, want to establish a rule by an aristocratic elite.
Shadia Drury, *Leo Strauss and the American Right*, St. Martin's Press, New York, 1997.

[129] Strauss had another proposal that any writer would find repulsive. He would argue that political philosophers could lie to their readers for the sake of the "social good". He saw the need for an external exoteric language directed at outsiders, and an internal esoteric language directed at ingroup members, in order to fool the masses.
Shadia Drury, *Ibid.*

[130] "Robert D. Kaplan on how the United States projects power around the world—and why it must.", *The Atlantic Monthly*, June 18, 2003.
Norman Mailer, *Why Are We at War?*, Random House, New York, 2003.

[131] Some go even further and adopt a strategy of linking anti-Semitism and anti-Americanism in order to direct U.S. foreign policy in a particular direction. For Jonathan Rauch, for example, writing in the *Atlantic Monthly* magazine, radical Arab Muslims are both anti-American and anti-Semitic: *"Increasingly and ominously, anti-Semitism and anti-Americanism are converging. The crafty Jews provide the brains, and the bullying Crusaders (Americans) provide the muscle. After 9/11, the mufti of Jerusalem preached, "Oh Allah, destroy America, for she is ruled by Zionist Jews!"...We Americans are all Jews now".*
Jonathan Rauch , "To Beat the Axis of Evil, Confront the Axis of Anti-Semitism —Increasingly and ominously, anti-Semitism and anti-Americanism are converging. We Americans are all Jews now", *The Atlantic Monthly*, June 28 2003.

[132] Even under the International Criminal Court, the U.S. would have the

option of negotiating bilateral agreements with countries which accept military assistance—as was the case with the Philippines and Columbia in 2002—protecting their soldiers from any criminal action that might be taken against them.

[133] In 2003, the parallel was striking: the U.S. occupied Iraq while Israel occupied Palestine.

[134] The International Criminal Court is comprised of 18 judges and one prosecutor. The first judges were named in September of 2002, and formally elected in the beginning of 2003. The Court therefore began its deliberations in 2003. In a concession to countries which have hesitated to participate (United States, Russia, China), the court will hear only crimes committed after July 1, 2002.

[135] According to the statutes of the International Criminal Court, a crime against humanity is defined as an act committed during a general or systematic attack against a civilian population and the knowledge of such an attack, including "inhuman acts", intentionally causing severe suffering, and the violation of physical integrity or assaults upon mental or physical health.
Genocide includes acts committed with the intention to destroy, completely or partially, a national, ethnic, racial, or religious group, including a violation of the physical or mental integrity of members of the group, or the intentional subjecting of such a group to conditions that would result in its total or partial physical destruction.

[136] Congress has adopted an anti-International Criminal Court law, which forbides the U.S. government from collaborating with the Court and authorized the president to use "all necessary and appropriate means" to free Americans held by the Court. Some people call this law the "Law to invade The Hague".
Marcus Gee, "U.S. vetoes Bosnia mission to protest new world court", *The Globe and Mail*, July 1, 2002, p.A1.

[137] The Bush Administration partially won its bluff against the ICC. The Security Council adopted a resolution proposed by Great Britain, Mauritius, and France asking the ICC to grant a 12-month delay before opening an inquiry or bringing an accusation against any Blue Beret who is a citizen of a country that has not ratified the treaty establishing the

Court. This exemption for American citizens was prolonged another twelve months on June 12, 2003. Indeed, Security Council Resolution 1487 was identical in its wordings to Resolution 1422 of July 12, 2002, and exempted Americans involved in peace missions from prosecution by the International Criminal Court for a period of twelve months, from July 1st to June 30th.

[138] In 2002, the U.S. had 704 soldiers among the 45,159 Blue Berets deployed throughout the world.

[139] The most widely accepted rules of international conflicts derive from the four Geneva Conventions of 1949, which govern a range of humanitarian issues arising in wartime, from aiming at civilians to the treatment of prisoners of war.
In 1977, a series of protocols were added to elaborate on the conventions, but although more than 150 nations have ratified the protocols, the United States has not.

[140] Quentin Peel, "An Empire in Denial Opts Out", *The Financial Times*, Aug. 19, 2002, p.11.

[141] The world has not forgotten that it was the United States, under Harry S. Truman, which was the first to use nuclear arms against civilians.
Like George W. Bush, Harry S. Truman was a weak president. He was the owner of a men's clothing store in Missouri who had the good luck to be chosen by Franklin D. Roosevelt as the vice presidential candidate in the 1944 elections. It was thus by accident that he became president, upon the death of Roosevelt, on April 17, 1945.
On August 6, 1945, Truman ordered the nuclear bombing of the Japanese city of Hiroshima, killing 140,000 people. On August 10, 1945, he ordered the nuclear bombing of the Japanese city of Nagasaki, killing 90,000 people. Since then, no other country has used nuclear arms to settle a dispute. The United States is the only one to hold this dubious honor.
Some Americans and some Japanese think these bombings of civilian populations were justified in order to persuade the Japanese wartime leaders to surrender.
Nicholas D. Kristof, "Blood on Our Hands?", *The New York Times*, August 5, 2003.

[142] Marlise Simons, "World Court for Crimes of War Opens in The Hague", *The New York Times*, March 12, 2003.

[143] Thirty five countries that refused to sign an immunity agreement with the United States, among them Brazil, Venezuela, Costa Rica, South Africa, Bulgaria and Slovakia, had their U.S. military aid suspended to the amount of $47 million for 2003.

[144] The 1945-46 Nuremberg trial was established in order to indict and prosecute 24 individuals and 6 organizations for crimes against peace, war crimes, and crimes against humanity. At the end of the trial, 11 were sentenced to hang. Field Marshal Hermann Goering committed suicide the night before the scheduled execution, and the remaining ten were hanged.

[145] Saddam Hussein, President of Irak, in Julia Preston, "Hussein, in a letter to General Assembly, Says Bush wants to control Middle East Oil"., *The New York Times*, September 20, 2002, p. A12.

[146] U.S. media like to take comfort in the idea that the reason that Americans are hated in many countries is because of jealousy. In reality, Americans are not hated because of what they are, but because of what they do outside their borders.

[147] George W. Bush was suspected of insider trading in 1990, when it is said that he acted on privileged information, reportedly making a quick profit of nearly a million dollars. His father was the president at the time.
Barrie McKenna, "Bush tangled in web of corporate wrongdoing", *The Globe and Mail*, July 5, 20902, p. B6.
Also, Allan Fotheringham, "Naughty capitalism familiar territory for Bush", *The Globe and Mail*, July 6, 2002, p. A2.
Also, Richard S. Dunham and Mike McNamee, "Bush Sr.'s Profitable Crossing", *Business Week*, March 4, 2002, p.12.

[148] Cheney, as well as his company, was accused of having manipulated the accounts to inflate profits by $445-million between 1999 and 2001.
Kelley Patrick, "Cheney set to become Bush's 2004 running mate", *The Globe and Mail*, May 8, 2003, p. A14.

[149] Donald H. Rumsfeld's motto on his desk is "Aggressive fighting for the right is the noblest sport the world affords."
Bill Moyers, "Now with Bill Moyers", *PBS*, Oct. 18, 2002.


[150] The National Security Council is chaired by the President. Its regular attendees (both statutory and non-statutory) are the Vice President, the Secretary of State, the Secretary of the Treasury, the Secretary of Defense, and the Assistant to the President for National Security Affairs. The Chairman of the Joint Chiefs of Staff is the statutory military advisor to the Council, and the Director of Central Intelligence is the intelligence advisor. The Chief of Staff to the President, Counsel to the President, and the Assistant to the President for Economic Policy are invited to attend any NSC meeting. The Attorney General and the Director of the Office of Management and Budget are invited to attend meetings pertaining to their responsibilities. The heads of other executive departments and agencies, as well as other senior officials, are invited to attend meetings of the NSC when appropriate.


[151] James Hamilton, "What is an Oil Shock?", *Journal of Econometrics*, April 2003, pp. 363-98.


[152] The report is titled "Reliable, Affordable, and Environmentally Sound Energy for America's Future", Report of the National Energy Policy Development Group, Washington, 2001.


[153] Edward L. Morse and Amy Myers Jaffe, "Strategic Energy Policy Challenges for the 21st Century", Report of an Independent Task Force Sponsored by the James A. Baker III Institute for Public Policy of Rice University and the Council on Foreign Relations, April 2001.


[154] BP, in particular, had plans to absorb some smaller Russian oil companies in order to create the third largest oil company in Russia, behind OAO Yukos and OAO Lukoil.
Jeanne Whalen and Bhushan Bahree, "BP in talks to create new Russian oil giant", *The Wall Street Journal*, February 10, 2003.


[155] "Strategic energy Policy Challenges for the 21st Century", op.cit.

¹⁵⁶ In 1907, the British and the Russians formally carved up Iran. The Russians got the northern regions while the British were ceded the Southern oil fields. Great Britain dictated what the price of Iranian oil would be for nearly a half-century, that is until Mohammad Mossadeq attempted to nalionalize Iranian oil.
See, Karl E. Meyers, *The Dust of Empire: The Race for Mastery in the Asian Heartland, Public Affairs,* New York, 2003.

¹⁵⁷ Citation drawn from Bob Woodward, *The Commanders,* Simon and Schuster, New York, 1991, p. 230.

¹⁵⁸ James Woolsey, former CIA Director (1993-95), "Spiking the Oil Weapon", *The Wall Street Journal,* Sept. 19, 2002, p.A16.

¹⁵⁹ Canada has enormous petroleum reserves—367 billion barrels. Its known reserves are even larger than the known reserves of Saudi Arabia. However, 84% of those reserves are in tar sands, which hold about 309 billion barrels of recuperable heavy oil. Tar sand oil is not easily accessible, is costly to extract, and requires that the world price of oil remain above $15 US to be profitable. Canada's conventional oil reserves are still important, at 58 billion barrels, nearly double Mexico's proven reserves of 32.6 billion barrels. It is expected that by 2005, half of all Canadian oil production will come from its tar sands projects.
Source: National Energy Board (NEB), Canadian Energy Supply and Demand to 2025.

¹⁶⁰ U.S. Department of Energy, Energy Information Administration.

¹⁶¹ Africa should be supplying more oil in the future. In particular, five countries (Nigeria, Angola, Gabon, Equatorian Guinea, and Chad) should see their production increase. Only Nigeria is a member of OPEC; Gabon left the organization in 1995.
James Dao, "In Quietly Courting Africa, White House likes Dowry: Oil", *The New York Times,* Sept.19, 2002.

¹⁶² In 2002, OPEC officially produced 21.7 million barrels of oil a day. However, the true production was 2 million barrels more. OPEC

produces a bit more than a third of the world's total production.
OPEC was created on September 10, 1960 by five countries: Saudi Arabia, Iran, Iraq, Kuwait and Venezuela. They were then responsible for 80% of worldwide oil exports.
Thaddeus Herrick, "OPEC is to Hold Oil Output Steady", *The New York Times*, September 20, 2002, p. A5.

[163] Since April 1998, Iraq does not participate in the allocation of OPEC oil quotas. In percentage terms, these production quotas of about 25.4 millions barrels per day are as follows: 32,5 % to Saudi Arabia, 14,7 % to Iran, 11,5 % to Venezuela, 8,7 % to the United Arab Emirats (UAE), 8,2 % to Nigeria, 8,0 % to Kuwait, 5,4 % to Libya, 5,2 % to Indonesia, and 3,2 % to Algeria.
Source: Bloomberg, — U.S. Energy Information Administration.

[164] In fact, in 2003, the Saudi government was planning to ask the United States to withdraw its forces from Saudi Arabia.
Patrick Tyler, "Saudis will disengage from U.S., princes hint", *The Globe and Mail*, February 10, 2003, p. 8.

[165] "Strategic Energy Policy Challenges for the 21st Century", op.cit.

[166] James Woolsey, op.cit.

[167] Four Russian oil companies (Loukoil, Sibneft, Tyumen Oil and Yukos) plan to build a pipeline to ship Russian oil through the arctic port of Murmansk. Some 584 million barrels a day could be transported to European and American markets, begining in 2007.

[168] *The Guardian*, June 5, 2003.

[169] "Strategic Energy Policy Challenges for the 21st Century", op.cit.

[170] Barbette Stern, "Le pétrole, l'autre enjeu du conflit", ["Oil is the other stake in the war"], *Le Monde*, September 19, 2002.

The New American Empire

---

[171] Known world oil reserves are around 1,000 billion barrels, while the Middle East has about 664 billion barrels.
U.S. Department of Energy, Energy Information Administration.


[172] The oil from the Caspian Sea is much more expensive to pump, around $7 or $8 a barrel and possibly $12 or $13 a barrel. Iraqi oil can be extracted for less than $1 a barrel, i.e. 70 cents a barrel. The known oil reserves in the Caspian Sea basin are around 30 billion barrels. However, the potential reserves could be around 235 billion barrels.
Babette Stern, *Le Monde*, op.cit.


[173] Patrick Brethour, "Iraq a field of dreams for big oil firms", *The Globe and Mail*, April 12, 2003, p. B1.


[174] Babette Stern, op. cit.


[175] Neela Banerjee, "Iraq Is Strategic Issue for Oil Giants, Too", *The New York Times*, February 22, 2003.


[176] Bob Herbert, "Ultimate Insiders", *The New York Times*, April 14, 2003.


[177] The members of this important Task Force were:

*Odeh Aburdene*, (Capital Trust S.A.);
*Graham Allison*, (Harvard University and Assistant Secretary of Defense for Policy and Plans in the Clinton administration);
*Joseph C. Bell*, (Hogan & Hartson and previously U.S. Designated Representative for the International Energy Agency);
*Patrick Clawson*, (Washington Institute for Near East Policy);
*Frances D. Cook* (Ballard Group LLC, and former ambassador, including twice to energy-exporting countries);
*Jack L. Copeland*, (Copeland Consulting International);
*Charles B. Curtis*, (NTI, a foundation organized to reduce the threat from weapons of mass destruction and former Deputy Secretary and Undersecretary of the U.S. Department of Energy and Chairman of the Federal Energy Regulatory Commission);
*Toby T. Gati*, (Akin, Gump, Strauss, Hauer & Feld, L.L.P. and former Assistant Secretary of State for Intelligence and Research in the Clinton

278

administration);
*Luis Giusti*, ("Shell" Transport and Trading, and former Chairman and CEO of Petróleos de Venezuela, S.A.);
*David L. Goldwyn*, (Goldwyn International Strategies, LLC, and former Assistant Secretary of Energy for International Affairs);
*Michel T. Halbouty*, (Earth scientist and engineer);
*Amy Myers Jaffe*, (senior energy advisor at the James A. Baker III Institute for Public Policy of Rice University and former senior economist for *Petroleum Intelligence Weekly*);
*Melanie A. Kenderdine*, (Gas Technology Institute and former Deputy Assistant Secretary at the Department of Energy);
*Joseph P. Kennedy II*, (Citizens Energy Corporation);
*Marie-Josee Kravis*, (Economist and Senior Fellow at the Hudson Institute and Ford Motor Company, Vivendi Universal, U.S.A. Networks, Hasbro Inc., Hollinger International, and CIBC board member);
*Kenneth Lay*, (Chairman and CEO of Enron Corporation).
*John H. Lichtblau*, (Chairman and CEO of Petroleum Industry Research Foundation, Inc. (PIRINC));
*John A. Manzoni*, (British Petroleum and former head of the BP side of the BP/Amoco merger directorate);
*Thomas F. Mclarty III*, (Kissinger McLarty Associates, and a former Chairman and CEO of Arkla, Inc);
*Eric D.K. Melby*, (Forum for International Policy and Scowcroft Group);
*Sarah Miller*, (Energy Intelligence Group);
*Steven L. Miller*, (Chairman and CEO of Shell Oil Company);
*Ernest J. Moniz*, ( M.I.T. and former Undersecretary for Energy, Science, and Environment in the Department of Energy [1997–2001]];
*Edward L. Morse*, (Hess Energy Trading Co., LLC, and chair of the joint Task Force);
*Shirley Neff*, (Economist for the Democrats on the Senate Energy and Natural Resources Committee);
*David O'Reilly*, (Chairman of the Board and CEO for ChevronTexaco);
*Kenneth Randolph*, (Secretary of Dynegy, Inc);
*Peter Rosenthal*, (Chief Correspondent on energy and commodities for Bridge News);
*Gary N. Ross*, (CEO of the PIRA Energy Group);
*Ed Rothschild*, (Podesta/Mattoon in Washington, D.C. and former Energy Policy Director of Citizen Action);
*Jefferson B. Seabright*, (Vice President of Policy Planning for Texaco Inc. and former Director of the Office of Energy, Environment & Technology);
*Adam Sieminski*, (Deutsche Banc Alex and Chairman of the Independent Petroleum Association's oil and gas supply/demand committee);
*Matthew Simmons*, (President of Simmons & Company International);
*Ronald Soligo*, (Rice University);

*Michael D. Tusiani,* (Chairman and CEO of Poten & Partners);
*Philip K. Verleger Jr.,* (President of PK Verleger LLC and a Principal with the Brattle Group);
*Enzo Viscusi,* (Group Senior Vice President and Representative for the Americas of ENI, an Italian-based integrated energy company);
*Chuck Watson,* (Chairman and CEO of Houston Dynegy Inc.);
*William H. White,* (President of the Wedge Group Inc.);
*Daniel Yergin,* (Chairman of Cambridge Energy Research Associates);
*Mine Yücel,(* Senior Economist and Assistant Vice President, Federal Reserve Bank of Dallas).

Source: "Strategic Energy Policy Challenges for the 21st Century", April 2001, Report of an Independent Task Force Sponsored by the James A. Baker III Institute for Public Policy of Rice University and the Council on Foreign Relations.

[178] Other Arab-Israeli wars have been:
- the "Suez-Sinai War" of 1949, during which the British and the French joined in on the side of the Israelis, presumably to punish Egyptian president Gomar Nasser for claiming control of the Suez canal;
- the "Six-Day War" of 1967 when Israel, backed by Western powers (primarily France), succeeded in destroying the Arab forces and claimed the Gaza Strip, the Sinai Peninsula, the Golan heights, East Jerusalem, and the West Bank from the neighboring countries of Syria, Jordan, and Egypt.

[179] The Organization of Petroleum Exporting Countries (OPEC) was formed in 1960. However, its strength and impact were not felt until 1973, when the cartel decided to cut back on oil exports and raise oil prices. During the "Six-Day War" in 1967, OPEC tried to impose an oil embargo, but without great success.
With the exception of Venezuela, most OPEC countries are Muslim countries.

[180] Prices rose significantly again (150%) in 1979 in the wake of the Iranian Revolution.

[181] The ultimate source of that threat lies, however, in the unresolved Palestinian-Israeli conflict.

[182] Testimony of Richard Spertzel in front of the House Armed Services Committee on the subjet of "Iraqi Weapons Capabilities", *C-SPAN*, Sept. 10, 2002.

[183] John Tagliabue, "Europeans Strive to Tighten Trade Ties with Iraq", *The New York Times*, Sept. 19, 2002.

[184] The other kind of contract, supplying of services, is less advantageous, since it does not have the same positive impact on the balance sheet, and is therefore less desirable.
Mark Roche, "Le lobbying intensif sur le pétrole est à la hauteur de l'enjeu", ["The intensive lobbying around oil is a reflection of its importance"], *Le Monde*, Oct.31, 2002.

[185] Tom Raum, "Bush administration's Iraq campaign includes behind-scenes bartering", *Associated Press*, Sept. 22, 2002.

[186] John Tagliabue, op.cit.

[187] Neil King, Jr. And John H. Fialka, "Balance of Power in Oil Fallout From an Iraq War, Iran could Gain, Saudis Lose", *The New York Times*, Sept. 19, 2002, p. A1.

[188] Reported by the Russian newspaper *Izvestia* and reviewed by the *Courrier international*, Oct. 4, 2002.

[189] *Courrier International*, "Irak: le pétrole, moteur de la guerre américaine", Sept. 28, 2002.

[190] Tom Fennell, "Not for Justice, but Oil", *Maclean's*, Oct. 7, 2002, p. 28.

[191] For a history of oil companies, see Anthony Sampson, *The Seven Sisters*. New York, Bantam Books, 1976.
The original "Seven Sisters" or "Majors" were five American companies (Gulf and Standard Oil—which merged in 1984 and formed Chevron—

Exxon, Mobil, and Texaco) plus two European companies, British Petroleum and Royal-Dutch Shell. The eighth sister could have been the French company "la Compagnie française des pétroles", ancestor of the company Total.

[192] Martin Smith, "Truth, War and Consequences", Frontline, *PBS*, October 9, 2003.

[193] Marc Roche, "Le lobbying intensif sur le pétrole est à la hauteur de l'enjeu", ["The intensive lobbying around oil is a reflection of its importance"], *Le Monde*, Oct. 31, 2002.

[194] Since 1993, the American firms Chevron-Texaco and Exxon-Mobil are part of a consortium, called TangizChevroil, with the Russian company LukArco and the Kazakhian company KazMunaiGaz, to develop the oil fields of Kazakhstan. Similarly, Royal Dutch/Shell Group and Exxon Mobil Corp. are also involved in a consortium to develop the Kashagan oil fields in the North Caspian Sea.
See, Peter Wonacott, "China oil firm shut out", *The Globe and Mail*, May 12, 2003, p. B8.
Sabrna Tavernise, "Kazakhstan Gets a Lesson in Oil Politics", *The New York Times*, November 16, 2002, p. B3.

[195] According to authors Jean-Charles Brisard and Guillaume Dasqui, George W. Bush tried to negociate the construction of a pipeline with the Taliban government in Afghanistan, before September 11, 2001. In exchange for an agreement for a free passage for Ossama bin Laden to Saudi Arabia, the pipeline would go from Kazakhstan to the Indian Ocean, passing through Afghanistan.
Jean-Charles Brisard and Guillaume Dasquie, *Ben Laden, la vérité interdite*, Gallimard, Paris, 2002.

[196] Numerous pipelines are planned: one towards the East and South, passing through Afghanistan to the Pakistani port of Multan on the Indian Ocean, would serve the Asian market; another pipeline, some 1,100 miles long, would go from Baku to Ceyhan on the Mediterranean Sea, transporting natural gas from Turkmenistan and crossing the Caspian Sea, Azerbaijan, and Georgia to Turkey; another would go west, linking the northern Caspian region to the Russian port of Novorossiysk on the Black Sea, with a portage across the Bosphorus Strait to European

and world markets.

[197] *The New York Times*, July 5, 2002. "Washington planifierait une attaque massive sur l'Iraq", *La Presse*, July 6, 2002, p. A9.

[198] For an analysis of the government collusion with the arms industry, see: Helen Caldicott, *The New Nuclear Danger: George W. Bush's Military-Industrial Complex*, The New Press, New York, 2002, 416 p. The principal armaments producers in the U.S. and their Pentagon contracts in 2002 (in parentheses) are: Lockheed Martin ($17 billion), Boeing ($16.6 billion), Northrop Grumman ($8.6 billion), Raytheon ($7.0 billion) and General Dynamics ($7.0 billion). *USA Today*, April 3, 2003, p. 1A.

[199] Remarks made on PBS in August 2002.

[200] Bloomberg Network, Aug. 16, 2002.

[201] Henry A. Kissinger, *The Washington Post*, Aug. 12, 2002, and affiliated newspapers.

[202] "Des blindés sont envoyés vers le golfe persique", *Le Devoir*, Sept. 5, 2002.

[203] Robert Burns, *Associated Press*.

[204] *Le Monde*, Oct. 9 and 12, 2002, respectively.

[205] On November 27, 2002, more than a year after the September 11 attacks, George W. Bush chose Kissinger, 79, to preside an independant panel to study the reasons the government's systems of prevention failed to sound the alarm. Unable to make public his contracts with companies and foreign governments, Kissinger resigned one month later.

[206] Among the most vociferous: *New York Times*' William Safire and *Washington Post*'s Charles Krauthammer.

[207] Bénédicte Mathieu, with Eric Leser, Marc Roche et Frédéric Therin, "L'empire de Rupert Murdoch au service d'une propagande pro-guerre ", [Rupert Murdock's media empire at the service of pro-war propaganda"], *Le Monde*, April 14, 2003.

[208] Andrea Mitchell, "A number of prominent Republicans are now publicly coming out against President Bush's plans for Iraq", *Newsweek*, Aug. 16, 2002.
This didn't prevent Senator Hagel from voting in favor of the Bush resolution allowing the use of force against Iraq.
David Firestone, "2 Critics of Bush Iraq Policy Say They'll Back Resolution", *The New York Times*, Oct. 10, 2002.
Also Michael Langan, "Un ex-secrétaire d'État de Bush père convie à la prudence au sujet de l'Irak", Agence France-Presse, *La Presse*, Aug. 26, 2002, p. A8.

[209] Agence France-Presse, "D'ex-généraux rejettent une guerre solitaire en Irak", *La Presse*, Aug. 31, 2002, p. A15.

[210] The Newshour, *PBS*, Aug.27, 2002.

[211] This was essentially the same as the proposition made by French President Jacques Chirac.

[212] James A. Baker III, "The Right Way to Change a Regime", *The New York Times*, Aug. 25, 2002.

[213] In the end, however, Congressman Armey sided with George W. Bush and voted for the resolution authorizing the use of military force against Iraq.
Mireille Duteil, Jean Guisnel, and Olivier Weber, "Irak: Comment les faucons préparent la guerre", *Le Point*, Aug. 16, 2002.

[214] Paul Koring, "Powell exposes split over Iraq invasion", *The Globe*

and Mail, Sept. 2, 2002.

[215] The problem for Colin Powell was that he wasn't the only Secretary of State in the Bush cabinet. Donald H. Rumsfeld, the Secretary of Defense, acted as if he were the Secretary of State. For example, it was Rumsfeld who publicly proposed attacking Iraq and changing the government.
Tom Raum, Associated Press, "Rumsfeld presses for action against Iraq", Sept. 19, 2002.

[216] In 1991, Joe Lieberman was among the handful of Democrats who supported the U.S. intervention against Iraq.

[217] Frank Rich, "It's the War, Stupid", The New York Times, Oct. 11, 2002.

[218] Jimmy Carter, "The Troubling New Face of America", The New York Times, Sept. 5, 2002, p. A31.

[219] In the middle of the campaign to persuade the American public to support a unilateral intervention in Iraq, the American Jewish Committee (AJC) launched a televised publicity campaign on CNN, Fox News, and MSNBC, to the tune of millions of dollars, spreading the message that "America and Israel share the same values, a vision of peace."
Agence France-Presse, "Un clip pro-Israel fait des remous aux É.-U.", La Presse, Oct. 3, 2002, p.B4.

[220] Robert Burns, "Bush given detailed plan for attacking Iraq", Associated Press, Sept. 22, 2002.

[221] Paul Krugman, "Toward One-Party Rule", The New York Times, June 27, 2003.

[222] Section 8 of the First Article of the U.S. Constitution states: The Congress shall have Power:...
To declare war...;
To raise and support Armies...;

To provide and maintain a Navy;
To make Rules for the Government and Regulation of the land and naval
Forces;...

[223] The tension between the Powell people and the Rumsfeld people may have been real. However, at a higher level, Powell and Rumsfeld were playing the "good cop-bad cop game", the former being perceived as more prudent and somewhat reluctant to go to war, while the latter projected a ruthless and reckless image.

[224] On October 12, 2002, when George W. Bush reluctantly accepted to pursue diplomatic channels through the United Nations in the conflict with Iraq, at the same time he reinforced the influence of Colin Powell and the State Department within the cabinet, against the Pentagon and the trio Cheney-Rice-Rumsfeld.

[225] Agence France-Presse, "Les extrémistes de retour en force en Afghanistan", *La Presse*, Sept. 16, 2002, p. A1.

[226] Stephanie Nolen, "Promises to Afghans lie in ruins a year later", *The Globe and Mail*, Oct. 7, 2002, p. A1.

[227] Indonesia is 90% Muslim and the most populous of Islamic countries. It shelters extremist fundamentalist Islamic groups, such as Jemaah Islamiyal and Laskar Jihad (Combattants for Islam). These extremist religious groups set up paramilitary training camps and resort to terror and subversion to introduce Islamic law in Southeast Asia. They are as dangerous as the Talibans in Afghanistan, before their expulsion by the U.S. military forces and their allies.

[228] Barton Gellman, "Report: Al Qaida gets nerve weapon", *The Washington Post*, Dec. 12, 2002.

[229] North Korea, another member of George W. Bush's *"Axis of Evil"*, admitted to possessing a program for producing nuclear weapons, in breach of a 1994 freeze agreement with the U.S. A troubling factor was that Pakistan had supplied the nuclear technology to North Korea in exchange for missile technology. It was out of the question, however, for

the U.S. to disarm North Korea by force. First, North Korea has no oil. Second, it was no threat to Israel. Third, there was a Chinese gorilla behind it.
David E. Sanger and James Dao, "U.S. Says Pakistan Gave Technology to North Korea", *The New York Times*, Oct. 18, 2002.

[230] The expression is from Jean-Pierre Chèvemenet, "L'Amérique veut se saisir d'une pompe à pétrole", ["The U.S. wants to grab an oil pump"], *Le Monde*, Oct. 12, 2002.

[231] Two researchers at the famous Brookings Institute offered a more somber view of the difficulties that lay ahead if Iraq were to be invaded militarily.
See: Philip H.Gordon and Michael E. O'Hanlon, "A Tougher Target: The Afghanistan model of warfare may not apply very well to Iraq", *The Washington Post*, December 26, 2001.

[232] The Israeli government went ahead building a 700-kilometre wall, most of it on expropriated Palestian land and costing $1.5 billion US to build. It also adopted a law forbidding Palestinians who marry an Arab Israeli from adopting Israeli citizenship. On October 14, 2003, the Bush administration vetoed a U.N. resolution declaring such a unilateral grab of Palestinian territory as being "illegal under international law", even though the resolution was supported by 10 countries, with 4 abstentions.
Timothy Appleby, "Israel to build 22 new settler homes", *The Globe and Mail*, Aug. 1, 2003.
Agence France-Presse, "Les Etats-Unis ont mis leur veto au projet de résolution sur le 'mur' israélien" [The U.S. vetoed a resolution on the Israeli 'wall' "], *Le Monde*, October 15, 2003.

[233] These new untested weapons, like the so-called "smart bombs", i.e. the Joint Direct Attack Munitions (JDAM), used high-energy electronic pulsations that could be launched using satellites or from remote-controlled Predator drones (un-manned planes). A new combat airplane, the F/A-18 super Hornet, the Longbow Apache helicopter, the Patriot missile and the Abrams M1A1 tank promised to be extremely useful.
Paul Koring, "Bombing Baghdad", *The Globe and Mail*, Oct. 12, 2002, p. F6.

[234] Matt Bai, "Rove's Way", *The New York Times Magazine*, Oct. 20,

2002.

235 Thomas L. Friedman, "Read My Lips", *The New York Times*, June 11, 2003.

236 George W. Bush proposed a $674 billion tax-cutting package for the 2003 budget. Greenspan's call to prudence was met by a demand that he resign by Senator Jim Bunning, a Republican from Kentucky.
Edmund L. Andrews,"Greenspan Throws Cold Water on Bush Tax Plan", *The New York Times*, February 12, 2003.

237 Paul Krugman, "Everything Is Political", *The New York Times*, August 5, 2003.
An indication of the extent of the problem: when John Snow, the Treasury Secretary, meets with Karl Rove, the political csar of the administration, the meetings take place in Mr. Rove's office.

238 The biggest concern was the control of the Senate. In order to name neo-conservative judges to the Supreme Court, the Bush Administration needed a Republican Senate. Although the House controls the budget, it is the Senate that must confirm nominations to the Supreme Court.

239 The Associated Press, "Iraq Becomes Presidential Issue", *The New York Times*, Oct. 12, 2002.

240 On this issue, George W. Bush asked the American public to make an act of faith. It was perhaps one of his "faith-based initiatives"!

241 During the first Persian Gulf War, in 1991, the government of Bush, Sr. employed a certain number of lies in order to kindle hate for Saddam Hussein. 1) The government said that Iraqi soldiers took newborns out of their hospital incubators, leaving them to die on the floor, and stole the incubators. This was false. It was all a hoax orchestrated by Hill and Knowlton, a public relations firm in New York. 2) The U.S. government said that military satellites showed Iraqi trooops were amassed on the border of Saudi Arabia, ready to invade. Private communication satellites showed no troop concentration on the Iraq/Saudi border.
John R. MacArthur, *Second Front: Censorship and Propaganda in the*

*Gulf*, 2002.

[242] Barry Levinson, Director, scenario by David Mame.

[243] William M. Welch, "Frayed tempers snap over politics, patriotism", *USA Today*, Sept. 26, 2002, p. 6A.

[244] David S. Broder and Helen Rumbelow, "War talk shapes fall elections", *The Washington Post*, Sept.29, 2002, p. A01.

[245] David S. Broder and Helen Rumbelow. Ibid.

[246] Dominique de Villepin, "Irak: ne pas brûler les étapes." [Iraq: Let us not rush things"], *Le Monde*, Analyses et forums, Sept. 30, 2002.

[247] These requirements were the same as those contained in the Security Council Resolution 1284, in December 1999.

[248] From mid-April to early June, temperatures are already inhospitably hot. In June, they may rise to 120°, and are acompanied by 50-mile an hour dust-filled winds. The "shamal" blows from mid-June to mid-September, forming dust storms that can rise several thousand feet. Dehydration and heat exhaustion threaten soldiers, even more vulnerable when they must carry protective equipment in case of chemical or biological attacks. Dust can clog engines and air filters, disable laser-guided weapons and even block gun sights.

[249] A majority of 9 out of 15 of the members is required to adopt a resolution, but only Great Britain, Bulgaria, Norway, Columbia, and Singapore were ready to support the aggressive U.S. resolution against Iraq.

[250] There was still the possibility of a reprimand from a majority of the Security Council, which didn't happen when NATO intervened in Kosovo. Russia's proposed reprimand was defeated 12 to 3.

[251] A former CIA analyst and Clinton Security Advisor on Iraq, Kenneth M. Pollack, put it succinctly enough, "...in the end, we [the U.S.] will have to act regardless of whether we have a pretext or not."
Kenneth M. Pollack, *The Threatening Storm; The Case for Invading Iraq*, Random House, New York, 2002, p. 365.


[252] David E. Sanger, Eric Schmitt and Thom Shanker,"War Plan in Iraq Sees Large Force and Quick Strikes", *The New York Times*, Nov. 10, 2002, p. YNE 1.


[253] The plan was titled "Shock and Awe" by the administration. It detailed how 300 to 400 Tomahawk cruise missiles would rip through Iraq on the first day of a U.S. assault, which is more than the number that were launched during the entire 40 days of the first Gulf War. On the second day, another 300 to 400 cruise missiles would be sent. *"There will not be a safe place in Baghdad,"* said one Pentagon official. *"The sheer size of this has never been seen before, never been contemplated before,"* the official said. One of the authors of the Shock and Awe plan stated the intent is, *"So that you have this simultaneous effect, rather like the nuclear weapons at Hiroshima, not taking days or weeks but in minutes."* CBS News January 27, 2003; *The New York Times*, February 2, 2003.


[254] In fact, months before the Bush administration went to the U.N., U.S.-led covert operations were going on inside Iraq with the purpose of destabilizing the country before a military invasion. The entire presentation to the United Nations was a side show and a smokescreen to the war preparations.
Douglas Jehl with Dexter Filkins, "U.S. Moved to Undermine Iraqi Military Before War", *The New York Times,* August 10, 2003.


[255] Ellen Hale, "Blair risking more than his popularity", *USA Today*, February 18, 2003, p. 9A.
For an inside account of Tony Blair's politics of deception about the Iraqi war, see Robin Cook, *Point of Departure*, Simon & Schuster, London, 2003, 432 p.


[256] Jack Kelley, "U.S. kills al Qaeda suspects in Yemen", *USA Today*, Nov. 5, 2002, p. 1A.

257 Republicans also reversed the balance in state elections, where they could be expected to lose 350 seats in a mid-term election. Instead, they won 200 additional seats.

258 Sylvie Kauffmann, "Des Américains pas tranquilles" ["Some Americans who are not subdued"], *Le Monde*, Dec. 22, 2002.

259 A good example of such a paralysis of the Security Council in the case of aggression by one its veto-carrying members was provided in October 1956, when the Soviet Union illegally invaded the newly-democratic country of Hungary, following the overthrow of the communist dictatorship. Because of the Soviet veto, the Security Council could do nothing. When, in March 2003, the United States illegally invaded Iraq, it could also do so with impunity. In both instances, neither the Soviet Union nor the United States were excluded from the United Nations.

260 Chapter VII of the Charter was again invoked for Somalia, in an even clearer case of "humanitarian reasons" for international intervention. Indeed, on December 3, 1992, the Security Council passed Resolution 794 and invoked Chapter VII of the Charter to authorise the use of "all necessary means" to establish a "secure environment for humanitarian relief".

261 For a detailed analysis of these issues, consult the report of the International Commission of the Intervention and the Sovereignty of States.

262 "To help the Iraqis [would not have been] a reason to put American kids' lives at risk, certainly not on the scale we did it."
Sam Tannenhaus, *Vanity Fair*, June, 2003.

263 Ron Fournier, "Bush challenges UN to confront Iraq", *Associated Press*, Sept. 13, 2002.

Between 1967 and 2002, there were 67 U.N. resolutions dealing with Iraq. The main U.N. resolutions regarding Iraq are the following:

Resolution 660 of August 2, 1990, condemns the Iraqi invasion of Kuwait and demands that Iraq withdraw immediately and unconditionally all its forces to their positions of August 1, 1990;

Resolution 661 of August 6, 1990, raises economic sanctions against Iraq with an embargo on all Iraqi imports, "except those supplies intended strictly for medical purposes, and, in humanitarian circumstances";

Resolution 678 of November 29, 1990, authorizes Member States to use all necessary means to uphold and implement resolution 660 (1990) and all subsequent relevant resolutions and to restore international peace and security in the area and sets a January 15, 1991, deadline for full Iraqi compliance;

Resolution 686 of March 2, 1991, demands that all Kuwaiti property seized by Iraq be immediately returned;

Resolution 687 of April 3, 1991, maintains the prohibitions against the sale or supply to Iraq of commodities or products, other than medicine and health supplies and foodstuffs, until Irak destroys "all chemical and biological weapons and all stocks of agents and all related subsystems and components and all research, development, support and manufacturing facilities, and all ballistic missiles with a range greater than 150 kilometres";

Resolution 986 of April 14, 1995, establishes an "Oil-for-Food" program and requests the Secretary General to establish an escrow account for the purposes of this resolution;

Resolution 1284 of December 17, 1999, decides to establish, as a subsidiary body of the Council, the United Nations Monitoring, Verification and Inspection Commission (UNMOVIC), which replaces the Special Commission established in 1991;

Resolution 1373 of September 12, 2001, increases cooperation and fully implements the relevant international conventions and protocols relating to terrorism;

Resolution 1441 of November 8, 2002, requires of the government of Iraq that it provide a currently accurate, full, and complete declaration of all aspects of its programs to develop chemical, biological, and nuclear weapons.

Resolution 1472 of March 28, 2003, authorizes the U.N. Secretary

General, during a renewable period of 45 days, to continue the "Oil-for-Food" program, as the situation permits.

[264] Michael Hedges, "Iraq agrees to allow weapons inpectors", *Houston Chronicle*, Sept. 17, 2002, p. 1A.

[265] Jooneed Khan, "Accord entre Bagdad et l'ONU sur le retour des experts", *La Presse*, Oct. 2, 2002, p. A12.

[266] *Le Courriel international*, Revue de presse, Sept. 30, 2002.

[267] One of the few people to make the connection publicly, early on, was the comedian Jon Stewart, who hosts the satirical "The Today Show". At the end of September, 2002, in conversation with George Stephanopoulos, President Clinton's former advisor recycled into a talk show host on ABC, Stewart asked if the Administration was planning a regime change in Iraq because the U.S. wanted to take control of Middle East oil. Stephanopoulos agreed that it was a possibility. "But who in this Administration is interested in the oil industry?", Stewart asked ingenuosly.
Simon Houpt, "The World According to Stewart", *The Globe and Mail*, Oct. 3, 2002, p. R1.
Another comedian, Bill Maher, host of the program "Poltically Incorrect", on ABC, suffered the wrath of Disney Co., owner of ABC, because he had said on the air, after September 11, 2001, that while it was cowardly for the terrorists to kill thousands of people, it was also cowardly to bomb people from 30,000 feet.
Isabelle Massé, "Pas du tout 'politically correct' ", *La Presse*, July 20, 2002, p. D10.

[268] Agence France-Presse, "Administration 'provisoire' plutôt qu"occupation', dit Washington", *Le Devoir*, Oct. 12, 2002.

[269] The U.S. and British governments claimed that they possessed proofs that Iraq had weapons of mass destruction, but despite their obligations under Security Council Resolution 1441 to transmit these proofs to the U.N. inspectors, they refused to do so.

[270] An Iraq divided into three parts—a Kurdish country in the North, a Sunnite country in the middle, and a Shiite country in the South—would be considerably weakened.

[271] Edward Epstein, "Firm linked to Cheney wins oil-field contract: Hussein may destroy facilities in event of war", *The San Francisco Chronicle*, March 8, 2003, page A12. The contract went to Kellogg Brown & Root Services, which is owned by Halliburton Co..

Even before the beginning of the war between the United States and Iraq, the U.S. Agency for International Development and the Army Corps of Engineers were taking bids from American companies for building contracts in postwar Iraq. Airports, schools, hospitals, roads, etc. would have to be rebuilt and U.S. companies such as Bechtel Group, Fluor Corporation, the Louis Berger Group and Washington Group International were well-positioned to receive such contracts.

However, if such public procurements contracts are not awarded in an open competitive bidding system, the United States could be in breach of the Convention on Public Procurements of the World Trade Organization (WTO) which was signed by 25 countries, including the United States,. See Alan Cowell, "British Ask What a War Would Mean For Business", *The New York Times*, March 18, 2003, p.W1.

[272] This was a prescription that the authors of the Versailles Treaty of 1919 forgot with disastrous consequences for the 20th Century.

[273] See, Richard Pierre Claude, and B.H., Weston, eds., *Human Rights in the World Community*, University of Pennsylvania Press, Philadelphia, 1992.

[274] An adaptation of this section has been published in the magazine *The Humanist*, in its May/June, 2003 issue. See Rodrigue Tremblay, "Just War Theory", *The Humanist*, May/June, 2003, pp 15-18.

[275] Judith Wagner DeCew, "Codes of Warfare." *Encyclopedia of Applied Ethics*, Volume 4. San Diego: Academic Press, 1998.

[276] Robert G. Clouse, *War: Four Christian Views*, Downers Grove, Intervarsity Press, 1991.

[277] Aquinas, Saint Thomas. "On War." *Summa Theologica*, Part II, Question 40.

[278] The U.S. military has thousands of nuclear bombs, the largest being the nine-megaton B-53 nuclear bombs.

[279] Cluster bombs are composed of 202 bomblets which are packed with razor-sharp shrapnel dispersed at super-high speed over an area as large as 22 football fields, ripping into human bodies. These weapons are banned by the Geneva Protocol Relating to the Protection of Victims of International Armed Conflicts, article 51.

[280] The idea of war varies greatly whether you are an American or a European. A poll conducted in June 2003, by the U.S.-based German Marshall Fund, asked the following question, "Under certain conditions, is war necessary to obtain justice?" The answer was yes for 55 percent of Americans, 35 percent of British citizens, 22 percent of the Dutch, but for only 12 percent of the French and of the Germans.
Laurent Zecchini, "La question de l'usage de la force et le rôle dominant des Etats-Unis divisent Américains et Européens", *Le Monde*, September 5, 2003.

[281] Reuters, "Pope Urges World to Avoid 'Dramatic Conflict'", *The New York Times*, March 5, 2003.

[282] See, Mister Thorne, "Atheists in Foxholes, Christians in Uniform, *The Humanist*, May/June 2003, pp 19-23.

[283] Neo-conservative Christians and U.S. televangelists are among the few who believe that offensive wars, such as the U.S.-led 2003 War against Iraq, are moral. One month before the war, televangelist Charles Stanley decreed that "God approves of war...and hates peaceniks".
Mister Thorne, op. cit

[284] Remark made Sunday, September 15, 2002, during a conversation with representatives of the trade union IG Metall, in Steven Erlanger "Bush-Hitler Remark Shows U.S. as Issue in Germany Election", *The New York Times*, September 20, 2002, p. A1.

[285] Philippe Pons "Les Etats-Unis, nouvel empire mongol?", ["The U.S.: A New Mongol Empire?"], *Le Monde*, Sunday, October 20, 2002.

[286] The Monroe Doctrine contained four points:
1- The American continents were no longer open to European colonization;
2- the United States would consider any increase in European political control in the Western Hemisphere to be a threat to its own security;
3- the United States promised not to intervene in the affairs of existing European colonies; and
4- the United States would not interfere in the domestic affairs of European countries.

[287] Bush also said, "The military must be ready to strike at a moment's notice in any dark corner of the world. All nations that decide for aggression and terror will pay the price."

[288] From the Project's founding *Statement of Principles*, Project For The New American Century, 1150 Seventeenth Street, N.W., Suite 510, Washington, D.C., 20036.

[289] Paul Wolfowitz and Lewis Libby, "Rebuilding America's Defenses. A Report of The Project for the New American Century", September 2000.

[290] Israeli military analyst Amos Gilboa cited by Noam Chomsky, "Hegemony or Survival", July 2001.

[291] For an analysis of the risks of preemption, see Ivo H. Daalder, James M. Lindsay, and James B. Steinberg, *Hard Choices: National Security and the War on Terrorism*, Current History, December 2002.

Also, Michael E. O'Hanlon, Susan E. Rice and James B. Steinberg, "The New National Security Strategy and Preemption", *The Brookings Institute* Policy Brief #113, December 2002. 8 p.

[292] According to the Caroline clause of 1837 of international law, still valid today, preventive actions are permissible only when "the immediate necessity of self-defense exists and is overwhelming and neither a choice of means nor a possibility of negotiations remains... A war to nip in the bud the appearance of a danger is prohibited... Preemptive war is *de facto* an offensive war."
See Jurgen Wagner "From Containment to Pax Americana:
The National Security Strategy of the US", Sozialismus, November 15 2002, (published in German under the title "Vom Containment zur Pax Americana:
Die nationale Sicherheitsstrategie der USA").
See also Robert Leicht, "With the Threat of a Unilateral Military Strike, George W. Bush Forces His War Goal on the United Nations", Die Zeit, 2002

[293] Karen Armstrong, *The Battle for God*, Alfred A. Knopf, New York, 2001, p. 216.

[294] *The Observer*, January 12, 2003.

[295] The Bush administration, with its preemption philosophy, was carrying out a frontal attack upon the United Nations.
See Jonathan Steele, "In a chilling U-turn, the US claims the right to strike pre-emptively", *The Guardian*, June 7, 2002.

[296] See Robert Leicht, "With the Threat of a Unilateral Military Strike, George W. Bush Forces his War Goal on the United Nations", *Die Zeit*, 2002.

[297] In 1950, world trade as a percentage of world output was less than 8 percent. In 2002, this percentage was approaching 30 percent. The greatest expansion of wealth in the history of mankind, during the second half of the 20th Century, was fueled mainly by this expansion in world trade.

[298] Maureen Dowd, "Warring Tribes, Here and There", *The New York Times*, April 2, 2003.

[299] Three lines of early warning radar stations were built:
— the Pinetree Line, which ran east to west just north of the US border and was completed in 1962; the Mid-Canada Line which was a Dopler radar fence and ran along the 55th parallel, and the arctic Distant Early Warning Line which followed the 66th parallel and was completed a few years later. Between 1985 and 1994,the DEW Line was upgraded with fifteen new FPS117 phased-array radars and re-named the North Warning Line, in order to protect against the threat of nuclear cruise missiles.

[300] In 2002 alone, the Pentagon spent $8.5 billion on its anti-missile program.

[301] Lawrence Kaplan, cited by Andrew Bacevich in *The National Interest*, Summer 2001.

[302] Cited by Noam Chomsky, "Hegemony or Survival", July 2001.

[303] Mikhail Gorbachev, *Memoirs*, Doubleday, New York, 1995, 769 p.

[304] See, J. Gallagher and R. E. Robinson, "The Imperialism of Free Trade", *Economic History Review*, 2nd series, VI, 1953.

[305] Some call the first America "Blue America", while the second, "Red America" is the America of the "red necks".
Doug Saunders, "Caught in the crossfire of the 'two Americas'", *The Globe and Mail*, Oct. 12, 2002, p. F3.

[306] From a speech given by George W. Bush at West Point on June 7, 2002.

307 When Canadians and Europeans are asked what they think of the American model of democracy, half admire it and half reject it. A worldwide poll conducted in 2002, by the Pew Research Center, revealed the following information about the perception of American democracy by citizens of other large democracies:

TABLE- American Ideas about Democracy:
Canada, Europe

|  | Like % | Dislike % | Don't know/Ref % |
|---|---|---|---|
| Canada | 50 | 40 | 10 |
| Germany | 47 | 45 | 7 |
| Italy | 45 | 37 | 18 |
| Great Britain | 43 | 42 | 15 |
| France | 42 | 53 | 5 |

Source: The Pew Research Center For The People & The Press, "What the World Thinks in 2002", December 4, 2002.

308 See the excellent article by Paul Krugman, "For Richer", *The New York Times Magazine*, Oct. 20, 2002.
Also, Kevin Phillips, *Wealth and Democracy*, New York, 2002.

309 The Pew Research Center for the People & the Press, "What the World Thinks in 2002", Dec. 4, 2002. (www.people-press.org)
Also, Adam Clymer, "World Survey Says Negative Views on U.S. are Rising", *The New York Times*, Dec. 5, 2002.

310 TABLE- Support toward using force to remove Saddam Hussein (poll conducted by The Pew Research Center-2002) (in percentages)

|  | U.S. | Britain | France | Germany | Russia | Turkey |
|---|---|---|---|---|---|---|
| Favor | 62 | 47 | 33 | 26 | 12 | 13* |
| Oppose | 26 | 47 | 64 | 71 | 79 | 83* |
| Don't know | 12 | 6 | 3 | 3 | 9 | 4* |
|  | 100 | 100 | 100 | 100 | 100 | 100 |

* Turkish respondents were asked about allowing the U.S. and its allies to use bases in Turkey for military action.
Source: The Pew Research Center For The People & The Press, "What the World Thinks in 2002", December 4, 2002.

[311] TABLE- Explanation of the motivation behind the American use of force against Iraq (poll conducted by The Pew Research Center-2002) (in percentages)

| | U.S. | Britain | France | Germany | Russia | Turkey |
|---|---|---|---|---|---|---|
| The U.S. believes Saddam is a threat | 67 | 45 | 21 | 39 | 15 | n/a |
| The U.S. wants to control Iraqi oil | 22 | 44 | 75 | 54 | 76 | |
| Don't know | 11 | 11 | 4 | 7 | 9 | |
| | 100 | 100 | 100 | 100 | 100 | |

Source: The Pew Research Center For The People & The Press, "What the World Thinks in 2002", December 4, 2002.

[312] "Views of a Changing World: 2003 War With Iraq Further Divides Global Publics", Pew Research Center for the People & the Press, Survey Reports, June 3, 2003.

[313] The American people have cooled on France and Germany as much as the French and Germans have cooled on the U.S. In 2003, 29 and 44 percent respectively of Americans had a favorable opinion of France and Germany, against 79 et 83 percent in February 2002.

[314] The Pew Research Center For The People & The Press, "What the World Thinks in 2002", December 4, 2002. Op.cit.

[315] For Europeans, the two principal "rogue" states threatening world peace are Israel and the United States. A poll taken all over Europe in October 2003 indicated that 59 percent of Europeans considered Israel the main threat to world peace, followed by the United States, North Korea and Iran at 53 percent.
BBC News, "Europeans believe Israel poses the biggest threat to world peace, just ahead of the United States", November 4, 2003.

[316] Saddam Hussein gave numerous key government positions to people from his native village, Takrit. Since they all have the same family name, al-Takriti, he forbade the use of family names in Iraq, pretexting that it is a Western custom.

317 A *Newsweek* article documented the military aid the U.S. gave Saddam during the 1980's. He used that aid to invade Kuwait in 1990. See "How We Created Saddam", *Newsweek*, Sept. 22, 2002.

318 Michael I. Niman, "What Bush Doesn't Want You to Know About Iraq", *The Humanist*, March-April, 2003.

319 Ali Babakhan, *Les Kurdes d'Irak, leur histoire et leur déportation par le régime de Saddam Hussein*, Paris, 1994, 352 p.

320 The Kurdish population is distributed as follows: 15 million in Turkey, 5 million in Iraq, 7 million in Iran, 1 million in Syria, and 350,000 in Armenia (ex-Soviet Republic).

321 Less known than the Kurdish tragedy, the fate of the Iraqi Shiites is none the less a similar human tragedy. More numerous than the Sunnite Arabs who rule the country, Iraqi Shiites have also born the brunt of persecutions and deportations by the regime of Saddam Hussein, especially after their uprising in 1991.
See Ali Babakhan, *L'Iraq: 1970-1990, déportations des Shi'ites*, Paris, 1996, 238 p.

322 In December 2002, the Under Secretary of Defense, Paul Wolfowitz, spoke to the newly-elected Turkish government, asking for permission for the U.S. to use Turkish bases to launch a possible air war against Iraq. Turkey was told that if the U.S. had to go to war without its help, it would harm relations between the two countries. A sign of what was to come was the remark of a high Administration official who warned, *"war plans have a momentum all their own. The Turks can't keep their options open until the last minute."*
Turkey was promised Patriot missiles, support for their candidacy into the European Union, and assistance in settling the conflict with Greece over the island of Cyprus. In return, Turkey would agree to let the U.S. use Turkish air and land bases for its attack against Iraq, even though 83% of the Turkish population was opposed to the forceful overthrow of Saddam Hussein.
Carla Anne Robbins and Greg Jaffe, "U.S. Keeps Pressure on Iraq, Seeks Turkey's Aid", *The Wall Street Journal*, Dec. 3, 2002, p. 2.

[323] Harmonie Toros, "Turkey says vote on U.S. troops likely Tuesday", *Associated Press*, February 24, 2003.

[324] Turkey has traditionally followed a very repressive policy towards its large Kurdish minority. The 15 million Turkish Kurds cannot give their children Kurdish names, they do not have their own primary school education system in their own language, and laws allowing Kurdish-language braodcasting have not been implemented.

[325] Initially, in order to secure Turkey's support, the Bush White House had made an offer of $26 billion in American aid—$6 billion in grants and $20 billion in loans — it was supposed to be "final."
The Turks knew they were in a strong negotiating position and requested more than twice that sum.
Despite their country's 50-year-old military alliance with the United States, Turkey's officials were citing polls showing that 96 percent of the Turkish people opposed the war.
Dexter Filkins with Judith Miller, "Proposal by Turkey Stalls U.S. Bid to Use Its Bases", *The New York Times*, Februay 18, 2003.

[326] Filkins, Dexter with C. J. Chivers, "U.S. in Talks on Allowing Turkey to Occupy a Kurdish Area in Iraq", *The New York Times*, February 7, 2003.

[327] The vote was 264 for to 251 against, with 19 abstentions. But to be adopted, the measure would have needed 267 positive votes. It was short by three votes.
Dexter Filkins, "Turkish Deputies Refuse to Accept American Troops", *The New York Times*, March 2, 2003.

[328] Before losing the election in November 2002, the ailing Prime Minister of Turkey, Bulent Ecevit, repeated Turkey's intransigent and colonialist position towards the Kurds. "We are absolutely opposed to a military operation (American) in our region." He added that if the Kurds in northern Iraq created an independant Kurdish state on the border with Turkey, "we would take the necessary measures".
Agence France-Presse, "L'incertitude persiste sur les conditions qui seront faites au retour de l'ONU en Irak" *La Presse*, Oct. 6, 2002, p. A3.

At the end of November 2002, George W. Bush met with Ahmet Necdet Sezer, the Turkish president, at a meeting of NATO. Bush assured him that the U.S. did not wish to see any changes in Iraq's frontiers, and confirmed the U.S. support for Turkey's admission into the European Union. See "Inside the Secret Campaign to Topple Saddam", *Time Magazine*, Dec. 2, 2002, p. 39.

[329] The Kurds claim to have an army of 100,000 soldiers, called "peshmerga".

[330] On Oct.7, 2002, George W. Bush made the committment to keep Iraq united.

[331] January 28, 2003, was also the date of the national elections in Israel.

[332] In 1991, shortly after the conclusion of the first Gulf War when asked his assessment of the number of Iraqi soldiers and civilians killed, which had been put at over 100,000, General Powell, then the United States' top military man, is reputed to have answered, "It's really not a number I'm terribly interested in."

[333] *Associated Press*, "Bush welcomes second U.N. resolution at Blair's urging", February 1, 2003.

[334] The Bush administration was suggesting these reprisals against countries opposed to its war against Iraq:
-Russia was told by the U.S.ambassador that energy cooperation and investment, joint work in security and anti-terrorism programs and partnership in space would be "casualties";
-Angola was told that $20 million in annual humanitarian aid might be reduced;
-Chile was told that a pending free-trade agreement with the U.S. could be delayed;
-Guinea and Cameroon, two poor African countries, were told that the United States might not push hard for loans those countries needed from international lenders...etc.
Laurence McQuillan and Tom Squitieri, "Arm-twisting on U.N.

resolution intensifies", *USA Today*, March 12, 2003, p. 4A.

[335] Eric Schmitt, "Japan Authorizes Troops for Iraq, *The New York Times,* July 27, 2003.

[336] A Mexican diplomat describing the hostile visit to Mexico by Undersecretary of State Marc Grossman and Kim Holmes, the Assistant Secretary of State for international organizations.
Dafna Linzer, "U.S.diplomats lean on undecided U.N. Security Council members", *Associated Press,* February 24, 2003.

[337] William Safire, "On Rewarding Friends", *The New York Times,* April 3, 2003.

[338] From 1946 to 2002, the Soviet Union and Russia have cast 121 veto votes, the United States 76 veto votes, Great Britain 32 veto votes, France 18 veto votes and China/Taiwan 5 veto votes.

[339] Paul Krugman, "Let Them Hate as Long as They Fear", *The New York Times,* March 7, 2003.

[340] A poll conducted nationally between February 12 and 18, 2003 by the Program on international Policy Attitudes at the University of Maryland and Knowledge Networks showed that 37 percent of Americans were supportive of a U.S. invasion of Iraq, 36 percent were against, and 25 percent disapproved but would still support it if it were to be launched. In Israel, polls showed 60 percent in favor of a war, 40 percent against, making this country the most war prone of all countries.
Frank Davies, "Floridians divided on war", *The Miami Herald,* February 22, 2003, p. 14A.

[341] "Les Français expriment une condamnation sans appel de la guerre", ["French people are overwhelmingly against the war"], *Le Monde,* April 1st, 2003.

[342] According to international law, the Bush administration had no right to give an ultimatum to the United Nations. In 1981, the U.S. government

reaffirmed the validity of the Caroline clause of international law that says that no country can launch an attack against another, merely because it is the stronger, if it is not in a situation of self-defense. Indeed, when Israel launched an attack against Iraq by bombarding the Iraqi nuclear reactor Tamuz 1 that was under construction, on June 7, 1981, there was a vote of condemnation at the UN Security Council. With the vote of the U.S., this pre-meditated attack was declared a clear violation of international law. Resolution 487 of June 19, 1981, condemning Israel, was adopted unanimously. It considered that the Israeli threats to attack nuclear facilities in Iraq and in other countries continue to endanger peace and security in the region and was contrary to international law, and a violation of the Charter of the United Nations.

[343] Steven R. Weisman with Felicity Barringer, "U.S. Seeks 9 Votes From U.N. Council to Confront Iraq", *The New York Times*, February 21, 2003.

[344] In February 2003, George W. Bush's overall job approval rating was down to 54 percent, which was sensibly the same level he enjoyed before the September 11, 2001, terrorist attacks.
Patrick E. Tyler and Janet Elder, "Poll Finds Most in U.S. Support Delaying a War", *The New York Times*, February 14, 2003.
Also, David Sanger with Elizabeth Bumiller, " U.S. Will Ask U.N. to State Hussein has not Disarmed", *The New York Times*, February 14, 2003.

[345] Patrick E. Tyler, "As Cold War Link Itself Grows Cold, Europe Seems to Lose Value for Bush", *The New York Times*, February 12, 2003.

[346] The White House had leaked to the medias damaging disinformation against France. The French ambassador to the United States feld obliged to write a letter to the White House and to members of Congress to denounce eight specific lies that the Pentagon was using to smear France in U.S. public opinion.
Andrea Koppel and John King, "France says it is victim of smear campaign", CNN Washington, *The New York Times*, May 17, 2003.

[347] Patrick E. Tyler, op. cit.

[348] Howard W. French,"U.S. Approach on North Korea Is Straining Alliances in Asia", *The New York Times*, February 24, 2003.

[349] After the war of invasion turned into a guerrilla war, during the summer of 2003, the Bush White House even resorted to character assassination against journalists who sent unfavorable reports. Indeed, it tried to discredit ABC News correspondent Jeffrey Kofman, by smearing him because in his private life he was gay and carried a Canadian passport. An American soldier in Iraq had told him, "*If Donald Rumsfeld was here, I'd ask him for his resignation.*"
Boston Globe columnist H.D.S. Greenway agreed and asked for the dismissal of Secretary of Defense Donald H. Rumsfeld and of his first assistant, Deputy Secretary Paul Wolfowitz, for incalculable damage to U.S. diplomacy.
Maureen Dowd, "Let's Blame Canada", *The New York Times*, July 20, 2003.
H.D.S. Greenway, "Give Rumsfeld and Wolfowitz the Boot", *The Boston Globe*, July 11, 2003.

[350] But the intervention which must have most upset the White House was that of Nelson Mandela. In a speech in Johannesburg, South Africa on January 30, 2003—a speech only sparsely reported in the U.S.—the 1993 Nobel Peace Prize winner lambasted the Bush administration for its war plans in the most severe terms. "*One power with a president who has no foresight and cannot think properly is now wanting to plunge the world into a holocaust...Who are they to decide now they are the policemen of the world? Why is the U.S. behaving so arrogantly?...All that he (Bush) wants in Iraq is oil. It is a tragedy what Bush is doing...If there is a country that has committed unspeakable atrocities in the world, it is the United States of America. They don't care for human beings.*"

Even Pope John Paul II entered the fray and joined the opponents to the Bush-Blair war against Iraq. "*In fact, neither the threat of war nor war itself should be allowed to alienate Christians, Muslims, Buddhists, Hindus and members of other religions...[We should find] a fair and peaceful solution, based on humanitarian and moral principles shared by all the religions of the world.*""

Frances D'Emilio, "Pope: War with Iraq would be tragedy for religion", *USA Today*, February 21, 2003. Also, Reuters, "Pope Urges World to Avoid 'Dramatic Conflict'", *The New York Times*, March 5, 2003.

351 Mister Thorne, "Atheists in Foxholes, Christians in Uniform, *The Humanist*, May/June 2003, pp 19-23.

352 Agence France-Presse, "Les Non Alignés rejettent une action militaire unilatérale des USA en Irak", *Le Monde*, February 23, 2003.

353 Salah Nasrawi, "Arab Summit: Nations reject any U.S. aggression on Iraq", *Associated Press*, March 2, 2003.

354 One U.S. publication which has consistently opposed the war against Iraq is the weekly magazine *The Nation*. See Jonathan Schell, "The Case Against the War", *The Nation*, March 3, 2003.

355 Dafna Linzer, "U.N. discussions end in bitter disagreement", *Associated Press*, February 28, 2003.

356 Agence France-Presse, "La Grande-Bretagne et les Etats-Unis lancent le compte à rebours pour une guerre en Irak", *Le Monde*, Dec. 20, 2002.

357 Kenneth T. Walsh, with Kevin Whitelaw, Mark Mazzetti, David S. Powell and William Boston, "Making The Case", *U.S. News & World Report*, February 10, 2003, p. 24.

358 Ron Fornier, "Bush: Overthrowing Saddam would encourage Mideast peace", *Associated Press*, February 27, 2003.

359 The disinformation coming from the Bush White House and the propaganda distilled by the U.S. media were so effective that in a Times/CBS News survey, 42 percent of Americans believed Saddam Hussein was personally responsible for the attack on the World Trade Center and the Pentagon, and in an ABC News poll, 55 percent believed he gives direct support to al Qaeda.
In a September 6, 2003, Washington Post poll, sixty-nine percent of Americans believed that Saddam Hussein was personally involved in the Sept. 11 attacks, two years after the events, even though there had been

no proof of a link between Iraq and the terrorists' attacks against the United States.
Maureen Dowd, "The Xanax Cowboy", *The New York Times*, March 8, 2003.
*Associated Press*, "poll suggests 69 percent believe Saddam, 9-11 link", September 7, 2003.

[360] Felicity Barringer with David E. Sanger, "U.S. Says Hussein Must Cede Power to Head Off War", *The New York Times*, March 1, 2003.

[361] Some were even advancing the possibility of a hundred-year war! Alan Freeman, "We are at the Start of a Hundred-year War", *The Globe and Mail*, February 14, 2003.

[362] Don Van Natta Jr. and Desmond Butle, "Calls to Jihad Are Said to Lure Hundreds of Militants Into Iraq", *The New York Times*, November 1, 2003.

[363] See Nocholas Lemann, "How It Came To War", *The New Yorker*, March 31, 2003, p.39.

[364] One of the people who was the most involved in war planning, Deputy Defense Secretary Paul Wolfowitz, has acknowledged that in the first weekend after September 11th *"the disagreement was whether [invading Iraq] should be in the immediate response or whether you should concentrate simply on Afghanistan first."*
See Deputy Secretary Wolfowitz' interview with Vanity Fair's Sam Tannenhaus, carried out on May 9, 2003, and published in *Vanity Fair*, June, 2003.

[365] Time.com, May 5, 2002.

[366] From mid-2002 to the first few months of 2003, American air war commanders carried out airstrikes on key command centers, radars and other important military assets in Iraq. The Bush administration was trying to weaken Iraqi air defenses in anticipation of a possible war already planned for 2003. Air war commanders were required to obtain the approval of Defense Secretary Donald H. Rumsfeld if any planned

airstrike was thought likely to result in deaths of more than 30 civilians. More than 50 such strikes were proposed, and all of them were approved. Michael R. Gordon, "U.S. Air Raids in '02 Prepared for War in Iraq", *The New York Times,* July 20, 2003.

367 Many journalists were "embedded" with the U.S.-led forces. For the others, it was made clear what was expected of them. One of them, veteran journalist Peter Arnett was dismissed by NBC News President, Neal Shapiro, for commenting about the war on a state-run Iraqi TV. Arnett had said that the U.S.-led coalition's war plan had failed because of Iraq's resistance.
Peter Johnson and Donna Leinwand, "TV Networks pull Arnett, Riviera", *USA Today,* April 1, 2003, p. 1A.

368 According to an article published on December 8, 2002, high-echelon military officers said the U.S. had enough tanks, warships, aircraft, bombs, and troops in the Persian Gulf region to launch an attack against Iraq in January.
Eric Schmitt, "Buildup Leaves U.S. Military Nearly Set to Start Attack", *The New York Times,* Dec. 8, 2002.

369 See Presidential speech, March 17, 2003.

370 Another reason for a spring 2003 war is that Bush did not want to start his 2004 reelection campaign while in the middle of a war.

371 An American journalist undertook to classify the 10 worst living dictators. He came out with the following list:1- Kim Jong II (South Korea), King Fahd and Crown Prince Abdullah (Saudi Arabia), Saddam Hussein (Iraq), Charles Taylor (Liberia), Than Shwe (Burma), Teodoro Obiang Nguema (Equatorial Guinea), Saparmurad Niyazov (Turmenistan), Muammar Al-Qaddafi (Libya), Fidel Castro (Cuba), and Alexander Lukashenko (Belarus). He could easily have added the name of Robert Mugabe (Zimbabwe), whom he reserved for special mention.
David Wallechinsky, "The 10 Worst Living Dictators", *Parade Magazine,* February 16, 2003, p. 4.

372 Under pressure from the League of Nations, Greece retreated from Albania after 9 days of occupation.

[373] Fearing a larger war, the League of Nations imposed no sanctions on Japan in 1931. In 1935, however, the League imposed a commercial embargo against Italy. Italy left the League of Nations and completed its occupation of Ethiopia. Italy had tried to conquer Ethiopia, "Africa's Switzerland", in1896, but it was repulsed by the army of the Emperor Menelek II. Emperor Haile Selassie I was less fortunate, and Ethiopia became an Italian colony in 1935, until British troops expelled the Italians in 1941.

[374] Patrick E. Tyler, "As Cold War Link Itself Grows Cold, Europe Seems to Lose Value for Bush", *The New York Times*, February 12, 2003.

[375] Paul Koring, "U.S. has double standard, Iraq says", *The Globe and Mail*, Dec. 31, 2002, p. A8.

[376] According to a report from UNICEF, published on Aug. 12, 1999, 500,000 Iraqi children less than 5 years old died between 1991 and 1998, partly because of the economic sanctions. From 1991 to 2002, this would mean 700,000 Iraqi children under 5 years old who have died.
See www.humanite.presse.fr/journal/international, "Les premières victimes de l'embargo ont moins de quinze ans", May 15, 2002.
Also, "Is U.S. really Cruel Toward Ordinary Iraqis?" *The Wall Street Journal*, Nov. 13, 2002, p. A25.

[377] For example, Israel, which is the only nuclear power in the region, is deemed to possess up to 100 nuclear bombs.
William J. Kole, "U.S. singles out Iraq while nukes spread", *Associated Press*, Sept, 11. 2002.

[378] On September 12, 2001, the Security Council adopted Resolution 1368, recognizing "the inherent right" of the United States to individual or collective legitimate defense, in conformity with the Charter. The resolution authorized the U.S. to pursue anti-American terrorists outside its borders. It did not, however, authorize the U.S. to attack other sovereign states nor to overthrow their leaders.
On February 5, 2003, at the U.N. Security Council, Secretary of State Colin Powell attempted to establish a terrorist connection between the Iraqi government and an al Qaeda affliate headed by Abu Musab ak-

Zarqawi. However, none of the key countries represented in the Council were swayed by the circumstantial evidence.
See Michael R. Gordon, "Powell's Case Against Iraq: Piling Up the Evidence", *The New York Times*, February 6, 2003.

[379] Philip Golub and Agnes Levallois, "Washington veut remodeler le Moyen-Orient", *Le Monde*, Sept. 19, 2002.

[380] On January 8, 1918, President Woodrow Wilson announced a policy that is still today considered to be of the greatest importance in the history of the United States. The Wilson program espoused the liberty of all peoples to determine their type of government, the freedom of the seas, and the creation of an international organism to preserve the peace, the League of Nations, the predecessor of the United Nations.

[381] USA Today/CNN poll done after the November, 2002, elections reported that 58% of Americans approved the invasion of Iraq to overthrow Saddam Hussein. Two thirds of the respondants, however, insisted that the U.S. should get the previous authorization from the U.N. before acting.
Richard Benedette, "Poll: Most support war as a last resort", *USA Today*, Nov. 26, 2002, p. 3A.

[382] John Stanton and Wayne Madsen, "The Emergence of the Fascist American Theocratic State", *Center for Research on Globalization*, Washington, D.C., Feb. 17, 2002.

[383] Bob Woodward, *Bush at War*, Simon & Schuster, New York, 2002, p. 302.

[384] For an analysis on how U.S. foreign policy is traditionally geared to guarantee economic growth, see Andrew J. Bacevich, *American Empire, The Realities and Consequences of U.S. Diplomacy*, Harvard University Press, Cambridge, 2003.

[385] Timothy Appleby, "Annan sees no reason for attack on Iraq", *The Globe and Mail*, Jan. 1, 2002, p. A1.

[386] Timothy Appleby, op.cit.

[387] It is a political reality that the Republicans profit more electorally from armed conflicts than the Democrats, on the order of 2 to 1. In September, 2002, for example, after falling to around 60%, Bush's approval rating rose to 67% and higher when he began talking again about Iraq.

See Will Lester,"Republicans have advantage on military issues, run even with Democrats on economy, poll says", *Associated Press*, Sept. 17, 2002.

[388] The Bush administration has been very adept in exploiting the September 11 massacre, for partisan political gain.

Paul Krugman, "Exploiting the Atrocity", *The New York Times*, September 12, 2003.

[389] What Ariel Sharon wanted above all was the exile of Yasser Arafat and a guardianship of the Palestinian Authority. An American war with Iraq could provide the necessary cover to put his plan to work.

Paul Adams, "Israel Operatives practice Abducting Arafat", *The Globe and Mail*, Oct. 4, 2002, p. A10.

[390] In bowing to their pressure, Bush played into the hands of Israel, which tremendously damaged U.S. credibility in the rest of the world.

An example of the close association between Israeli and U.S. interests is the fact that the Bush government was planning joint military operations for the Israeli and American armies in Iraq.

Associated Press, "U.S.Considers Israeli Plan on Iraq", *The New York Times*, Oct. 19, 2002.

[391] Irving Kristol, "The Neoconservative Persuasion," *The Weekly Standard*, August 25, 2003.

[392] In order to exploit, to the maximum, the national trauma of Sept. 11, Bush's advisors drafted a re-election strategy around the third anniversary of the Sept. 11 attacks, in September 2004. For maximum effects, they planned to stage the 2004 Republican Convention in

New York City, from August 30 to September 2. These dates were chosen so the partisan event would flow into the commemorations of the third anniversary of the World Trade Center and Pentagon attacks. They planned to spend the record amount of $200 million on Bush's re-election— twice the amount of his first campaign — even though George W. Bush would face no serious opposition for his party's nomination in 2004.
Adam Nagourney and Richard W. Stevenson, "Bush's Aides Plan Late Campaign Sprint in '04", *The New York Times*, April 22, 2003.

[393]   Quoted in Patrick Jarreau, Sylvie Kauffmann and Mouna Naïm, "Irak: comment l'Amérique s'est enlisée", ["Iraq: How America got entangled."], *Le Monde*, September 17, 2003.

[394]   With the media distracted, Israel could go on building a long wall to carve up and annex huge areas of Palestinian territory.
Greg Myre, "Israel Approves an Expanded Security Barrier", *The New York Times*, October 2, 2003.

[395]   The North Atlantic Treaty Organization (NATO) is a political military defense organization created on April 4, 1949, in order to defend the security of its members and to defuse political crises. In 2003, it had 19 members. However, 7 additional countries were scheduled to join it in 2004.
In 2003, the Bush administration attempted to turn the defensive alliance into an offensive military organization.
Filkins Dexter, "Turkey Backs United States Plans for Iraq", *The New York Times*, February 6, 2003.

[396]   In a Radio-Canada/CBC broadcast on June 9, 2002, two Islamic clerics in London, Abu Qatada and Abu Hamza, admitted that they encouraged the murder of Americans and of Muslims who opposed their jihad.
*CBC/The National*, "The Recruiters", June 9, 2002.

On January 20, 2003, Scotland Yard staged a nighttime raid on the great mosque in Finsbury Park. Several people who were suspected to be in possession of the mortal poison ricin were arrested. Police found a stun gun and canisters of CS gas.
Agence France-Presse, "Raid dans une mosquée londonienne", *Le Monde*, le 20 janvier 2003.

See also Don Van Natta Jr., "London Imam Is Removed as Leader of Mosque",
*The New York Times*, February 5, 2003.

[397] Ed Johnson, "Al-Qaida has 'substantial presence' in Britain, London police chief says", *Associated Press*, February 17, 2003.

[398] Ed Johnson, "Muslims debate their role in the West", *Associated Press*, Sept. 16, 2002.

[399] Marc Roche, "Le lobbying intensif sur le pétrole est à la hauteur de l'enjeu", *Le Monde*, Oct. 31, 2002.

[400] Agence France-Presse, "Moscou menace de lâcher l'Irak", *La Presse*, Dec. 14, 2002, p. B8.

[401] Robert Cottrell and Krishna Guha, "Concern in Washington over Russsian Trade Deal with Iraq", *The Financial Times*, Aug. 19, 2002, p.1.

[402] Carola Hoyos, "Russia Drives Hard Bargain on Iraq Oil", *The New York Times*, Oct. 3, 2002.
Also, Greg Hitt, "Bush and Putin Vow to Support Energy Ventures", *The Wall Street Journal*, Nov. 25, 2002, p. A13.

[403] Germany entered the Security Council at the same time, as a non permanent member, replacing Norway, a traditional U.S. ally. The other new members for the year 2003, were Angola, Chili, Pakistan, and Spain. The countries which were beginning their second year on the Council were Bulgaria, Cameroon, Guinea, Mexico, and Syria.
Germany took over the presidency of the Security Council for the month of February 2003.

[404] Agence France-Presse, "Bras de fer sur l'Irak à l'OTAN", *Le Monde*, February 12, 2003.

[405] In a meeting on February 11, 2003, in New York City, the United States National Security Advisor, Condoleezza Rice, had urged the chief weapons inspectors to present a tough report on Iraq, arguing that time was running short.
Julia Preston with Steven R. Weisman, "France Offering Plan to Expand Iraq Arms Hunt", *The New York Times*, February 12, 2003.

[406] "I have my detractors in Washington. There are bastards who spread things around, of course, who planted nasty things in the media."
Helena Smith, "Blix lashes out at critics, 'bastards' who thwarted work", *The Globe and Mail*, June 11, 2003, p. A13.

[407] Nicholas D. Kristof, "Let me give the White House a hand", *The New York Times*, June 13, 2003.

[408] Louis Charbonneau, "'Proof' that Iraq sought uranium was fake", Reuthers, March 7, 2003.
Nevertheless, this did not stop Vice President Cheney, on March 16, 2003 on "Meet The Press", to declare that "*We believe he [Saddam Hussein] has, in fact, reconstituted nuclear weapons. I think Mr. El Baradei frankly is wrong.*"
Similarly, President George W. Bush himself, on September 12, 2002, in his speech to the UN General Assembly, asserted that "*Right now, Iraq is expanding and improving facilities that were used for the production of biological weapons... Iraq has made several attempts to buy high-strength aluminum tubes used to enrich uranium for a nuclear weapon.*"

[409] The U.S. could block such a peace plan by using its veto.
Thom Shanker, "Rumsfeld Rebukes U.N. and NATO on Approach to Baghdad", *The New York Times*, February 9, 2003.

[410] Phillippe Le Cœur, "Les parlementaires semblent se résoudre à l'idée d'une intervention américaine en Iraq", *Le Monde*, Jan. 3, 2003.

[411] As a manifestation of his insensibility towards Europe, in 2001, George W. Bush appointed a new ambassador to France, Howard Leach, who did not speak French. One can imagine the uproar if this had been the reverse.
Vivienne Walt, "French see Bush as the ugly American", *USA Today*,

February 14, 2003, 13A.

[412] The conference at Yalta, in February 1945, saw the three victorious leaders of World War II—Franklin D. Roosevelt (USA), Winston Churchill (Great Britain), and Joseph Stalin (Soviet Union)—divide up Europe and take the reponsibility, with France, of governing vanquished Germany.

[413] The U.S.-Britain duo could not obtain the necessary 9 votes out 15 at the Security Council, and two permanent members, Russia and France, publicly indicated they were ready to veto any resolution calling for a military invasion of Iraq.

[414] Ever since the days of Harry Truman, who was the first president to go to war (against Korea) without congressional approval, modern-day presidents have interpreted articles of the Constitution vesting the President with executive power and making him commander-in-chief as giving him sole war-making authority.

[415] David Stout with Timothy O'Brien, "In Rebuff to U.N., President Says U.S. and Allies Have No Choice", *The New York Times*, March 17, 2003.

[416] In America's 1.4 million-strong military, visible minorities are overrepresented and the wealthy and the upperclass are essentially absent. While whites account for three out of five soldiers, the U.S. military has become a powerful magnet for blacks, and black women in particular, who now outnumber white women in the Army with 46 percent of all women in the military.
See, David M. Halbfinger and Steven A. Holmes, "Military Mirrors Working-Class America", *The New York Times*, March 30, 2003.

[417] "Shock and Awe" was the name given to the U.S. military strategy to conquer Iraq.

[418] At the March 23, 2003, 75th annual Academy Awards, author Michael Moore had the courage to state the obvious, "Our fictitious president... conducting a war for fictitious reasons." He was booed and

hissed.
William Keck, "Heaven and war politics move the spirit awards", *USA Today*, March 24, 2003, p. 2D.

[419] Dexter Filkins, "In Baghdad, Free of Hussein, a Day of Mayhem", *The New York Times*, April 12, 2003.

[420] "Move to dissolve Iraqi army has fueled unrest, some say ", *Los Angeles Times,* August 24, 2003.
See also: David Rieff, "Blueprint for a mess", *The New York Times*, November 2, 2003.

[421] As an indication of U.S. priorities, the National Museum of Iraq was left unprotected against looting, after the collapse of civil authorities in Baghdad, but the Bush administration made sure the Iraqi Oil Ministry building was protected by an entire company of Marines, along with a half dozen amphibious assault vehicles. The same military protection was quickly provided to shield the Iraqi oil wells. Precious heirlooms, books and artifacts from a 7,000-year-old civilization were lost. The Bush administration ignored repeated requests of scholars and archaeologists that the occupying forces must protect Iraqi history in the museum as zealously as they protected Iraqi wealth in the oil wells.
David Keyes, "History's Treasure House in Ruins", *The Globe and Mail*, April 15, 2003, p.R1.

[422] Editorial, "War and Peace: Anarchy in the Streets", *The New York Times*, April 12, 2003.

[423] Associated Press, "Maintaining civil order a duty, UN tells U.S. and Britain", *The Globe and Mail,* April 11, 2003.

[424] President Bush, in his 2003 State of the Union address, had described a vast Iraqi weapons program and talked about several mobile labs, 30,000 munitions, 500 tons of chemical weapons, 25,000 liters of anthrax and 38,000 liters of botulinum toxin. These weapons had supposedly been deployed all over Iraq and had been given to field commands to use in combat.

[425] Robert Burns, "U.S. defends intelligence on Iraq arms", *Associated Press*, June 7, 2003.

[426] This is because the deleted pages were so embarrassing. Indeed, these pages explained in detail how the United States supplied Iraq with biological and chemical weapons, during the 1980's, and the involvement of twenty-four U.S-based corporations and key American political figures in the Reagan and Bush I administrations.
Michael I. Niman, "What Bush Doesn't Want You to Know About Iraq", *The Humanist*, March-April, 2003.

[427] Jeff Sallot, "Iraqi nuclear plant searched, public may be at risk, UN says", *The Globe and Mail*, April 100, 2003, p.A4.

[428] Amazingly, four months after the war, in a press conference on the 14th of July, 2003, George W. Bush went so far as to deny that the U.N. inspection teams were in Iraq. "*We gave [Saddam Hussein] a chance to allow the inspectors in, and he wouldn't let them in. And, therefore, after a reasonable request, we decided to remove him from power . . . *"
Inspectors were, of course, on the ground in Iraq for over three months, until they were pulled out because the U.S. was going to war.
See, "President reaffirms strong position on Liberia", White House, July 14, 2003.

[429] On Oct. 8, 2002, as reported by Knight Ridder newspapers, U.S. intelligence officials charged that "*the administration squelches dissenting views, and that intelligence analysts are under intense pressure to produce reports supporting the White House's argument that Saddam poses such an immediate threat to the United States that pre-emptive military action is necessary.*"
Paul Krugman, "Who's Unpatriotic Now?", *The New York Times*, July 22, 2003.

[430] Paul Krugman, "Passing It Along", *The New York Tmes*, July 18, 2003.

[431] Barton Gellman, "Search in Iraq Fails to Find Nuclear Threat", *The Washington Post*, October 26, 2003.

[432] These teams inspected more than 350 suspected sites in Iraq but to no avail. No stockpiles of unconventional weapons were found. Judith Miller, "A Chronicle of Confusion in the Hunt for Hussein's Weapons", *The New York Times*, July 20, 2003. Also, David E. Sanger, "A Reckoning: Iraqi Arms Report Poses Political Test for Bush", *The New York Times*, October 3, 2003.

[433] *The Los Angeles Times*, June 7, 2003.

[434] Editorial, "The Quest for Illicit Weapons", *The New York Times*, April 18, 2003.

[435] Elisabeth Bumiller, "Cold Truths Are Lurking After Pomp on Carrier", *The New York Times*, May 2, 2003.

[436] On May 1, 2003, PBS's Newshour even had a guest, a military novelist, who argued that civilians of countries attacked by the United States are "guilty civilians", and they should be attacked and killed just as the military. "I wonder if precision bombing is doing enough damage to a country", said the guest novelist. ..."The justification for killing so many [Germans and Japanese during World War II] was because ...they weren't innocent civilians. They were guilty civilians. Precision bombs avoid civilian casualties and there's a theology built up around this, and I'm not sure that wars are going to be won with precision bombs that can be carried into pieces that mean anything."
"Lessons of War", Newshour, *Public Broadcasting System (PBS)*, May 1, 2003.

[437] Kurt Eichenwald, "U.S. Indicts 11 Former Enron Executives", *The New York Times*, May 2, 2003.

[438] British Prime Minister Tony Blair had given his support for a war against Iraq as soon as April 2002, when he met George W. Bush at his ranch in Crawford, Texas.
See Jean-Pierre Langellier, "M. Blair a donné son accord à la guerre en Irak dès avril 2002" [Mr. Blair gave his go-ahead for a war against Iraq as early as April 2002], *Le Monde*, September 19, 2003.
See also: Sheryl Gay Stolberg and Adam Nagourney, "Democrats Split

on Challenging Iraq Arms Hunt", *The New York Times*, June 14, 2003.

[439] Bush's speech on the the USS Abraham Lincoln aircraft carrier, on May 1st, 2003.

[440] James Risen and Douglas Jehl, "Expert Said to Tell Legislators He Was Pressed to Distort Some Evidence", *The New York Times*, June 25, 2003.
Douglas Jehl, "Agency Disputes View of Trailers as Labs", *The New York Times*, June 26, 2003.

[441] Paul Krugman, "Matters of Emphasis", *The New York Times*, April 29, 2003.

[442] In June 2001, a meeting was held at the Washington Carnegie Endowment for Peace Institute (CEIP) with representatives of most of the key U.S. governement, military and security agencies and departments. Iraq's weaponry was discussed and the conclusion was that such weapons posed no urgent global threat. Iraq had no nuclear capability and little in the way of chemical and biological weapons. The little Iraq had was deemed to be of "limited military effectiveness."
Sunil Ram, "No Weapons and a Funeral", *The Globe and Mail*, August 6, 2003, p. A13.

[443] Wolfowitz added another tactical reason to invade Iraq: the need to withdraw U.S. troops from Saudi Arabia, where their presence has been one of al Qaeda's biggest grievances, and to control Arab Middle East from the centrallly located Iraq. Indeed, as the U.S. presence in Saudi Arabia and Turkey became more problematic, Iraq appeared a well situated place to relocate American Middle Eastern military bases.

There were four official reasons given by Wolfowitz to go to war against Iraq, "there have always been three fundamental concerns. One is weapons of mass destruction, the second is support for terrorism, the third is the criminal treatment of the Iraqi people. Actually I guess you could say there's a fourth overriding one which is the connection between the first two...The third one by itself, as I think I said earlier, is a reason to help the Iraqis but it's not a reason to put American kids' lives at risk, certainly not on the scale we did it".
Basically, however, the alleged existence of weopons of mass destruction

was the main justification for war that could be sold to Congress, to the U.S. public, to allies and to the 15 members of the United Nations Security Council.
Sam Tannenhaus, *Vanity Fair*, June, 2003.
See also the declarations of former Treasury Secretary Paul H. O'Neill in Ron Suskind's book, *The Price of Loyalty*, 2004.


444  Besides having been the chief architect of the U.S-led invasion of Iraq, Paul Wolfowitz also carried a quasi judicial responsability, that was to select among the 680 prisoners held at the Guantanamo base those who can be indicted and accused before U.S. military courts. Mr. Wolfowitz was also entitled to choose the members of the tribunals.
See, "Aux Etats-Unis, des juristes s'indignent de la situation des prisonniers de Guantanamo" ["In the U.S., lawyers are scandalized by the prisoners' fate at Guantanamo base"], *Le Monde*, June 30, 2003.
Neil A. Lewis, "Six Detainees Soon May Face Military Trials", *The New York Times*, July 4, 2003.


445  As an example of how badly U.S. medias informed Americans about the war against Iraq, most national newspapers, with the notable exception of the *Washington Post* and of the *Washington Times*, failed to report Rumsfeld's confession.
Dana Milbank and Mike Allen, "Bush and Rumsfeld Defend Use of Prewar Intelligence on Iraq ", *The Washington Post*, July 10, 2003.
Stephen Dinan, "9/11 spurred war, Rumsfeld says", *The Washington Times*, July 10, 2003.
Julian Borger, "Rumsfeld shifts stance on Iraq weapons", *The Guardian*, July 10, 2003.


446  Nicholas D. Kristof, "16 Words, and Counting", *The New York Times*, July 15, 2003.


447  James Risen, "Iraq Said to Have Tried to Reach Last-Minute Deal to Avert War", *The New York Times*, November 6, 2003.


448  "Guiding Principles for U.S. Post-Conflict Policy in Iraq", Report of an Independent Working Group Cosponsored by the Council on Foreign Relations and the James A. Baker III Institute for Public Policy of Rice University, December 2002.
The report advised the Bush administration not to impose a too heavy

hand on Iraq, because the impression could last that the Iraqi people had not been liberated but defeated, and that the entire operation against Iraq was undertaken for imperialist, rather than disarmament, reasons.

[449] Douglas Jehl and Judith Miller, "Draft Report Said to Cite No Success in Iraq Arms Hunt", *The New York Times*, September 25, 2003.

[450] For an account of how Vice-president Dick Cheney, his chief of staff Lewis Libby, and Defense hard-liners Paul Wolfowitz and Douglas Feith, built up the case to invade Iraq, see, Tamara Lipper, Richard Wolffe and Roy Gutman, "How Dick Cheney sold the War", *Newsweek*, November 17, 2003.

[451] For an excellent assessment of the case, see: Spencer Ackerman and John B. Judis, "The First Casualty", *The New Republic*, June 19, 2003.

[452] Carl Hulse and David E. Sanger, "New Criticism on Prewar Use of Intelligence",*The New York Times,* September 29, 2003.

[453] See David Corn , *The Lies of George W. Bush: Mastering the Politics of Deception*, Crown Publishers, 2003.

[454] Paul Krugman, "You Say Tomato", *The New York Times,* July 29, 2003.

[455] Remarks by the President After Meeting with Members of the Congressional Conference Committee on Energy Legislation, September 17, 2003. Saddam Hussein was captured on December 13, 2003.

[456] On August 28, 2003, President George W. Bush signed Executive Order 13315, giving complete control of Iraq's state assets to the U.S. Treasury. It was published in the Federal Register on September 3, 2003.

[457] It was left to pro-administration journalists to attempt, after the fact, to outline "good" reasons to launch a war of choice without a United Nations mandate. These so-called good reasons were: 1- that Saddam

Hussein was a bad dictator who could one day acquire weapons of mass destruction; 2- that there was a need to make Iraq a more "decent" place; and 3- that a "message" had to sent to neighboring countries not to encourage suicide bombers and fanatical religious extremists. None of these "good" reasons would have allowed a military invasion of Iraq under international law.
Thomas L. Friedman, "The War Over the War", *The New York Times*, August 3, 2003.

[458] A CBS News survey conducted in July 2003 indicated that 56 percent of those polled believed the Bush administration overestimated Iraq's weapons of mass destruction and less than a majority said the war would be worth its costs if such weapons were not found.
James Dao, "Iraq Questions Shake Even Some of Bush's Faithful", *The New York Times*, July 17, 2003.

[459] In the months leading to the war, President Bush said that Iraq was able to deliver biological weapons via unmanned aerial vehicles (UAVs). This also was propaganda overkill. Declassified Air Force intelligence estimates indicate that such a threat was nonexistent.
David Rogers, "Bush Oversold Drove Threat", *The Wall Street Journal*, September 10, 2003, p. A4.

[460] There were personal tragedies connected with the scam. For instance, British Weapons Advisor David Kelly committed suicide, after appearing before a Parliamentary committee in mid-July, 2003 to face questions over a British Broadcasting Corp. report that British government aides doctored intelligence on Iraqi weapons to strengthen the case for war.
The Associated Press, "British Weapons Advisor Reported Missing", *The New York Times*, July 18, 2003.

[461] As a comparison, here are the costs of other wars in billions of 2002 dollars: World War I (1914-18) $191 billion; World War II (1939-45) $2,896 billion; Korean War (1950-53) $336 billion; Vietnam War (1964-73) $494 billion; Persian Gulf War (1990-91) $76 billion.
Source:Center for Strategic and Budgetary Assessments.

[462] The Director of the Office of Management and Budget, Mitchell E. Daniels Jr., calculated that the fiscal cost of a war with Iraq would be between $50 and $60 billion.

Elizabeth Bumiller, "White House Cuts Estimate of Cost of War with Iraq", *The New York Times*, Dec. 311, 2002.

[463] "Calculating the Consequences", *The Economist*, Nov. 30, 2002, p. 63.

[464] The costs that the United States would have to shoulder as an occupying power in Iraq are analysed in James Fallows, "The Fifty-First State?", *The Atlantic Monthly*, November 2002, p. 53-64.

[465] Agence France Presse, "U.S. said divided on Iraqi oil future", *The Globe and Mail*, February 10, 2003.
Because of the need for oil revenues in Iraq, it is unlikely that the U.S. government would let oil prices plummet after the planned increase in Iraqi oil production. It would rather persuade Saudi Arabia to decrease its production in order to maintain oil prices.

[466] "Study: War with Iraq could cost U.S. $2 trillion over a decade", *Associated Press*, Dec. 8, 2002.

[467] Bloomberg News, "U.S. economy shows no sign of 'double dip' back into recession", *The Gazette*, Dec. 18, 2002, p. B5.

[468] Face the Nation, *CBS*, Sunday, February 16, 2003.

[469] Coincidentally, the 54-year Kondratieff cycle was scheduled to hit its trough in 2003, having followed its long wave of inflation-disinflation-deflation since 1949.

[470] The amounts saved in lower energy costs for the U.S. economy, as a result of a military take-over of Iraq, can be calculated as follows. It can be postulated that the U.S. economy will continue consuming 20 million barrels of oil a day indefinitely, or 7,3 billion barrels yearly, and will continue importing a minimum of 50 percent of this amount. At a base price of $20 a barrel, the annual cost of oil consumption is $146 billion and the imports amount to $73 billion.
In the absence of a U.S. take-over of Iraqi oil reserves, we initially

assume that the world price of crude will rise to $40 within a decade and will remain at this level indefinitely. At this price, U.S. consumers would have to pay $400 million more for oil each day, and imports cost $200 million more daily.
On a yearly basis, U.S. imports of oil would increase, at a minimum, by $73 billion. Therefore, a base price of $20 a barrel rather than $40, and taking a discount rate of 5%, translates into a net total discounted savings of $1,460 billion for the U.S. economy.
If the real price for petroleum were to reach $50 a barrel on average over the entire 21st Century (without military intervention), and assuming that the United States will have to increase its imports of crude to 75 percent of total consumption, the additional import cost of oil would be $375 million a day or $136,875 billion on a yearly basis. A $20 base price rather than $50 for a barrel of oil would translate into a net total discounted savings of $3,285 trillion or $3,285 billion, for the U.S. economy.

[471] "Several of the companies involved in the closed-door bidding, allowed in times of a national crisis under federal procurement laws, have close ties to the White House or were major contributors to the Bush presidential campaign. "
Stephen J. Glain and Robert Schlesinger, "Halliburton unit expands war-repair role", *The Boston Globe*, July 10, 2003.

[472] There was also an oil bonus for Israel. An Iraqi oil pipeline passing through Jordan and ending in Israel, and which had been closed by the government of Saddam Hussein, was going to be reopened after a victorious U.S.-led war against Iraq.

[473] For estimates of direct military costs of a U.S.-led war against Iraq and the post-war occupation of that country, see Steve Kosiak, "Potential Cost of a War with Iraq and Its Post-War Occupation", Center for Strategic and Budgetary Assessments, Washington D.C., February 25, 2003.

[474] Scott Taylor, "Gulf War Syndrome: The weapon we gave Iraq", *The Globe and Mail*, February 17, 2003, p. A11.

[475] "Collateral Damage: The health and environmental costs of war on Iraq", Report, Medical Association for the Prevention of War on the

"Health and Environmental consequences of a new war against Iraq", 2002. (www.medact.org/tbx/pages/sub.cfm?id=556)

[476] Agence Science-Presse, "Des scientifiques contre la guerre", *La Presse*, Dec. 15, 2002, p. F6.

[477] Eric Schmitt and Elisabeth Bumiller, "U.S. General Sees Plan to Shock Iraq Into Surrendering", *The New York Times*, March 5, 2003.

[478] Tristan Péloquin, "Les soldats irakiens meurent par milliers", *La Presse*, April 6, 2003, p. A6.

[479] Matthew L. Wald, "Senator Questions Security at Nuclear Arms Laboratories", *The New York Times*, June 23, 2003. Also, "Senate Votes To Lift Ban On Producing Nuclear Arms", *The New York Times*, May 21, 2003.

[480] The inhuman character of modern weapons is highlighted by a report from Human Rights Watch. Cluster bombs are particularly devastating. They are dropped from an airplane, and at a precise altitude, they let loose a cluster of 202 smaller bombs which fall to the ground on small parachutes. They explose when they hit the ground, sending deadly fragments, capable of killing people and even penetrating tanks or personnel transport vehicles over an oval surface of 120 meters by 250 meters. When the little bombs don't explode, they become *de facto* anti-personnel bombs.
According to Human Rights Watch, 69% of the victims of these bombs in Afghanistan in 2001-2002, were children.
Vernon Loeb, "U.S. accused of illegal bombing in Afghanistan", *Associated Press*, Dec. 18, 2002.

[481] Patrick E. Tyler, "Baghdad Bombed; Desert Skirmishes Stretch 350 Miles", *The New York Times*, March 28, 2003.
According to Iraqbodycount.org, the U.S.-led coalition killed 2,500 civilians during the 2003 Iraq War and thousands of Iraki soldiers.

[482] Alan Freeman, "U.S. soldiers fire on Iraqis, killing several", *The Globe and Mail*, April 30, 2003, p.A8.

<sup>483</sup> Kenneth Roth, "Give Iraqis real justice—not a U.S. puppet show", *The Globe and Mail*, April 10, 2003, p. A19.

<sup>484</sup> Indictments for war crimes and for crimes against humanity can be presented at the International Criminal Court by any of the 89 countries which have ratified the creation of the court. In Belgium, courts used to be empowered to judge alleged war crimes. In March 2003, for example, the representatives of seven Iraqi families filed a complaint naming George H. Bush, Colin Powell, Dick Cheney and Norman Schwarzkopf for unlawful deaths of loved ones during the 1991 Gulf War, even though the latter was legal under the U.N. Charter. In June 2003, accusations were also levied against George W. Bush and Tony Blair for war crimes in Iraq. On July 12, 2003, however, a new Belgian government, under pressure from Washington and under the threat of having NATO's Headquarters moved, modified the 1993 law of "universal competence" to make it apply only to Belgian residents.
See Dan Bilefsky, "Bushes on Trial in Belgium? It is Unlikely, but Brussels Still Worries", *The Wall Street Journal*, March 28, 2003, p. A11.

<sup>485</sup> In 1946, Judge Robert Jackson considered the initiation of a war of aggression a "supreme international crime".
Karim Benessaieh, "Bush et Rumsfeld traités de criminels de guerre", *La Presse*, 2 mai 2003, p. A7.

<sup>486</sup> Edmund L. Andrews and Susan Sachs, "Iraq's slide into lawlessness squanders good will for U.S.", *The New York Times*, May 18, 2003.

<sup>487</sup> Jack Beatty, "A war against Iraq could be the most catastrophic blunder in U.S. history", *The Atlantic Monthly*, February 5, 2003.

<sup>488</sup> Doug Saunders, "U.S. in guerrilla war, general says", *The Globe and Mail*, July 17, 2003.

<sup>489</sup> See, "Army chief: Force to occupy Iraq massive", *USA Today*, February 25, 2003.
Also, David Rieff, "Blueprint for a mess", *The New York Times*,

November 2, 2003.

[490]   The initial cost of the invasion was $20 billion, with another projected cost of $12 billion until the September 30 end date for fiscal year 2003, for a total of some $32 billion in direct outlays. It was also estimated that keeping an occupation force of 75,000 troops in Iraq would cost the United States another $17 billion a year.


[491]   The Defense Department comptroller, Dov Zakheim, estimated that military operations had cost more than $10 billion, personnel and personnel support costs had approached $7 billion, and munitions and equipment costs had topped $3 billion.
Richard W. Stevenson with Felicity Barringer, "Bush Urging U.N. to Lift Sanctions Imposed on Iraq". *The New York Times*, April 17, 2003.


[492]   Nassan Hafidh, "Iraqi start talks on choosing new oil minister", *The Globe and Mail,* April 21, 2003, p. B5.


[493]   Agence France-Presse, "Saddam renversé, un général américain sera placé à la tête du pays", *La Presse,* April 5, 2003, p. A12.


[494]

Associated Press, "Putin says Iraq invasion illegal", *The Globe and Mail,* April 12, 2003.


[495]   Douglas Jehl with Jane Perlez, "Pentagon Sending a Team of Exiles to Help Run Iraq", *The New York Times*, April 26, 2003.


[496]   Felicity Barringer and Neela Banerjee, "Who'll Control Iraq's Oil?", *The New York Times,* April 9, 2003.


[497]   Bhushan Bahree, "No crash seen for oil", *The Globe and Mail*, April 10, 2003, p. B11.


[498]   It seems that the bidding to rebuild Iraq's oil industry was rigged in favor of Halliburton, the company formerly headed by Vice President

Dick Cheney.
Influence peddling seemed indeed to be rampant in Bush's White House.
Mr. Joe M. Allbaugh, President Bush's campaign manager in 2000 and the director of the Federal Emergency Management Agency until March 2003, headed a company, New Bridge Strategies, whose purpose was to be a middleman to advise other companies that seek taxpayer-financed business, especially contracts in Iraq, a country that represented "... *opportunities of such an unprecedented nature and scope*".
Douglas Jehl, "Washington Insiders' New Firm Consults on Contracts in Iraq", *The New York Times*, September 30, 2003.
Neela Banerjee, "Rivals Say Halliburton Dominates Iraq Oil Work", *The New York Times*, August 8, 2003.
Also, "Halliburton, principal bénéficiaire de la reconstruction de l'Irak" ["Halliburton is the main beneficiary of reconstruction contracts in Iraq"], *Le Monde*, June 20, 2003.

[499] In 2003, Iraq's reconstruction remained firmly under White House control. This was in sharp contrast to what President Harry S. Truman did at the time of the Marshall Plan. Truman was very concerned about profiteering in the name of patriotism. To insure that the plan would not become a boondoggle, the Marshall Plan funds were administered by an agency independent of the White House.
Paul Krugman, "Who's Sordid Now?", *The New York Times*, September 30, 2003.

[500] Felicity Barringer with Steven R. Weisman, "U.S. Will Ask U.N. to Back Control by Allies in Iraq", *The New York Times*, May 9, 2003.

[501] Patrick Brethour, "Iraq a field of dreams for big oil firms", *The Globe and Mail*, April 12, 2003, p. B1.

[502] Patrick Brethour, ibid.

[503] In Germany, in 1945, the country was divided into four sectors and was under military rule during four years. In 1949, Germany was divided into two countries and both countries, East and West Germany, recovered their full sovereignty in 1955.

[504] Laurent Zecchini, "La perspective d'une intervention de l'Alliance

atlantique en Irak se précise", *Le Monde*, April 29, 2003.
After Kosovo, on August 11, 2003, NATO accepted a new mission outside of Europe and took over the command of security forces in Kabul, in Afghanistan.

505 See the excellent documentary by Martin Smith, "Truth, War, and Consequences", *PBS, Frontline,* October 9, 2003.

506 Ms Bodine lasted only three weeks on the job before being replaced. Neil King Jr., "U.S. to Utilize Iraqi Soldiers in Rebuilding Postwar Nation", *The Wall Street Journal,* March 12, 2003, p. A6.

507 *Agence France-Presse,* op. cit.

508 Kellogg Brown & Root (KBR), a subsidiary of Halliburton, obtained a contract from the U.S. Army Corps of Engineers, on March 24, 2003, without a bidding process, and only four days after the beginning of the war, in order to extinguish any fire in Iraqi oil fields. The contract also gave the Halliburton group a concession on Iraqi oil.
General Robert Flowers, head of the Army Corps of Engineers confirmed that KBR was not only expected to put outany fire, but was also granted the responsability of *"administering the oil facilities and of selling future oil outputs"*.
Patrick Jarreau, "Halliburton a obtenu la concession d'une partie du pétrole irakien" [Halliburton has been granted part of Iraqi oil"] , *Le Monde*, May 9, 2003.

509 Thom Shanker and Eric Schmitt,"Pentagon Expects Long-Term Access to Four Key Bases in Iraq", *The New York Times*, April 20, 2003.

510 In May 2003, the U.S. opposed the project of an Arab-backed U.N. resolution ridding the Middle East of weapons of mass destruction.
Israel is widely believed to have nuclear weapons and is not party to global treaties aimed at controlling the spread of nuclear, chemical or biological weapons. On Iraqi bases, it is likely U.S. forces would maintain weapons of mass destruction.
Associated Press, "Powell Rejects Syrian Weapons Proposal", *The New York Times*, May 3, 2003.

[511] In the Middle East as elsewhere, the possibility of perpetual war is present. A new war could be launched each year by the United States, no matter the damage that such instability would do to the world economy. Since the demise of the Soviet Union, the balance of power as a means of containing conflict has been upset, allowing the United States, as the sole surviving empire, to launch military incursions wherever and whenever it wished." Citing the bombing of the United Nations headquarters in Baghdad two days before, which had killed 23 people, the Bush administration made a move, on August 21, 2003, to have the Security Council authorize other nations to send troops to Iraq, but without the U.S. relinquishing one inch of control over the country. France's deputy ambassador, Michel Duclos, gave an answer, *"Sharing the burden and responsibility in a world of equal and sovereign nations also means sharing information and authority."*
Felicity Barringer, "U.S. Presses U.N. Members to Bear More of Iraq Burden", *The New York Times*, August 22, 2003.

[512] Jeff Gerth, "Report Offered Bleak Outlook About Iraq Oil", *The New York Times*, October 5, 2003.

[513] Initially, the Coalition Provisional Authority in Iraq, managed by Paul Bremer, was able to operate partly on seized Iraqi banking assets, and the hope was that future oil revenues would cover future expenditures. However, with widespead sabotage and looting in the Iraki oil industry, expected oil earnings were clearly insufficient to rebuild the country and cover the costs of repair and of protection of the oil infrastructures at the same time.
Regarding the cost of maintaining a permanent American military force in Iraq, estimates varied between $19 billion a month for 106,000 troops and $29 billion if two new divisions had to be created.

[514] Anxious not to lose too much public support for its war in Iraq, the Bush administration ordered that there should be no media coverage nor ceremonies surrounding the arrivals of dead U.S. soldiers at air bases. News coverage and photography of dead soldiers' homecomings were formally forbidden.
See, Dana Milbank, "Curtains Ordered for Media Coverage of Returning Coffins ", *The Washington Post,* October 21, 2003, p. A23.

[515] Many books have also documented the official lies advanced during

the Vietnam War. See Neil Sheehan, *A Bright Shining Lie,* 1988.

[516] A quick precipated American exit from Iraq could either plunge that country into open civil war, or insure that the country turns theocratic, with Islam as state religion.
See, Steven R. Weisman and Carl Hulse, "In U.S., Fears Are Voiced of a Too-Rapid Iraq Exit", The New York Times, November 14, 2003.

[517] Douglas Jehl, "U.S. Now Signals It Might Consider U.N. Force in Iraq", *The New York Times*, August 28, 2003.

[518] Brian Knowlton, "At U.N., Bush Stands Firm on Iraq, but Also Asks for Help", *The New York Times*, September 23, 2003.

[519] Timothy Appleby, "Turkey agrees to send troops to Iraq", *The Globe and Mail,* October 7, 2003.
Finally, the Turkish government elected not to send troops to Iraq.
David E. Sanger, "With a U.S. Nod, Turkey Says It Won't Send Force to Iraq", *The New York Times*, November 8, 2003.

[520] At the time, there were 24,000 non-American troops in Iraq, but almost half of them were British.

[521] Felicity Barringer with David E. Sanger, "U.S. Drafts Plan for U.N. to Back a Force for Iraq", *The New York Times*, September 4, 2003.

[522] Russia indicated it could be accommodating if some Iraqi oil contracts were to be forthcoming and could even be persuaded to send troops to Iraq to "protect" its oil specialists in the country.
Neela Banerjee, "Russia Sends Message to U.S. About Iraqi Oil Contracts", *The New York Times,* September 27, 2003.

[523] Felicity Barringer, "Unanimous Vote by U.N.'s Council Adopts Iraq Plan", *T.he New York Times,* October 17, 2003.

[524] David E. Sanger, " Bush Thanks Japan for Iraq Aid", *The New York*

*Times*, October 18, 2003.


[525] Editoral, "Presidential Character", *The New York Times*, September 9, 2003.


[526] Brent Scowcroft and George H. Bush, *A World Transformed,* 1998. Quoted by Andy Rooney, "If I Were Bush's Speechwriter", *CBS* 60 Minutes, November 2, 2003.


[527] Richard T. Cooper, "General Casts War In Religious Terms", *The Los Angeles Times,* October 16, 2003.
Suzanne Goldenberg, "US defends role for evangelical Christian," *The Guardian,* October 17, 2003.


[528] The zealots of the Southern Baptist Convention prepared to walk in the bloody steps of soldiers to profit from the disarray and fear of the newly conquered people. Thus, political imperialism risked being twinned with some sort of religious imperialism.
At the same time, far from becoming a free and peaceful society after the U.S.-led invasion, occupied Iraq shows tendencies to change from a largely secular nation into a totalitarian and radically fundamentalist Islamic country. For instance, under the previous dictatorship, Christians were allowed to sell alcohol and were protected from Muslim religious extremists who wanted to apply Sharia laws. Since the U.S.-led occupation, such tolerance is disappearing. In Shiite southern Iraq, in particular, almost every liquor shop has been forcibly closed. And even worse, people selling liquor are summarily executed by self-appointed Islamist vigilantes." Nicholas D. Kristof, "Cover Your Hair", *The New York Times,* June 24, 2003.


[529] Suzanne Goldenberg, "Abduction, rape drive the women of Iraq indoors", *The Globe and Mail,* October 11, 2003, p. A12.


[530] Nicholas D. Kristof, op. cit.
See also: Rémy Ourdan, "Les Irakiennes, premières victimes du chaos politique et social de l'après-Saddam", ["Women, the first victims of the political and social chaos in post-Saddam Iraq"], *Le Monde,* September 17, 2003.

[531]   Neil MacFarquhar, "Long Ruthlessly Secular, Iraq Sees Fervent Islamic Resurgence", *The New York Times,* October 24, 2003.


[532]   For a description of the workings of Nazi Germany, see: William L. Shirer, *The Rise and Fall of the Third Reich: A History of Nazi Germany,* Touchstone Books, 1990 (First edition, 1960).
Also, Albert Speer, *Inside the Third Reich: Memoirs,* Simon and Schuster, 1997.


[533]   On May 10, 1933, in Germany, the Nazis undertook the auto-de-fe of "forbiden and prohibited books", under the leadership of the minister of Information and Propaganda, Joseph Goebbels. Adoph Hitler had gained power on January 30, 1933.


[534]   In early 2003, Natalie Maines, lead singer for the Dixie Chicks, criticized President Bush for his war plans against Iraq. Heeding the call of far-right radio stations, a crowd gathered in Louisiana to watch a 33,000-pound tractor smash a collection of Dixie Chicks CD's, tapes and other paraphernalia.
Since 1996, when the Telecommunications Act of 1996 removed many restrictions on media ownership, many U.S. radio stations have been taken over by neo-conservative chains, some of them owning more than one thousand local stations, such as Cumulus Media and Clear Channel Communications. As a consequence, the U.S. population is subjected to an unprecedented barrage of unbalanced politico-religious propaganda.


[535]   President Bush, like his father, is a member of the secret Masonic society Skull and Bones. In his book *A Charge to Keep,* Bush wrote that he joined the Skull and Bones during his last year at Yale. He mentioned that he couldn't say more about it than that he had made 14 new friends.
George W. Bush, *A Charge to Keep,* Morrow, New York, 1999.
— Skull and Bones is a charitable tax-exempt secret society. Its purpose is to give favors to members for jobs and influence. President Bush Jr. named five fellow members to his administration.
Morley Safer, "Skull & Bones", *CBS 60 Minutes,* October 5, 2003.
Ron Rosenbaum, "At Skull and Bones, Bush's Secret Club Initiates Ream Gore ", *The New York Observer,* April 23, 2001.
Also, Alexandra Robbins, *Secrets of the Tomb: Skull and Bones, the Ivy League and the Hidden Paths of Power,* Little, Brown and Company, 2002.

[536] Paul M. Kennedy, *The Rise and Fall of Great Powers: Economic Change and Military Conflict from 1500-2000*, Vintage Books, New York, 1989.

[537] On this subject, see the excellent book by Joseph A. Tainter, *The Collapse of Complex Societies*, 1988.

[538] Originally the term "barbarian" meant someone who could not speak Greek.

[539] Robert Mantran, (dir.) *Histoire de l'empire Ottoman*, Fayard, Paris, 1989, 810 pages.

[540] The empire which lasted the longest was the Byzantine or Eastern Roman Empire. It began in 330 A.D. when Emperor Constantine, newly converted to Christianity, moved the headquarters of the Roman Empire from Rome to Constantinople. This empire ended in 1453 when Constantinople felt to the Turks. The date 330 A.D. also marks the transformation of the Roman Empire into a divine right monarchy. Its golden "Hellenic" age, however, lasted from 641 to 1204, the latter date being that of its overrun by the barons of the 4th Catholic Crusade, which marked the beginning of its decadence.

[541] Paul M. Kennedy, op. cit.

[542] It can be argued that the two largest religions, Christianity and Islam, destroyed two great civilizations, the Roman civilization and the Arab civilization, and replaced them with more mediocre and more primitive religious civilizations.
In 380 A.D., the Roman emperor Theodosius I opened a Pandora's box which paved the way for the advent of the Middle Ages and which held back the Christian world for more than a thousand years. He decreed that Christianity was the only official religion of the Roman Empire and, as a corollary, that the emperors held power by divine right, under the authority of God. The Church and the State were one.
Similarly, Islam is a religion profoundly anchored in the traditions of a 7th Century peasant society. It denies the right to freedom of conscience

and of religion, refuses the principle of religious tolerance, and tramples the democratic principle of the equality of the sexes, while rejecting the democratic principle of the separation of Church and State. By introducing religious and anti-scientific governments, Islam has held back the Arab world for centuries. From 750 to about 1000 A.D., science and technology in the Arab world were much more advanced than in Christian Europe. Then Arab science was declared heretic by religious fanatics. For militant Islam, all truth had to be "revealed" from God (Allah) and didn't need to be researched.

[543] For an analysis of the positive and negative contributions of religions to society, see: Rodrigue Tremblay, *L'Heure juste, le choc entre la politique, l'économique et la morale,* Éditions Stanké Internationales, 2001, chapter 4.

[544] The Enlightenment, in the 18th Century, was a European philosophical movement characterized by rationalism, scientific learning, religious skepticism and political empiricism in social and political thought.

[545] See David Landes, *Richesse et pauvreté des nations,* Albin Michel, Paris, 1998.

[546] In most countries where Islam is dominant, the Islamic clergy considers science to be a Western invention and "irreligious". They see scientific and economic progress as a menace to their reactionary conservatism. Their greatest desire is to revive the primitive Middle Ages, when populations were uneducated and could be more easily manipulated by the political-religious class. Without the aid of scientific and technological progress, the populations in Muslim countries are condemned to material inadequacy and underdevelopment.

[547] For a history of the limited-liability companies, see: John Micklethwait and Adrian Wooldridge, *The Company, A Short History of a Revolutionary Idea,* Modern Library, 2003.

[548] In France, René Descartes (*Discours de la méthode,* 1637) wrote the definitive description of the scientific method.

[549] Leonard Dudley, *The Word and the Sword: How techniques of information and violence have shaped our world,* Blackwell, Cambridge, Mass., 1991, chap. 4, p.134, p.122.

[550] A. Maddison, "Phases of Capitalist Development", Banca Nazionale Del Lavoro, *Quarterly Review,* June 1977, pp. 103-137.

[551] Thom Shanker, "New Top General Tells Legislators U.S. Will Probably Need a Larger Army", *The New York Times,* July 30, 2003.

[552] Worldwide military expenditures exceeded $800 billion in 2002.

The top military spenders (in billions) were:
United States $343.2
Russia $60
China $42
Japan $40.4
United Kingdom $34
Saudi Arabia $27.2
France $25.3
Germany $21
Brazil $17.9
India $15.6
Italy $15.5
South Korea $11.8
Source: Data compiled by the Nuclear Age Peace Foundation.

[553] This is a record. And it keeps getting larger. The U.S. defense budget is scheduled to reach $451 billion in 2007.

The first victim of the financial crisis that looms will be the U.S. dollar. As soon as a political or economic shock reverses the net flow of capital toward the U.S., the dollar will cease to dominate international financial markets. People forget that foreigners own $1.5 trillion in U.S. equities and another $1.4 trillion in U.S. bonds."

In 2002, foreigners owned 11 percent of U.S. stocks and 42 percent of treasury bonds.

---

[554] Oswald Spengler, *The Decline of the West*, 2 Vols., trans. Charles Francis Atkinson, Alfred A. Knopf, New York, 1922.

[555] See Dwight Perkins, "China's future: economic and social development scenarios for the Twenty-first Century." In OECD, *China in the 21st Century*. OECD, 1996.

[556] For a review of economic and policy requirements for export-led growth, see Rodrigue Tremblay, "The Canada-U.S. Trade Arrangements for Export-Led Growth", *Review of North American Economics and Finance*, 1991, 14 p.

[557] In George Orwell's novel *1984* the world was divided into three countries: Oceania, Eurasia, and Estasia. Alliances were constantly shifting among the three, always pitting two countries against the third, in varying combinations.
George Orwell, *1984*, Signet Classic, re-issue 1990, originally published in 1948.

Table-1

Gross domestic products of the principle economic blocks
(trillions of US dollars, adjusted to purchasing power parities)

|                   | 2002 | 2007 | 2012 | 2017 |
|-------------------|------|------|------|------|
| United States     | 10,4 | 13,7 | 18,0 | 23,8 |
| European Union*   | 9,3  | 12,3 | 14,9 | 18,2 |
| Greater China**   | 7,8  | 12,4 | 19,7 | 31,3 |
| Japan             | 3,3  | 4,2  | 5,3  | 6,8  |

---

* For the EU, the year 2002 includes 15 countries; afterwards, 25 countries.
** Greater China includes the economies of Hong Kong and Taiwan.
Sources:
For 2002 and 2007: *Business Week*, Dec. 9, 2002, p. 51.
For 2012 and 2017, author's projections.

[558] U.S. companies dominate the rostrum of top brand names around the world. In 2002, the 100 Best Global Brands ratings placed 62 American companies in the top 100, and 8 of them (Coca Cola, Microsoft, IBM, GE, Intel, Disney, McDonald's, and Marlboro) were among the top ten.

[559] See Martin Rees, *Our Final Century: The 50/50 Threat to Humanity's Survival*, 2003.

# BIBLIOGRAPHY

N.B.: In general, articles in daily and weekly publications are not included in this section, but are fully cited in the endnotes.

Abbott, Elizabeth, *A History of Celibacy*, Scribner, New York, 2000, 493 pages.

Abrams, Elliot, *Faith or Fear: How Jews Can Survive in a Christian America*, The Free Press, New York, 1997.

Adams, Michael, *Fire and Ice, the United States, Canada, and the myths of converging values*, Penguin, Toronto, 2002.

Adler, Alexandre, *J'ai vu finir le monde ancien*, Grasset, Paris, 2002, 335 pages.

Ahmed, Rashid, *Taliban: Militant Islam, Oil and Fundamentalism in Central Asia*, Yale University Press, New Haven, 2001.

Ali, Tariq, *The Clash of Fundamentalisms*, Verso Books, New York, 2003.

Alterman, Eric, *Who Speaks for America?*, Cornell University Press, Ithaca, 1998.

Amuzegar, J., *Managing the Oil Wealth: OPEC's windfalls and Pitfalls*, London, 1999.

Ardant, G., *Histoire financière de l'Antiquité à nos jours*, coll. Idées, Paris, 1976.

Armstrong, Karen. *The Battle for God*, Knoff, New York, 1996, 448 pages.

Attali, Jacques, *Les Juifs, le monde et l'argent*, Fayard, Paris, 2002, 638 pages.

Babakhan, Ali, *Les Kurdes d'Irak, leur histoire et leur déportation par le régime de Saddam Hussein*, Paris, 1994, 352 pages.

Bacevich, Andrew J., *American Empire, The Realities and Consequences of U.S. Diplomacy*, Harvard University Press, Cambridge, 2003.

Baer, Robert, *See No Evil: The True Story of a Ground Soldier in the C.I.A.'s War on Terrorism*, Crown Publishers, 2002.

Balencie Jean-Marc and Arnaud de La Grange, *Mondes rebelles—Guerres civiles et violences politiques*, Paris, 1999.

Barber, Benjamin R., *Fear's Empire: War, Terrorism, and Democracy in an Age of Interdependence*, Norton, New York, 2003.

Barker, Dan. *Losing Faith in Faith: From Preacher to Atheist*, Annie L. Gaylor (Designer), Freedom From Religion Foundation, Inc, Madison, 1992, 392 pages.

Barkun, Michael, *Religion and the Racist Right: The Origins of the Christian Identity Movement*, Chapel Hill, N. C., 1994.

Barrett, B. David, *World Christian Encyclopedia*, Oxford University, 2001, 800 pages.

Barzun, Jacques, *From dawn to decadence: 500 years of western cultural life, 1500 to the present*, HarperCollins, New York, 2000, 877 pages.

Bauer, Julien, *Le système politique israélien*, Collection "Que sais-je?", Paris, 2002.

Beit-Hallahmi, Benjamin, *Original Sins: Reflections on the History of Zionism and Israel*, Olive Branch Press, 1993.

Berlin, Isaiah, *Freedom and its Betrayal*, Princeton, 2002, 182 pages.

Bibby, Reginald, *Restless Gods*, 2002.

Bordonove, Georges, *La tragédie cathare*, France Loisirs, Paris, 1992.

Bougeant, Father Guillaume Hyacinthe, S.J., *Histoire du traité de Westphalie, ou des négociations qui se firent à Münster et Osnaburg, pour rétablir la paix entre toutes les puissances de l'Europe*, Paris, Mariette, 1744.

Braver, Adam, *Mr. Lincoln's Wars*, Morrow, New York, 2002, 320 p.

Brisard, Jean-Charles et Guillaume Dasquie, *Ben Laden, la vérité interdite*, Gallimard, Paris, 2002.

Brzezinski, Zbigniew K., *The Grand Chessboard: American Primacy and Its Geostrategic Imperatives*, Basic Books, New York, 1998.

Bruni, Frank, *Ambling Through History*, New York, 2001.

# Bibliography

Buchanan, Patrick J. *A Republic, Not An Empire*, Regenery Publishing, Washington, 1999.

Bush, George H., *All the Best*, and George Bush, *My Life in Letters & Other Writings*, Simon & Schuster, New York, 2000.

Bush, George W., *A Charge to Keep*, Morrow, New York, 1999.

Caldicott, Helen, *The New Nuclear Danger: George W. Bush's Military-Industrial Complex*, The New Press, New York, 2002, 416 pages.

Camel, Camilleri, *Chocs des cultures: concepts et enjeux pratiques*, L'Harmattan, Paris, 1989, 398 p.

Canetti, Elias, *Crowds and Power*, 1960.

Chace, James and Caleb Carr, *America Invulnerable: The Quest for Absolute Security from 1812 to Star Wars*, Summit Books, New York, 1988.

Challand, G., *La question Kurde*, Maspero, Paris, 1961.

Chambost, Édouard, *Guide des paradis fiscaux*, 7th edition, Éditions Favre, Lausanne, 1999, 730 p.

Chesnais, Jean-Claude, *Le crépuscule de l'Occident: dénatalité, conditions des femmes et immigration*, R. Laffont, 1995, Paris, 366 pages.

Chomsky, Noam, *The Fateful Triangle: The United States, Israel & the Palestinians*, South End Press, 1983.

Cirincione, Joseph, et al, *Iraq: What Next*, Carnegie Endownment for International Peace, January 2003.

Claude, Richard Pierre, and B.H. Weston, eds., *Human Rights in the World Community*, University of Pennsylvania Press, Philadelphia, 1992.

Clouse, Robert G., *War: Four Christian Views*, Downers Grove, Intervarsity Press, 1991.

Conason, Joe, *Big Lies*, Thomas Dunne Books, New York, 2003.

Cook, Robin, *Point of Departure*, Simon & Schuster, London, 2003, 432 pages.

Cooley, John K., *Unholy Wars: Afghanistan, America and International Terrorism*, Stylus Publishing, LLC., New York, 2000.

Corn, David, *The Lies of George W. Bush: Mastering the Politics of Deception*, Crown Publishers, New York, 2003.

Crossen, Cynthia, *The Rich and How They Got That Way*, Crown Business, New York, 2000, 287 p.

Darwin, Charles, *The Descent of Man*, 1871.

De Cues, Nicolas, *Du non-autre, Le guide du penseur*, Préface, les Éditions du Cerf, Paris, 2002, 142 p.

Delpech, Thérèse, *Politique du chaos*, La République des Idées, Seuil, Paris, 2002.

Diamond, Jared, *Guns, Gems and Steel*, W.W. Norton & Company, New York, 1997.

Didion, Joan, *Political Fictions*, Alfred A. Knopf, New York, 2001, 338 pages.

Dommanget, M., *Le curée Meslier, athée, communiste et révolutionnaire sous Louis XIV*, Paris, 1965.

Drury, Shadia, *Leo Strauss and the American Right*, St. Martin's Press, New York, 1997.

Dudley, Leonard, *The Word and the Sword: how techniques of information and violence have shaped our world*, B. Blackwell, Cambridge, Mass., 1991.

Dulait, André, et François Thual, *Bagdad 2000: l'Avenir géopolitique de l'Irak*, and, Ellipses, collection l'Orient politique, Paris, 1999.

Duvernoy, Jean, *Le catharisme: L'Histoire des Cathares*, Éditions Privat, Toulouse, 1992.

Eisenhower, Dwight D., *Farewell Address*, 1960.

El Fadl, Abou, *The Place of Tolerance in Islam*, Beacon Press, 2002.

Eliade, Mircea, *Traité d'histoire des religions*, edition revised and corrected, Payot, Paris, 1974, 393 pages.

Ellsberg, Daniel, *Secrets: A memoir of Vietnam and of the Pentagon papers*, Penguin USA, 2002.

Enderlin, Charles, *Le rêve brisé: Histoire de l'échec du processus de paix au Proche-Orient, 1995-2002*, Éditions Fayard, Paris, 354 pages.

Fallaci, Oriana, *La Rage et l'Orgeuil*, Plon, Paris, 2002.

Fergerson, Niall, Empire, *The Rise and Demise of the British World Order and the Lessons for Global Power*, Basic, New York, 2002, 396 pages.

# Bibliography

Fernando-Armesto, Felipe, *The Americas: A Hemispheric history*, The Modern Library, 2003, 235 pages.

Feuerbach, Ludwig, *Contre le dualisme du corps et de l'âme, de la chair et de l'esprit* (II), Paris, 1990.

Feuerbach, Ludwig, *Pensées sur la mort et l'immortalité*, publié en 1830 et reproduit par les Éditions du CERF, Paris, 1991.

Finkelstein Norman, *L'Industrie de l'Holocauste*, La Fabrique, Paris, 2001, 160 pages.

Forman, Ira, *Jews in American Politics*, New York, 2001, 512 pages.

France, Anatole (Anatole-François Thibault), *Les dieux ont soif*, Calmann-Lévy, Paris, 1912.

Franken, Al, *Lies and the Lying Liars Who Tell Them: A Fair and Balanced Look at the Right*, Penguin Books, New York, 2003.

Fromkin, David, *A Peace to End All Peace: Creating the Modern Middle East, 1914-1922*, Vintage Books, New York, 2000.

Frum, David, *The right man: The Surprise Presidency of George W. Bush*, Random House, 2003.

Gauchet, Marcel, *La Religion dans la démocratie*, Gallimard, Paris, 1998.

Gibbon, Edward, *The History of the Decline and Fall of the Roman Empire*, Peter Fenelon Collier, New York, 1899.

Gibbon, Edward, and David Womersley, *The History of the Decline and Fall of the Roman Empire*, (Abridged), Penguin Classics, 2003.

Gorbachev, Mikhail, *Memoirs*, Doubleday, New York, 1995, 769 p.

Gould, Steven Jay, *The Structure of Evolutionary Theory*, New York, 2002.

Gresh, Alain, *Irak, la faute*, Cerf, Paris, 1999.

Hall, Stephen S., *Merchants of Immortality. Chasing the Dream of Human Life Extension*, Houghton Mifflin, Boston, 2003, 439 p.

Halsell, Grace, *Forcing God's Hand*, Crossroads International Publishing, Washington DC, 1999.

Halsell, Grace, *Prophecy and Politics: Militant Evangelists on the Road to Nuclear War*, Lawrence Hill & Company, Westport, CT, 1986.

Halsell, Grace, *Prophecy and Politics: The Secret Alliance between Israel and the US Christian Right*, Lawrence Hill & Company, Westport (CT), 1989.

Hart, D. G., *That Old-Time Religion in Modern America*, Ivan R. Dee, 2002, 246 p.

Hart, Jeffrey, *Smiling Through the Cultural Catastrophe*, Yale University Press, New Haven, 2001.

Hatfield, J.H., *Fortunate Son: George W. Bush and the Making of an American President*, third edition, introduction by Mark Crispin Miller, preface by Greg Palast, Soft Skull Press, New York, 2003.

Hawking, Stephen, *The Universe in a Nutshell*, Bantam, New York, 2001, 216 pages.

Held, David, *Democracy and the Global Order*, Stanford University Press, Stanford, 1995, 324 p.

Herzl, Theodor, *The Jewish State, An Attempt at a Modern Solution to the Jewish Question*, ed. Jacob M.Lakow, New York, 1896.

Hirsh, Michael, *At War With Ourselves, Why America Is Squandering Its Chance to Build a Better World*, Oxford University Press, New York, 2003, 288 p.

Hobsbawm, Eric J., *The Age of Empire, 1875-1914*, Vintage Books, New York, 1989.

Hobson, J.A. , *The Economic Bases of Imperialism*, Allen and Unwin, London, 1902, 1948.

Hoyle, Fred, Geoffrey Burbidge, and Jayant Vishnu Narlikar, *A Different Approach to Cosmology: From a Static Universe Through the Big Bang Towards Reality*, Cambridge University Press, 2000, 357 pages.

Huffington, Arianna S., *Pigs at the Trough: How Corporate Greed and Political Corruption Are Undermining America*, Crown Publishing Group, New York, 2003, 275 pages.

Hull, Edward, *The Wall Chart of World History, From Earliest Times to the Present*, DAG Publications LTD., London, 1999.

Huntington, Samuel P., "Generations, Cycles, and Their Role in American Development", in R. J. Samuels, ed., *Political Generations and Political Development*, Lexington Books, Lexington Mass., 1977.

Hume, David, *Dialogues concerning natural religion in focus*, London, 1779.

# Bibliography

Hurtig, Mel, *The Vanishing Country: Is it too late to save Canada?* McClelland & Stewart, Toronto, 2002. 433 pages.

Ignatieff, Michael, "The Burden", *New York Times Magazine*, January 5, 2003.

Ivins, Molly and Lou Dubose, *Bushwhacked: Life in George W. Bush's America*, Random House, 2003, 347 pages.

*Jews for Justice in the Middle East, Origin of the Palestinian-Israel Conflict*, P.O. Box 14561, Berkeley, California, 2000. See also the site: http://www.nowarforisrael.com/

Johnson, Chalmers, *Blowback. The Costs and Consequences of American Empire*, Owl Book, Hudson, 2001.

Kagan, Robert, "Power and Weakness,", Policy Review, No. 113, Hoover Institution, June 2002.

Kampfner, John, *Blair's Wars*, Free Press, London, 2003, 384 pages.

Kaplan, Robert, D., *Warrior Politics, Why Leadership Demands a Pagan Ethos*, Random House, New York, 2001, 198 p.

Keegan, John, *A History of Warfare*, Alfred A. Knopf, London, 1993.

Kennedy, Paul M., *The Rise and Fall of Great Powers: Economic Change and Military Conflict from 1500-2000*, Vintage Books, New York, 1989.

Kennedy, Paul M., *Preparing for the Twenty-First Century*, Random House, New York, 1993, 429 p.

Kepel, Gilles, *Jihad, expansion et déclin de l'islamisme*, Gallimard, Paris, 2000/tr. Jihad, *The Trail of Political Islam*, Harvard University Press, 2003.

Kepel, Gilles, *La Revanche de Dieu*, Paris, 1991.

Kepel, Gilles, (éd), *Les politiques de Dieu*, Éditions du Seuil, 1993, coll. L'idée du Monde, Paris, 300 pages.

King, Jane and Malcolm Slesser, *Not by Money Alone: Economics as Nature Intended*, Jon Carpenter Publishing, Oxford, 2002.

Kissinger Henry, *Diplomacy*, Simon and Schuster, New York, 1984.

Klare, Michael T., *Resource Wars, the new landscape of global conflict*, Metropolitan Books, New York, 2001, 291 pages.

Knelman, F.H., America, *God and the Bomb: The Legacy of Ronald Reagan*, New Star Books, Vancouver, 1987, 478 pages.

Koenig, Harold G., and Michael E. McCullough, *Handbook of Religion and Health*, Oxford University Press, 2001.

Krakauer, Jon , *Under the Banner of Heaven: A Story of Violent Faith*, Doubleday, New York, 2003.

Lapham, Lewis, *Theater of War*, The New Press, New York, 2002.

Le Roy Ladurie, *Emmanuel, Montaillou*, Paris, 1975.

Lester, Toby, "Oh, Gods!", *The Atlantic Monthly*, February, 2002.

Levine, Allen, *Scattered Among the Peoples: The Jewish Diaspora in Ten Portraits*, McClelland & Stewart, Toronto, 2002, 410 pages.

Lewis, Bernard, *What Went Wrong?*, Oxford University Press, 2001, 192 pages.

Lind, Michael, *Made in Texas, George W. Bush and the Southern Takeover of American Politics*, A New America Book/Basic Books, New York, 2002, 201 pages.

Lipset, Seymour Marton and Earl Raab, *Jews and the New American Scene*, Harvard University Press, Cambridge, 1994.

Lomborg, Bjorn, *The Skeptical Environmentalist*, 2001.

Luizard, Pierre-Jean, *La Question irakienne*, Fayard, Paris, 2002.

Maalouf, Amin, *Les croisades vues par les arabes*, J.C. Lattès, Paris, c.1983.

MacArthur, John R., *Second Front: Censorship and Propaganda in the Gulf War*, Hill & Wang, New York, 1992, (also Berkeley, CA, University of California Press, 1992), 260 pages.

Mackey, Sandra, *The Reckoning: Iraq and the Legacy of Saddam Hussein*, Norton, WW & Company, Inc., New York, 2002, 416 pages.

Mandelbaum, Michael, *The Ideas that Conquered the World: Peace, Democracy and Free Markets in the Twenty-first Century*, Public Affairs, New York, 2002.

Martin, Hans-Peter et Harald Schumann, *Le Piège de la mondialisation*, Édition Solin acte sud, 1997.

Marty, Martin E. and R. Scott Appleby, editors, *The Fundamentalism Project, 1991-2002*, University of Chicago Press, Chicago, 2002,

McNeil, W. H., *The Pursuit of Power: Technology, Armed Forces and Society since 1000 A.D.*, Chicago, 1983.

# Bibliography

McNeil, W. H., *The Rise of the West,* Chicago, 1967.

Mantran, Robert, (dir.) *Histoire de l'empire Ottoman,* Fayard, Paris, 1989, 810 pages.

Mead, Frank S. (revision par Samuel S. Hill), *Handbook of Denominations in the United States,* 9th edition, Abingdon Press, Nashville, Tennessee.

Micklethwait, John and Adrian Wooldridge, *The Company, A Short History of a Revolutionary Idea,* Modern Library, 2003, 227 p.

Minois, Georges, *Histoire de l'athéisme,* Fayard, Paris, 1998, 671 p.

Miquel, Pierre, *Les Guerres de Religion,* Fayard, Paris, 1980.

Mitchell, Billy, *Winged Defense,* 1925.

Michels, Robert, *Political Parties,* Free Press, New York, 1968.

Moore, Michael, *Dude Where Is My Country?,* Warner, New York, 2003.

Moore, Michael, *Stupid White Men- and other sorry excuses for the state of the nation!,* Regan Books, New York, 2001, 277 pages.

Morgan, David, *The Mongols (Peoples of Europe),* Blackwell, London, 1990, 256 pages.

Morse, Edward L. and Amy Myers Jaffe, *Strategic Energy Policy Challenges for the 21st Century,* report by an independent committee created by the James A. Baker III Institute for Public Policy, Rice University, April 2001.

Meyers, Karl E., *The Dust of Empire: The Race for Mastery in the Asian Heartland,* Public Affairs, New York, 2003, 272 pages.

Naipaul, V. S., *Among the believers: an Islamist journey,* Penguin Books, Toronto, 1981.

Naipaul, V. S., *Beyond belief: Islamic excursions among the converted peoples,* Little, Brown, London, 1998.

Nataf, André, *Les libres-penseurs,* Bordas, Paris, 1995, 255 pages.

Nelli, René, *Ecritures Cathares,* updated and reedited by Anne Brenon, Éditions du Rocher, Paris, 1994.

Newberg, Andrew, and Eugene d'Aquili, *Why God Won't Go Away: Brain Science & the Biology of Belief,* Ballantine, New York, 2000.

Neitzsche, Friedrich Wilhelm, *The Will to Power,* 1901, new trans. by Walter Kaufmann and R. J. Hollingdate, Vintage Books, New York, 1968.

North, Douglas C., *Structure and Change in Economic History*, Norton, New York, 1981.

North, Douglas C., *Institutions, Institutional Change and Economic Performance*, Cambridge University Press, Cambridge, 1990.

O'Donohue, Maura and Marie McDonald, Reports, *National Catholic Reporter Weekly*, 1995 and 1998.

Orwell, George, *1984*, Signet Classic, re-issue 1990, originally published in 1948.

O'Shea, Stephen, *The Perfect Heresy: The Revolutionary Life and Death of the Medieval Cathars*, Walker & Company, New York, 2000.

Palast, Greg, *The Best Democracy Money Can Buy*, Penguin, New York, 2002.

Panek, Richard, *Seeing and Believing: How the Telescope Opened Our Eyes and Minds to the Heavens*, Viking, New York, 1998.

Parsons, Albert R., *What is Anarchism*, 1887.

Paul, Don, *'9/11', Facing our Fascist State & What a Plot*, Irresistible Revolutionary, San Francisco, 2002, 144 pages.

Pelson, Robert Young, *The World's most Dangerous places*, Amazon Books, 2002.

Pew Research Center For The People & The Press, Report:"What the World Thinks in 2002", December 2002.(www.people-press.org)

Phillips, Kevin, *Wealth and Democracy: A Political History of the American Rich*, Broadway Books, New York, 2002, 474 pages.

Pinker, Steven, *The Blank Slate: The Modern Denial of Human Nature*, Viking, 2002, 509 pages.

Pipes, Daniel, *The Hidden Hand: Middle East Fears of Conspiracy*, St. Martin Press, 1996.

Pitt, William Rivers, with Scott Ritter, *War on Iraq: What Team Bush doesn't Want You to Know*, Context Books, New York, 2002.

Pollack, Kenneth M., *The Threatening Storm: The Case for Invading Iraq*, Random House, New York, 494 pages.

Posner, Richard A., *Public Intellectuals: A Study of Decline*, Harvard University Press, 2002, 416 pages.

Power, Samantha, *A Problem for Hell: America and the Age of Genocide*, Basic, New York, 2001.

# Bibliography

Quigley, John, *Palestine and Israel: A Challenge to Justice*, Duke University Press, 1990.

Rashid, Ahmed, *Taliban: Militant Islam, Oil and Fundamentalism in Central Asia*, Yale University Press, 2001.

Rees, Martin, *Our Final Century: The 50/50 Threat to Humanity's Survival*, Heinemann, London, 2003, 236 p.

Reinhart, Tanya, *Israel/Palestine, How to End the War of 1948*, Seven Stories Press, New York, 153 pages.

Renan, Ernest, *Histoire du peuple d'Israël*, five volumes, Paris, 1887-1893.

Renan, Ernest, *L'Histoire de l'origine du christianisme*, Paris, 1863-1881.

Rifkin, Jeremy, *The Hydrogen Economy: The Creation of the World-Wide Energy Web and the Redistribution of Power on Earth*, J P Tarcher, New York, 2002.

Ritter, Scott, *Endgame: Solving the Iraq Problem, Once and for All*, Simon & Schuster, New York, 1999 .

Robbins, Alexandra, *Secrets of the Tomb: Skull and Bones, the Ivy League, and the Hidden Paths of Power*, Little, Brown and Company, New York, 2002, 240 pages.

Roberts, Adam, ed., *Documents on the Laws of War*, Oxford University Press, 1999.

Roquebert, Michel, *L'Epopée Cathare*, (4 vols.), Éditions Privat, Toulouse, 1989.

Rougier, Louis, *Le Génie de l'Occident*, Histoire de L'Humanité, Laffont-Bourgine, Paris, 1969.

Rufin, Jean-Christophe, *L'Empire et les nouveaux barbares*, Éditions

Lattès, Paris 1991, reedited by Les Éditions Jean-Claude Lattès, Paris, 2001.

Rushdie, Salman, *The satanic verses*, London, 1989.

Said, Edward W., *The Question of Palestine*, Vintage Books, New York, 1992.

Sampson, Anthony, *The Seven Sisters*, Bantam Books, New York, 1976, 395 pages.

Schama, Simon, *A History of Britain: The Fate of Empire 1776-2002*, New York, 2002.

Schlesinger Jr, Arthur M., "America and Empire," in *The Cycles of American History*, Houghton Mifflin, Boston, 1986.

Schlesinger Jr, Arthur M., *The Imperial Presidency*, Houghton Mifflin, New York, 1973, 550 pages.

Schlesinger, Stephen, *Act of Creation, The Founding of the United Nations: A Story of Super Powers*, Westview Press, London, 2003, 392 pages.

Schmidt, Charles, *Histoire et Doctrine des Cathares*, Éditions Jean de Bonnot, Paris, 1996.

Schwartz, Stephen, *The Two Faces of Islam, the house of Sa'ud, from tradition to terror*, Doubleday, New York, 2002.

Scowcroft, Brent and George H. Bush, *A World Transformed*, Knopf, New York, 1998.

Shahak, Israel, *Jewish History, Jewish Religion: The Weight of 3000 Years*, London, 1994.

Shapiro H. R., *Total State; USA*, Manhattan Communications, 1990, 779 p.

Shawchuck, Norman and P. Kotler, B. Wren et G. Rath, *Marketing for Congregations*, Abingdon Books, Nashville, 1992, 424 pages.

Sheehan, Neil, *A Bright Shining Lie*, Random House, New York, 1988, 861 pages.

Shirer, William L., *The Rise and Fall of the Third Reich: A History of Nazi Germany*, Touchstone Books, New York, 1990, first edition 1960, 1264 pages.

Skinner, Quentin, *The Foundations of Modern Political Thought*, 2 Vols., Cambridge University Press, Cambridge, 1978, 405 pages.

Smith, Hedrick, *The Power Game, How Washington Works*, Ballantine Books, New York, 1988, 789 pages.

Snyder, Jack, *Myths of Empire: Domestic Politics and International Ambition*, Cornell University Press, Ithaca, 1991.

Sobel, Dava, *Galileo's Daughter: A Historical Memoir of Science, Faith, and Love*, Walker, New York, 1999.

Solomon, Norman and Reese Erlich, *Target Iraq: What The News Media Didn't Tell You*, with an introduction by Howard Zinn and an afterword by Sean Penn, Context Books, New York, 2003.

Speer, Albert, *Inside the Third Reich: Memoirs*, trans. Eugene Davidson, Simon & Schuster, New York, 1997, 596 pages.

# Bibliography

Spencer, Robert, *Islam Unveiled: Disturbing Questions About the World's Fastest Growing Faith*, foreword by David Pryce-Jones, Encounter Books, New York, 2002, 214 pages.

Spengler, Oswald, *The Decline of the West*, 2 Vols., trans. Charles Francis Atkinson, Alfred A. Knopf, New York, 1922.

Stark, Rodney and Roger Finke, *Acts of Faith, Explaining the Human Face of Religion*, University of California Press, Berkeley, 2000.

Stark, Rodney, *The Rise of Christianity*, 1996.

Stephens, James, *Francis Bacon and the Style of Science*, University of Chicago Press, Chicago, 1975.

Stiglitz, Joseph, *Globalization and Its Discontents*, W.W. Norton & Company, New York, 2002.

Summers Jr, Harry C., *The Vietnam War Almanach*, Presidio Edition, Novato CA, 1999.

Tainter, Joseph, A., *The Collapse of Complex Societies*, Cambridge University Press, New York, 1988, 250 p.

Taylor, Philip N., *War and the Media: Propaganda and Persuasion in the Gulf War*, Manchester University Press, New York, 1992.

Todd, Emmanuel, *Après l'empire*, Gallimard, Paris, 2002, 233 p.

Toffler, Alvin, and Heidi Toffler, *War and Anti-War: Survival at the Dawn of the 21st Century*, Diane Publishing Co, 1993.

Tremblay, Rodrigue, *Le Québec en crise*, Éditions Sélect, Montreal, 1981, 447 pages.

Tremblay, Rodrigue, *Les grands enjeux politiques et économiques du Québec*, les Éditions Transcontinental, Montreal, 1999, 339 pages.

Tremblay, Rodrigue, *L'Heure Juste, le choc entre la politique, l'économique et la morale*, Stanké international, Montreal, 2001, 352 pages.

Tremblay, Rodrigue, *Pourquoi Bush veut la guerre*, Les Intouchables, Montreal, 2003, 277 pages.

Trifkovic, Serge, *The Sword of the Prophet: Islam-History, Theology, Impact on the World*, Regina Orthodox Press, 2002.

Turcotte, Marc, *Histoire de la civilisation occidentale*, 2nd ed., Décarie éd., Montreal, 1996, 1999, 466 pages.

Van Creveld, Martin, *La transformation de la guerre*, Editions du Rocher, Paris/Monaco, 1998.

Van Wagoner, Richard S., *Mormon Polygamy: A History*, Signature Books, Salt Lake City, 1989.

Vidal, Gore, *Dreaming War: Blood for Oil and the Cheney-Bush Junta*, Thunder's Mouth/Nation Books, 2003, 197 pages.

Vidal, Gore, *Perpetual War for Perpetual Peace*, Avalon Publishing Group, New York, 2002.

Walzer, Michael, *Guerres justes et injustes: argumentation morale avec exemples historiques*, (Just and Injust Wars), Belin, Paris, 1999.

Weis, René, *The Yellow Cross: The Story of the Last Cathars*, 1290-1329. Knopf, 2000.

Wilson, Edward O., *Consilience, the unity of knowledge*, Thordike Press, 1998.

Wilson, James Q., *The Marriage Problem*, Harper Collins, 2002, 274 pages.

Winterer, Caroline, *The Culture of Classicism*, John Hopkins, 244 pages.

Witham, Larry A., *Where Darwin meets the Bible, Creationists and Evolutionists in America*, Oxford, New York, 2002.

Woodward, Bob, *Bush at War*, Simon & Schuster, New York, 2002, 376 pages.

Woodward, Bob, *The Commanders*, Simon & Schuster, New York, 1991, 398 pages.

Wright, Robert, *Nonzero: The Logic of Human Destiny*, 1998.

Zakaria, Fareed, *The Future of Democracy, Illiberal Democracy at Home and Abroad*, W.W. Norton, New York, 2003, 286 pages.

# TABLE-1

TWENTY LARGEST NATIONAL ECONOMIES- 2000
(billions of dollars)

| Rank | Country | Value added |
|------|---------|-------------|
| 1 | United States | $ 9,810 |
| 2 | Japan | 4,765 |
| 3 | Germany | 1,866 |
| 4 | United Kingdom | 1,427 |
| 5 | France | 1,290 |
| 6 | China | 1,080 |
| 7 | Italy | 1,074 |
| 8 | Canada | 701 |
| 9 | Brazil | 595 |
| 10 | Mexico | 575 |
| 11 | Spain | 561 |
| 12 | Rep. of Korea | 457 |
| 13 | India | 457 |
| 14 | Australia | 388 |
| 15 | Netherlands | 370 |
| 16 | Taiwan | 309 |
| 17 | Argentina | 285 |
| 18 | Rep. of Russia | 251 |
| 19 | Switzerland | 239 |
| 20 | Sweden | 229 |

Source: 2002 United Nations Conference on Trade and
Development (UNCTAD), Geneva.

# TABLE-2

RELATIVE STANDARDS OF LIVING :
REAL GDP per person
1950-2001, (USA:100)

| Countries | 1950 | 1989 | 2001 |
|---|---|---|---|
| Australia | 78.5 | 74.0 | 77.6 |
| Austria | 41.4 | 75.4 | 74.6 |
| Belgium | 60.4 | 76.8 | 75.9 |
| Canada | 81.9 | 87.5 | 77.9 |
| France | 53.2 | 74.2 | 69.7 |
| Germany | NA | 81.4 | 69.7 |
| Greece | 22.1 | 48.2 | 47.2 |
| Ireland | 38.1 | 49.9 | 82.1 |
| Italy | 38.5 | 73.0 | 69.1 |
| Japan | 20.2 | 78.2 | 72.9 |
| New Zealand | 88.8 | 61.2 | 55.8 |
| Spain | 26.2 | 53.5 | 56.4 |
| Sweden | 70.9 | 76.7 | 71.0 |
| Switzerland | 100.6 | 96.9 | 81.9 |
| Turkey | 16.3 | 18.9 | 17.8 |
| United Kingdom | 71.0 | 70.0 | 68.2 |
| United States | 100.0 | 100.0 | 100.0 |

Source: Groningen Growth and Development Center,
Netherlands.

# INDEX OF NAMES AND SUBJECTS

Maude, F. S. (Gen.) 171
McCain, John 175
McNamara, Robert 108
Mexico 80, 172-173
Middle Ages 129
Middle East 83-86, 178-179, 207
military-industrial complex 90-91
Milosevic, Slobodan 120
Monroe, James 133
Monroe Doctrine 134
Mossadeq, Muhammad 78
multilateralism 248
Murdoch, Rupert 94-95
Muslim countries 223
Muslim Empire (the) 228
Myers, Richard 209

**N**
National Bureau of Economic Research 205
NATO 175, 237
neo-conservative movement 65-66
Nietzsche 36-37
North Korea 183
nuclear bombs 47, 183
Nuremberg (trial of) 67

**O**
Odom William 187
oil 14-15, 61-62, 73-91, 187, 211-221
oil companies 78, 88-89, 183
"Oil-for-Food" (U.N. program of) 167
Omar, Mohammed (Mollah) 100
O'Neill, Paul H. 74-75
OPEC 85, 90

Orwell, George 243, 245
Ottoman (Turkish) Empire 165, 228

**P**
Pakistan 51, 161
Pearl Harbor, 93, 184
Pentagon (the) 205, 217
Perle, Richard 58-59, 93
Persian Gulf War (the 1991) 167
Pew Research Center (the) 157-163
Pilgrims (the) 25-26
Pledge of Allegiance (the) 43
Pope Gregory IX 231
Pope John Paul II 130
Pope John XXIII 130
Pope Pius XII 130
Powell, Colin 74, 97, 172
Preemption (theory of) 61, 138-139
"Project for the New American Century" 61-62, 134-135, 150
Putin, Vladimir 182, 190-191

**R**
Reagan, Ronald 18, 150
reconstruction contracts 216
Rees, Martin 349
religions 12-13, 29, 41-45, 65
Republican Party (the) 12, 34-35, 103-104, 115-116, 187, 199-200
"Resolution 1441" 113, 171
Rice, Condoleezza 60, 75, 134
Ridge, Tom 206

Ritter, Scott 81, 63, 197
Robertson, Pat 34-35
Roman Empire (the) 35, 128, 228
Rove, Karl 103, 208
Rumsfeld, Donald 73-74, 83, 99, 107, 174-175, 195-196, 217
Russia 41-42, 81-82, 87, 110-115, 189, 214

**S**
Saudi Arabia 65, 80-81, 90
Schwarzkopf, Norman. 174-175
Scopes, John 48-49
Scowcroft, Brent 96
Security Council 70, 110-115, 113, 167, 171, 174, 214
separation of Church and State 33-34, 49-50, 248
"September 11, 2001" 10, 184-185, 248
Sharon, Ariel 94
Shawcross, Sir Hartley 194
Shia Muslims 166
Shias 168, 119
Shinseki, Eric (Gen.) 211
Shultz, George 83
Solzhenitsyn, Alexander 25
Southern Baptist Convention 222
Soviet Union (the) 37-38, 139, 152-155, 222, 237
Spain 161
Spengler, Oswald 240
Spertzel, Richard 82
St. Augustine 128
"Star Wars" system 149-152
Strauss, Leo 65-66
Sub-Sahara Africa 54-55

Suez Crisis (the) 76
supremacy (ideology of) 65-66, 145, 223
Syria 59

**T**
Talibans (the) 45, 99
terrorism (Islamist) 100-101, 184-185
Thirty Years War (the) 127
Torquemada, Tomás de 18
totalitarianism 234
Truman, Harry S. 18, 42, 249
Turkey 46, 77, 161, 168-170, 220
Turner, Ted 55, 94, 176

**U**
United Nations 15, 109-110, 118-119, 130-131, 140-142, 211-221, 249
United Nations Charter 98, 118-119, 124-125
U.S. constitution 27
U.S. foreign policy 66, 76-77
United States 37-38, 138-139, 157-163

**V**
values 229-234
Venezuela 80
Vidal, Gore 98
Vietnam War 95, 108-109, 223

**W**
Wag the Dog (film) 107
war 45, 48, 127-131, 193-225,

Printed in the United States
33179LVS00009B/39

9 780741 418876